# INSTANT ACCESS GUIDE

## World Class Manufacturing

# World Class Manufacturing

Edited by
Thomas F. Wallace
and Steven J. Bennett

## omneo

An Imprint of Oliver Wight Publications, Inc.
85 Allen Martin Drive
Essex Junction, VT 05452

Copyright © 1994 by Thomas F. Wallace and Steven J. Bennett
Icons copyright © New Vision Technologies Inc.

Published by Oliver Wight Publications, Inc.

All rights reserved. This book or any parts thereof may not
be reproduced without permission from the publisher.

Oliver Wight Publications books may be purchased for educational,
business, or sales promotional use. For information, please call
or write: Special Sales Department, Oliver Wight Publications, Inc.,
85 Allen Martin Drive, Essex Junction, VT 05452.
Telephone: (800) 343-0625 or (802) 878-8161; FAX: (802) 878-3384.

Library of Congress Catalog Card Number: 93-060672

ISBN: 0-939246-42-2

Text design by Irving Perkins Associates

Printed on acid-free paper.

Manufactured in the United States of America.
2   4   6   8   10   9   7   5   3   1

# CONTENTS

*Introduction* ix
*Problem-Solving Index* xiii

## Part I—Strategic and Tactical Planning
*Introduction* 3

1. Hallmarks of Excellence  *Robert W. Hall* — 5
2. Time-Based Competition  *Joseph D. Blackburn* — 15
3. Linking Customers to Strategies via Quality Function Deployment (QFD)  *Thomas F. Wallace* — 25
4. Hoshin Planning: Breakthrough Tool for Strategy Deployment  *Charles J. Cormier* — 35
5. Sales and Operations Planning: Top Management's Handle on the Business  *Thomas F. Wallace* — 45
6. Resource Planning: For Manufacturing, the Business, and the Enterprise  *Darryl V. Landvater* — 59

## Part II—Customers and Products
*Introduction* 73

1. Being a World Class Customer  *Patricia E. Moody* — 75
2. Understanding the Voice of the Customer  *William Barnard* — 85

3. Efficient Consumer Response (ECR) *André J. Martin*   93
4. Forecasting Systems to Support World Class Competitiveness *Stephen A. DeLurgio, Sr.*   105
5. New Approaches to New Product Development *Douglas Daetz*   117
6. Quality Function Deployment: Breakthrough Tool for Product Development *William Barnard*   129

## Part III—People
*Introduction*   143

1. Building a Learning Organization *Daniel R. Tobin*   145
2. Making Employee Empowerment Work *Steven R. Rayner*   153
3. Energizing Your Workforce with High Performance Teams *Grace L. Pastiak*   163
4. Crossing Boundaries with Teamnets *Jessica Lipnack and Jeffrey Stamps*   173
5. Organizational Communication *Eric K. Hatch*   181
6. Compensation for the High Performance Enterprise *Donna R. Neusch and Alan F. Siebenaler*   193

## Part IV—Continuous Improvement
*Introduction*   207

1. Total Quality Management (TQM) *Joseph Colletti*   209
2. Tools for Total Quality Management (TQM) *Bill Montgomery*   225
3. Benchmarking the Best-in-Class *Pete Landry*   257
4. Just-in-Time: Driver for Continuous Improvement *William M. Boyst, Jr. (III)*   267
5. The Malcolm Baldrige National Quality Award Program *Stephen George*   281
6. ISO 9000: The International Quality Standard *Robert L. Jones and Joseph R. Tunner*   293
7. Discovering Improvement Opportunities Through Quality Auditing *Greg Hutchins*   305

## Part V—Infrastructure and Technology
*Introduction* 315

1. Automation  *Wayne Ralph*  317
2. Information Technology in Manufacturing
   *Gyanendra (Jerry) Singh*  329
3. The Focused Factory  *Thomas L. Niehaus*  343
4. Manufacturing Process Choice  *Peter T. Ward*  351
5. Converting to Just-in-Time Production Flow
   *Alfred W. Webber*  365
6. Plant Scheduling for High Customer Service
   *Ray Reed*  377

## Part VI—Supply Chain
*Introduction* 389

1. Enterprise Logistics Management (ELM)
   *Thomas G. Gunn*  391
2. Supplier Quality Management (SQM)
   *Kenneth J. Stork*  401
3. Supplier Scheduling: Linking Suppliers with
   Costumers  *Alfred W. Webber*  409

## Part VII—Measurements
*Introduction* 421

1. Measuring Customer Satisfaction  *Charles O'Neal*  423
2. Performance Measurements That Support World
   Class Manufacturing  *Thomas E. Vollmann*  435
3. One Set of Numbers: Integrating Operating Data and
   Financial Systems  *Jim Burlingame*  449
4. Activity-Based Costing: Driver for World Class
   Performance  *Peter B. B. Turney*  461

*Index*  471

# INTRODUCTION

TQM, ECR, QFD. It seems that every few months new three-letter acronyms appear in the lexicon of business thinking and practice, particularly in the manufacturing sector. But are Total Quality Management (TQM), Efficient Consumer Response (ECR), and Quality Function Deployment (QFD) merely passing fads—management techniques "de jour"? The weight of the evidence indicates that they are not. In fact, the "alphabet soup" of modern management concepts contains powerful "nutrients" that can help companies build competitive strength, shed costly fat, fortify the bottom line, and tone operations for world class performance.

Unfortunately, keeping up with the latest management techniques gets more difficult all the time, given the accelerating pace of innovation in the workplace and in academic institutions. It's difficult for busy executives and managers to keep current with what they must know about new approaches and techniques for improving processes and performance; building effective and loyal workforces; streamlining costs; aligning with suppliers, customers, and business partners; and attaining world class status.

*The Instant Access Guide for World Class Manufacturing* is designed to fill the breach by providing a "satellite's-eye view" of innovative yet proven management techniques that can benefit your company. The book is divided into seven parts, each a topic essential to improving performance and gaining a lasting competitive edge:

- Strategic and Tactical Planning
- Customers and Products
- People
- Continuous Improvement
- Infrastructure and Technology
- Supply Chain
- Measurements

Each part contains chapters written by leading experts and practitioners. With only a few exceptions, these chapters are organized in the following sections:

**In a Nutshell** describes the particular technique or management approach that is the subject of the chapter. Here the authors provide concise descriptions of their respective topics and explain why a particular technique or approach is critical to business success. Many chapters offer a brief history of the technique or management approach and its context in contemporary business practice.

The mechanics and practical applications of a particular technique or approach are explained with examples and illustrations of key points. The benefits and, in many cases, the costs involved in implementing the process are also set forth. Issues and roadblocks to successful implementation are explained concisely.

**Key Concepts** defines some of the terminology specific to the subject. If you need a quick explanation of "kanban," "Activity-Based Costing," "ISO 9000," or other terms, you'll find it here.

**Action Steps** presents concise measures for adopting the techniques or approach in your company.

**Problem-Solving** uses a question-and-answer format to tackle the problems common to many companies. These problems may relate to issues in your own company and are intended to give you a sense how the techniques and approaches can be applied.

**Summary, Information Resources,** and **Internal Cross-Reference** are found at the end of each chapter. These recap the key points, point to sources that you can use to gain greater understanding of the topic, and indicate other related chapters within the book that may prove helpful.

Please note: this book contains many leading-edge concepts and techniques. Because of this newness, some terminology and definitions are still evolving. Thus, you may find one author define a term or describe a concept in one way and another author define that same term or concept somewhat differently. As your editor, I have not attempted to force fit these differences into uniformity. Rather, each author's chapter has been allowed to stand on its own, using terms in a manner that best supports the author's message.

*The Instant Access Guide for World Class Manufacturing* is designed to be used in a number of ways, depending on your time constraints and specific needs. You can read it from cover to cover or "cherry pick" within individual chapters. You may scan it as a random access guide, making use of the cross-references contained within the chapters, or use the Problem-Solving Index on page xiii to hone in on issues of particular relevance to your company. This chart defines key problem areas and directs you to the chapters that address them.

No matter how you use this guide, I believe that you'll find it a valuable resource, and an easy way to grasp the broad range of powerful management concepts and techniques that have proven themselves in many industries.

Your suggestions for the inclusion of new topics in future editions and personal accounts of problem-solving using cutting-edge management techniques are welcomed. Please write to me at Oliver Wight Publications, Inc., 85 Allen Martin Drive, Essex Junction, Vermont 05452. I would be delighted to hear from you.

Thomas F. Wallace
Cincinnati, Ohio
September 1994

# PROBLEM-SOLVING INDEX

| If You Have These Problems | Refer to These Chapters |
|---|---|
| Ineffective strategic planning | I–1, I–2, I–3, I–4, IV–1 |
| Poor communications of strategic plans | I–4, III–5 |
| Strategic plans not focused on customers | I–3, II–2 |
| Late deliveries to customers | I–6, II–3, II–4, IV–1, IV–4, VI–1 |
| High backorders | I–6, II–3, II–4, IV–1, IV–4, V–2, VI–1 |
| Poor understanding of customer needs | II–1, II–2 |
| Long lead times for shipments to customers | I–2, I–5, II–3, IV–1, IV–4, V–1, V–4, V–5, V–6, VI–3 |
| Erratic customer requirements | II–1, III–4, VI–3 |
| Lack of teamwork | I–3, I–5, III–1, III–2, III–3 |
| Poor employee relations | III–1, III–2, III–5, III–6 |
| Low employee morale and motivation | III–1, III–2, III–3, III–5, III–6 |
| Inadequate employee training | III–1, IV–1, IV–3 |
| Ineffective pay plans | III–6 |
| Inadequate flow of new products | II–5, II–6 |

xiii

| | |
|---|---|
| New products not well accepted | II–2, II–6 |
| Long product-development time | II–5 |
| New products difficult to manufacture | II–5 |
| Poor quality | IV–1, IV–2, IV–3, IV–5, IV–6, IV–7, VI–2 |
| Processes that need streamlining | V–1, V–2, V–5, V–6 |
| High obsolescence | I–6, II–5, II–6, IV–4, V–6 |
| High scrap and rework | IV–1, IV–2, IV–4, IV–7, V–1, V–3, V–5 |
| Excessive customer returns | II–6, IV–1, IV–2, IV–7 |
| Adversarial relationships with suppliers | II–1, III–4, IV–1, V–2, VI–2 |
| Late supplier deliveries | I–6, VI–2, VI–3 |
| High material shortages | I–6, V–6, VI–3 |
| Excessive finished-goods inventories | I–5, I–6, II–4, IV–4 |
| Excessive work-in-process inventories | I–6, IV–4, V–4, V–5, V–6 |
| Excessive inventories | I–6, IV–4, V–6, VI–3 |
| Inadequate plant capacity | I–6, IV–4, V–6 |
| Inaccurate data | I–6, II–4, IV–2, IV–4, VII–3, VII–4 |
| Misleading performance measurements | I–1, VII–1, VII–2, VII–3, VII–4 |
| Invalid product costs | VII–4 |

# PART I
# STRATEGIC AND TACTICAL PLANNING

**1. Hallmarks of Excellence**
*Robert W. Hall*

**2. Time-Based Competition**
*Joseph D. Blackburn*

**3. Linking Customers to Strategies via Quality Function Deployment (QFD)**
*Thomas F. Wallace*

**4. Hoshin Planning: Breakthrough Tool for Strategy Deployment**
*Charles J. Cormier*

**5. Sales and Operations Planning: Top Management's Handle on the Business**
*Thomas F. Wallace*

**6. Resource Planning: For Manufacturing, the Business, and the Enterprise**
*Darryl V. Landvater*

**S**UPERIOR PLANNING ENABLES superior execution. As complexity increases and the rate of change accelerates, there is a geometric increase in the need for robust planning processes at both the strategic and tactical levels.

Most manufacturing enterprises are complex and operate in a constantly changing environment. They must be good at planning for the future—no matter how flexible their operations—or they will sooner or later lose the competitive race to those who are.

The first chapter in Part I—**Hallmarks of Excellence** by Bob Hall of the Association for Manufacturing Excellence—sets the "high bar" for true excellence in manufacturing. Next, Joe Blackburn from Vanderbilt University posits an approach to leapfrog the competition in **Time-Based Competition**. The following two chapters discuss breakthrough tools for strategic planning, originally developed in Japan, now used by North American companies with superb results. These chapters are **Linking Customers to Strategies via Quality Function Deployment** by your editor, Tom Wallace, and **Hoshin Planning: Breakthrough Tool for Strategy Deployment** by Charles Cormier from Boeing.

Part I concludes with a focus on linking strategic plans to ongoing operations in **Sales and Operations Planning: Top Management's Handle on the Business**, also by Tom Wallace, and effective planning at the tactical level in **Resource Planning: For Manufacturing, the Business, and the Enterprise** by Darryl Landvater, CEO of Oliver Wight Publications.

# Hallmarks of Excellence
## Robert W. Hall

**IN A NUTSHELL**

Ever since Tom Peters and Robert Waterman published their bestselling book *In Search of Excellence,* business owners, managers, consultants, and Wall Street have tried to codify the characteristics of the truly excellent company. But an absolute standard of business excellence is hard to come by—perhaps because business excellence, like beauty, is in the eye of the beholder.

And there are many "beholders" of business excellence. Every company has a set of stakeholders, and each has its own criteria for excellence. Outside stockholders are concerned with reported earnings, dividends, and stock price performance first and foremost. Suppliers look for a close relationship in the development of new products and a clear set of specifications and schedules. Employees think of stability and Employee Empowerment as hallmarks of the excellent company. Customers judge a company by the quality and reliability of its products. Communities place high marks on employment stability and corporate citizenship.

With so many viewpoints, what, then, is an excellent company? Here we must conclude that *an excellent company is one that performs well from the viewpoint of all stakeholders.* Intuitively, we know that very few companies fit this description, although many are dedicated to the Continuous Improvements that have excellence as a fundamental goal. Improvement—even Continuous Improvement—does not, however, signify or necessarily lead to excellence. Soviet industry under Stalin could correctly report improved output year after year, but this did little to change the fact that Soviet industry was light-years away from the standards of industrial excellence at that time. And Western industry was improving at a faster rate—broadening the gap between Soviet industrial performance and world class industrial excellence.

Merely being on the road to improving operations, then, does not connote excellence, nor does it ensure a successful journey. Further, no company can achieve excellence in a vacuum. While many companies begin their quest for improvement by focusing on their own processes and practices, they eventually learn that they must also look outward, to improve their suppliers and even their own behavior as customers of those suppliers.

Nor can companies seeking excellence improve everything at once. As we will see, they must set priorities emphasizing one or two major improvement categories, called "drivers," while avoiding backsliding in other areas.

## *The Improvement Process*

What propels companies to the category of "excellence" and what makes it possible for excellent companies to stay on top is a well-conceived and well-managed *improvement process*. Neither the identification of the critical drivers of company performance nor the development of a comprehensive set of performance measurements is of any value unless it is associated with an improvement process.

An improvement process is a total organizational effort to correct problems and improve performance. Sometimes it is called Continuous Improvement, which takes the form of small, incremental but unending steps toward the goal of excellence. Other times the process seeks improvement through larger steps—"reengineering" being a currently popular example. Whatever the name, an improvement process must include a coordinated effort that analyzes processes and improves them in terms of one or more performance measures. Usually, this is a combination of improvements: technology, technique, material flows, information flows, and, most important, the development of broader and deeper skills among the total workforce.

## *Excellence Requires Balanced Performance*

Anytime we work toward improving performance there is a danger of concentrating on one area to the neglect of others. Genuine improvement is an advance in at least one dimension of performance without slipping on other dimensions:

*External Quality* Value-adding performance for customers in ways they did not expect. Examples of measurements: repeat sales, warranty return rates, independent customer-satisfaction surveys, complaints, service wait times.

*Internal Quality* Processes that are as defect-free as possible. Examples of measurements: yields, defect rates, error rates, process capabilities, percent of processes with fail-safe mechanisms or procedures.

*Dependability* Never failing to make good on promises in production, service, and other functions. Examples of measurements: product reliability, on-time delivery to customer (just *shipping* on time means little to customers), on-time arrivals from suppliers, work-to-schedule deviations.

*Resource Use* Eliminating waste and nonvalue-adding steps. Examples of measurements: economy of products in use, labor productivity ratios (using total headcounts), output per square foot, inventory in days-on-hand (the lower the number, the more effectively many kinds of resources are being used), percentage of time equipment is ready for use, costs.

*Flexibility* The ability to make changes quickly and to respond to customers quickly; now sometimes called "agility." Examples of measurements: concept to customer-time to bring out a new product, customer order lead times, special order lead times, engineering change lead times, setup times, supplier lead times to make changes, time delay to increase/decrease production levels.

*Human Resource Improvement* Acting on the principle that people are the most important asset; not just employees, but people in customer and supplier organizations. Examples of measurements: training time given to customers, training effectiveness, percentage of employees cross-trained, training hours per year per employee, average number of positions in which an employee is qualified to work, suggestion rates (and adoption rates), literacy rates, attendance rates, and other morale indicators.

*Innovation* Always advancing in the application of product and process technology without waste. Examples of measurements: percentage of product line turnover, time-to-market indicators for product introduction, product feature comparisons with competitors, percentage of products with replacement innovations in pipeline, numbers of patents.

*Environmental Soundness* Operating all phases of the business without damage to the environment. Examples of measurements: levels of effluents or emissions from product manufacturing and from product use, recycling percentages, percentage of parts remanufactured or that can be used in remanufacture, total injuries and lost-time accidents, percentage of workforce subjected to potential long-term health hazards, illness rates.

*Financial Results* Sustaining a rate of return pleasing to financial supporters. Examples of measurements: the normal profit-and-loss statements, financial ratios, and pro forma projections; trends on actual costs (less confusing than comparisons using variances).

Each of these dimensions of performance is important to the excellent company. Most of the examples of performance measurements associated with these dimensions are aggregated; but a company's system of measurement should apply in detail to specific items produced or to specific workstations. Aggregate measurements should be built up from specific, detailed measures.

[Be sure to see chapters VII–1 and VII–2 for detailed treatment of performance measurements.]

## *The Overarching Performance Driver*

No one can pay attention to a blizzard of performance measures. An improvement process that aims for company excellence must have clarity and focus, otherwise the finite energies and attention of personnel will be quickly dissipated. Better companies go through extended campaigns to improve performance using a single and commanding performance driver. Former Hewlett-Packard CEO John Young used this approach with his periodic and successful "stretch goals," like the Ten-X program, which aimed to create a tenfold reduction in the H-P warranty failure rate over a ten-year period. A better-known example is Motorola's Six Sigma goal for quality improvement.

Other aspects of performance are not neglected in these single-driver improvement programs if the drivers have overarching characteristics, and if the programs are well executed. Improvement in the right driver usually pulls along improvement in a number of other categories. For example, some companies use lead time (or cycle time) as the driver. Concentrating on lead times also forces people to pay attention to quality and to other aspects of performance in order to reduce lead times.

## *Comparisons: How to Know if You Are Good*

No performance outcomes can be evaluated without a reference point, just as an athletic team that has never played a game has never been tested. There are roughly five ways to make comparisons:

1. *Standards.* These involve comparison with accepted norms, such as are set by regulatory bodies. Meeting the Good Manufacturing Practice criteria set by the Food and Drug Administration (FDA) is an example of such a standard.

2. *Prior performance.* This is the most common because the data

is internally available and can be historically compiled. A simple timeline graph is a good way to do it. Show the trend in performance along with the future goal.

3. *Customer expectations.* Only measures of external performance can be compared this way, but the information is vital. A company may have improved greatly by internal comparisons yet still not meet customer expectations or understand that it is falling short.

4. *Similar operations.* This is the benchmarking approach. How do operations compare with best-in-class, or best-known performance of similar operations elsewhere? Comparisons with competitors are needed, but may not be possible in detail. Separate parts of operations can be benchmarked against excellent examples from completely different industries. Actually finding and gathering the benchmarking data is a skill in itself, but data is of little value unless one understands how others' performance was achieved. Learning how others' performance was achieved is ultimately more valuable than data.

5. *Ultimate standards.* This is the "zero errors" standard. Setting up an ultimate standard as a goal is depressing unless people believe they know how to reach it. Otherwise there's no way to achieve the desired level of performance. A few companies have actually achieved a status of shipping no "known" defects. Even so, merely shipping "no known defects" does not ensure satisfaction with the product or service, but only that you are perfectly executing what you set out to do.

## *KEY CONCEPTS*

**Accuracy**: How closely the output of a measurement process will replicate a known standard. *See* **Precision**.

**Balanced measurements**: A set of measurements or performance assessments that covers the total scope of a company's activity.

**Benchmark**: The best-known performance by someone in an area in which you would like to improve.

**Best-in-class**: A best-known example of performance in a particular operation. One needs to define both the class and the operation to avoid using the term loosely.

**Business strategy**: The overall plan or direction for a total business.

**Cycle time**: The time between recurring events. For example, the time between completing parts on a machine is a machine cycle time. Often used as a synonym for "lead time."

**Driver**: A measurement or indicator used for goal setting in an improvement process, or as its "driver." (In cost accounting some processes are also referred to as "drivers" of certain costs.)

**Indicator**: The outcome of a measurement that suggests a condition indirectly. For example, absenteeism is often considered an indicator of workforce morale, but morale is not directly measured. Many performance measurements are indicators used to infer conclusions not directly addressed by the data.

**Lead time**: The elapsed time required for a process. The process may or may not recur. *See* **Cycle time**.

**Maturity index**: A system of performance rating in which performance indicators are established in levels. As a result, people can see where they are and where they need to go.

**Precision**: The degree to which separate measurements of the same phenomena will replicate each other. Measurements are often termed "accurate," when what is meant is that they are "precise." A number calculated using many insignificant digits may seem to be precise when it isn't.

**Relevance**: The property of being related to the subject or attribute of interest. A measurement can be either precise or accurate and still not be relevant. Cost figures are a common example, but a more common way is to simply accept measurements based on available data and stretch the inferences beyond relevance. An example is assuming that because customer complaints are near zero, they are pleased with products and services.

## ACTION STEPS

- Senior management must rid the organization of references to old performance drivers that divert attention from the new direction. An example is the continued use of individual machine efficiencies when machines are being grouped into cells. The use of performance measures is as important as the measurements themselves.
- Collect baseline data according to new performance measurements considered relevant to the new direction. This is necessary to chart progress measured against one's past.
- Senior management should develop a simple driving measurement (or small set of them) to guide the improvement process. This assumes that a business strategy and improvement strategy have been devised.
- Keep the performance measurements for an improvement process simple in the beginning. People cannot pay attention to many measurements and indicators. In addition, if the use of a few provides all the grist needed to keep the process moving, nothing more elaborate is needed.
- Develop a balanced set of performance measurements. This may take several years, but it is part of everyone's learning process about what excellent performance entails.
- Use the measurement system to help chart the course of business strategy and improvement strategy.

## PROBLEM-SOLVING

*"We need to determine what world class performance is all about."*

No easily obtained data reveals such a status. Though much abused, the phrase "world class" does denote a level of performance comparable to the best known anywhere in the world. Benchmarking is a tool for comparing your performance in particular operations with companies anywhere in the world that are recognized as being among the best in those same operations.

*"Our company pays exclusive attention to financial results."*

Unless financially minded people conclude that indicators of other performance are associated with long-term financial performance, their focus will not change. That reflects a larger mind-set problem. Generally, there must be a demonstration that reduction of lead times decreases investment and other costs; this is often best done through construction of time-cost profiles. A similar approach can be taken with quality; most companies call this "cost of quality." A number of beginning level world class measurements have a financial side to them so that people can be weaned from overdependence on financial indicators.

*"How do we initiate the use of nonfinancial measurements to guide performance? How are they incorporated in people's performance assessments?"*

The first step is to stop the use of performance measurements that direct attention to prior modes of behavior and performance. The rest starts to come together as organizations develop their improvement processes and reorganize to carry them out. If Top Management institutes an overall performance driver for improvement processes, the new system begins to take shape. Such a change is not executed unless Top Management creates the setting for it.

## SUMMARY

- An excellent company is one that performs well from the viewpoint of all stakeholders.
- What propels companies to the category of excellence and what makes it possible for excellent companies to stay on top is a well-conceived and well-managed *improvement process*.
- An improvement process is a total organizational effort to correct problems and improve performance. An improvement process must include a coordinated effort that analyzes processes and improves them in terms of one or more performance measures.
- An improvement process that aims for company excellence

must have clarity and focus, otherwise the finite energies and attention of personnel will be quickly dissipated. Better companies go through extended campaigns to improve performance using a single and commanding performance driver.

- Other aspects of performance are not neglected in single-driver improvement programs if the drivers have overarching characteristics. Improvement in the right driver usually pulls along improvement in a number of other categories.

## INFORMATION RESOURCES

*Performance Measurement for World Class Manufacturing*, Brian Maskell, Productivity Press, 1991.

*Measure Up! Yardsticks for Continuous Improvement*, Richard L. Lynch and Kevin F. Cross, Basil Blackwell, 1991.

*Measuring Up: Charting Pathways to Manufacturing Excellence*, Robert W. Hall, H. Thomas Johnson, and Peter B. B. Turney, Business One Irwin, 1991.

## INTERNAL CROSS-REFERENCE

Your understanding of this topic may be enhanced by the following chapters:

VII–1. Measuring Customer Satisfaction

VII–2. Performance Measures That Support World Class Manufacturing

---

### About the Author

Robert W. Hall is professor of operations management at Indiana University and director of education for the Association for Manufacturing Excellence. He is best known as the author of *Zero Inventories; Attaining Manufacturing Excellence*; and, more recently, *The Soul of the Enterprise*.

# 1-2

# Time-Based Competition
## Joseph D. Blackburn

**IN A NUTSHELL**

The essence of Time-Based Competition is the adage "Time Is Money": save customers time and they will give you *more* money. This is simple to say, obvious to everyone, and yet elusive to many manufacturers.

Time has emerged as a dominant dimension of global competition, fundamentally changing the way organizations compete. Leading firms are showing that quick response to customer demands—the distinguishing trait of the time-based competitor—provides a powerful, sustainable competitive advantage in the marketplace. The traditional cost-based competitor is defenseless against firms that can provide products with the most value for the lowest cost with the fastest response time.

This sounds like a contradiction. Doesn't haste make waste? Conventional wisdom maintains that in pursuing speed, the time-based competitor must incur higher costs or lower quality because the low-cost producer is shielded by an unavoidable tradeoff and the quicker competitor will be forced to charge higher prices. Unfortunately, there is more convention than wisdom in this line of thinking. Time-based competitors are changing the rules by developing reengineered processes that are simpler, faster, and have world class quality. And they are delivering products at prices comparable to those of traditional manufacturers.

## *Origins in Just-in-Time*

How is time-based capability developed? The fundamental tactics of process reengineering were first perfected in factory-floor operations. Toyota, through its Toyota Production System, developed and refined the process now better known as Just-in-Time (JIT) (see chapter IV–4). By focusing on the basic work processes, Toyota rethought the process and, in so doing, redefined the way manufacturing is viewed. As it sharpened and simplified the JIT process, productivity, quality, and flexibility increased. Not coincidentally, manufacturing costs also sharply declined.

The basic principles of JIT are central to the time-based reengineered process. Many of the benefits derive not from doing tasks faster, but from attacking waste and isolating those essential activities that deliver value to the customer and eliminate the rest. Another source of time delays and quality problems is large-batch production. Firms produce in batches to avoid costly changeovers and achieve economies of scale. Therefore, a concentrated effort to reduce changeover times and batch sizes is essential to JIT. As setup times and batch sizes are reduced, opportunities for parallel, rather than sequential, processing arise and are seized. As cycle times and batch sizes are reduced, new, compact layouts can be designed to speed and simplify the work flow.

## *From Just-in-Time to Time-Based Competition*

JIT on the factory floor and in the supply chain is necessary, but not sufficient, to be a time-based competitor. To their chagrin, many firms have found that despite slicing major chunks of time out of the manufacturing cycle, customers rate their response as slower than that of the industry leaders.

Why? To customers, what matters is the total time in the chain from expressed need to satisfaction, or from order entry to order fulfillment. For most firms, the manufacturing cycle is a small and shrinking part of that value-delivery chain. Customers are unimpressed by short-cycle manufacturing that takes only hours when the firm needs days to enter the order or weeks to pick and ship the product.

In many industries, the critical time measure is speed in the time-to-market process: bringing the latest features, designs, and technologies to customers. Speed in manufacturing cannot compensate for slow product development because an obsolete product, made quickly, has little value in the marketplace.

The time-based competitor asks the same question of all the processes by which customers are served: How can we simplify the process and provide the quickest possible response? Fortunately, the secret lies in taking the principles of Just-in-Time, proven on the factory floor, and using them to reengineer the other processes of the firm—white-collar processes as well as those of the blue collar. Our experiences with processes as diverse as order entry and new product development strongly suggest that sequential batch processing is just as prevalent in administrative processes (and just as detrimental) as it is in the factory.

Just-in-Time can be a powerful weapon for the firm that learns to master it. The time-based competitors are showing by example that much of that power can come from broad-band use of JIT within the organization; it is more than a technique for lean manufacturing. JIT provides the key to a lean, responsive organization.

## *Benefits*

True time-based competitors—the ones that set the standards in their industries—reap substantial benefits in the marketplace because customers will pay for the quickest response to their demands. Speed is a convertible currency, convertible into higher prices, faster growth, and greater market share. In basic industries such as plastic injection molding and electrical panel boards, our research found that the manufacturers that can deliver on demand garner price premiums of up to 30 percent. Other studies by George Stalk and his colleagues at Boston Consulting Group provide a rule of thumb that the fastest firms in most industries tend to be growing two to three times faster than the competition and have the largest market share.

Internally, the reengineered processes of time-based competitors have increased productivity, high quality, and costs that are comparable to, if not better than, the competition's.

The cost of ignoring the reengineering imperative is prohibitive. Traditional manufacturers that assume this to be a passing fad face an exodus of customers and diminished market share. The result is often a drastically downsized business, if not outright financial ruin.

Although the cost of implementing a time-based strategy is small relative to the benefits, management should not underestimate the cost of reengineering the corporation. The greatest cost (and the greatest obstacle) is in top-level management time. Top Management must develop a total commitment to the effort; it must be willing to fund the cultural change, to put new cycle time incentives in place, and to restructure the organization.

One way to control costs is to learn the how-tos of time compression. The firm that never learns but continues to bring in cadres of consultants to do the process reengineering and then leave will face exorbitant, escalating costs. Consultants have an important role to play, but primarily in the initial stages when they can help firms gain insights and commitment, and put proper performance measures in place. Companies must learn from these experiences and develop the knowledge and skill to replicate the reengineering process and continue the process of change.

## *Becoming a Time-Based Competitor*

How does a firm become a time-based competitor? Benchmarking of leading-edge firms reveals several key differences between time-based and conventional firms:

1. Time-based firms focus on processes rather than functions. Their key concern is in sharpening the critical processes that deliver

value to customers; functional expertise serves only to support those processes.

2. Time is used as a metric for performance throughout the total organization. The leading firms not only measure manufacturing cycle times but also order-entry cycles, new product development cycles, the time to respond to customer inquiries, and the time to close the books at the end of the month. Time performance measures should be reported on charts visible in every work area (as is becoming standard practice for quality measures in firms dedicated to Total Quality Management).

3. In the time-based firms, managers are evaluated and rewarded on the basis of their time metrics. Tying time performance into the reward system is the best way for Top Management to show its commitment to the concept. As the TQM experience has shown, in firms that fail to link performance into the incentive system, managers ignore the new initiative and return to the old way of doing things. Time is viewed as another trendy technique that will soon pass, to be supplanted by a new "flavor of the month."

4. Just-in-Time is the key to speed on the factory floor.

5. Speed on the factory floor by itself is not enough.

6. Reengineering based on JIT concepts is the key to speed in all the firm's processes. Reengineering is the engine of Time-Based Competition.

How is Time-Based Competition different from reengineering? Many companies are engaged in reengineering efforts, but for a large proportion of these the goal is merely to cut fat from the organization, not to be the fastest firm in the industry. The best reason for reengineering is not to make do with less, but to win new customers and grow the business—if your purpose is simply to get rid of people, you miss a major market opportunity. You win customers with fast response and high-quality products and services; the real time-based competitors know this. Firms that are just downsizing will end up with a diminishing slice of the pie and downsized revenues.

## KEY CONCEPTS

**Just-in-Time**: Principles that are fundamental to Time-Based Competition—waste elimination, process simplification, setup and batch-size reduction, parallel (rather than sequential) processing, and layout redesign are critical skills in every facet of the lean organization.

**Process analysis**: This is the basic tool of process improvement. A detailed process chart (or "road map") is essential to understanding the process and in guiding the subsequent analysis.

**"Quick Response"**: This is what the apparel industry calls Time-Based Competition. Partnerships of textile manufacturers, apparel producers, and mass-market retailers have worked together to shrink time in the supply chain and information-processing chain to move the entire process closer to customers and lower the risk for all members of the partnership.

**Reengineering**: The engine that drives Time-Based Competition. To gain speed, firms must apply the principles of reengineering to rethink and redesign every process and move it closer to the customer.

**Setup-time reduction**: Time compression in microcosm. All the actions necessary to time compress a process are captured in the setup-reduction activity. Most time-based competitors have mastered this quick changeover process.

**Time-to-market**: A key metric for the time-based competitor. The time required to complete the product development cycle.

**Value-added analysis**: With this activity, a process improvement team strips the process down to its essential elements. The team isolates the activities that in the eyes of the customer actually add value to the product or service. The remaining nonvalue-adding activities ("waste") are targeted for extinction.

**Value-added ratio**: A critical process improvement metric, it is computed as the ratio of value-added time in a process to the total cycle time.

## ACTION STEPS

- Make a commitment to change. Top Management must be committed to speed, to measure every process, and to offer rewards based on performance with respect to time.
- Identify key processes, particularly those that are critical to serving customers.
- Assign managers process (rather than functional) responsibility. Each manager should have a process improvement team ("tiger teams," "time bandits," "speed demons," etc.).
- Reengineering teams should be given carte blanche to rethink, redesign, and knock down walls—symbolic or otherwise.
- Measure team performance, make the results visible to everyone, and close the loop by rewarding people on the basis of performance.

## PROBLEM-SOLVING

*"We've been working on cycle-time reduction, but several days are required to take orders and transmit them to the distribution center."*

In a time-based environment, speed in the order-entry process is equally important as speed on the factory floor. The techniques of cycle-time reduction—process mapping, value-added analysis, waste elimination, and small-batch processing—are as applicable in order entry as on the factory floor. Process analysis and reengineering are required to simplify and speed order entry. Management must give high priority to this effort.

*"We are always playing catch-up with new products. Our competitors always seem to be beating us to the market with new features and new technology."*

Time-based firms are fast in new product development as well. The reason is that they have recognized the importance of JIT in this area. Conventional new product development is like conventional manufacturing: sequential, batch, and slow. In development, information (rather than product) is processed in large batches and transferred "over the wall." This leads to long, costly redesign cycles that extend the development time and delay market entry. In firms that apply JIT to product development, design information is processed and transferred in small batches. This stimulates overlapping, or concurrent, activities managed by a co-located team. Although some time compression is achieved by overlapping the activities, the most significant reductions derive from reducing the frequency and severity of redesign cycles. As on the factory floor, small-batch processing tends to improve quality and reduce rework through earlier exposure of problems.

*"Management keeps pressuring us to increase our customer fill rate, and then they get on our case because inventory turns are too low."*

This is a classic time trap. With long cycle times, the only way to provide better customer service is to increase finished-goods inventories, with larger production runs that increase cycle times. Management must understand that the only way to cut the vicious cycle is to reduce cycle times. Many time-based manufacturers have escaped by achieving the ultimate solution: develop the speed and flexibility to move to a make-to-order environment.

*"Management wants speed and efficiency, but it shoots down every automation proposal we make."*

Automation should usually be the last step in a time-compression campaign. Research by Ed Hay, of Hay Associates, and others has shown that in setup time reductions 75 percent of the time can typically be removed without resorting to expensive capital outlays. Most of the time reduction simply comes from reengineering the process—simplifying, coordinating, and removing waste. This principle of simplify first, then automate, is proving to have wide application in white-collar processes as well as on the factory floor.

## SUMMARY

- Time is money. Saving time for customers through faster response is the essence of a time-based strategy.
- There are many barriers to speed in the typical organization. Functional organizations impede speed. Pursuit of lowest cost production often leads to false economies, ponderous processes.
- Reengineering is the engine of Time-Based Competition. Just-in-Time provides the basic physics.
- Speed on the factory floor is not enough.
- The time-based firm focuses on all the processes that deliver value to its customers.

## INFORMATION RESOURCES

*Time-Based Competition: The Next Battleground in American Manufacturing*, Joseph D. Blackburn, Business One Irwin, 1991.
*Competing Against Time*, George Stalk and Thomas Hout, The Free Press, 1990.
*Reengineering the Corporation: A Manifesto for Business Revolution*, Michael Hammer and James Champy, Harper Business, 1993.
*Process Innovation: Reengineering Work Through Information Technology*, Thomas H. Davenport, Harvard Business School Press, 1993.
*Competitiveness Through Total Cycle Time*, Philip R. Thomas, McGraw-Hill, 1990.
*Improving Performance: How to Manage the White Space on the Organization Chart*, Geary A. Rummler and Alan P. Brache, Jossey-Bass, 1990.
*Time-Based Manufacturing*, Joseph A. Bockerstette and Richard L. Shell, McGraw-Hill, 1993.

## INTERNAL CROSS-REFERENCE

Your understanding of this topic may be enhanced by the following chapters:

- II–3. Efficient Consumer Response (ECR)
- II–5. New Approaches to New Product Development
- IV–4. Just-in-Time: Driver for Continuous Improvement
- VII–1. Measuring Customer Satisfaction

### About the Author

Joseph D. Blackburn is the James A. Speyer Professor of Production Management and director of the Operations Roundtable at the Owen Graduate School of Management, Vanderbilt University. He is the author of *Time-Based Competition: The Next Battleground in American Manufacturing*, and has published numerous papers on Time-Based Competition, MRP, inventory management, and new product development. His current research and consulting interests are in process-improvement techniques for Time-Based Competition and the management of new product development process.

# Linking Customers to Strategies via Quality Function Deployment (QFD)
## *Thomas F. Wallace*

### IN A NUTSHELL

Quality Function Deployment (QFD) is emerging as an important tool for developing business strategies with a high degree of customer focus. It enables Top Management teams to capture the "voice of the customer" and to embed that voice into their strategic plans.

For many companies, the process of developing business strategies has major shortcomings. These include:

- Overemphasis on financial matters to the exclusion of other important issues
- A tendency to institutionalize the status quo
- An ineffective planning process
- Difficulty in obtaining broad-based commitment to the strategy within the business unit

More important, today's strategic planning processes lack the intense customer focus that is the basis for competitive success in the 1990s. Lack of customer focus causes companies to miss the breakthrough discoveries that make it possible to leapfrog competitors.

QFD enables businesses to eliminate these problems, to make customers the core of their strategic plans, and to make important discoveries regarding the future direction of their customers and markets.

## *Origins*

QFD originated as a tool for product development and is best known for its use in that area. Its first known application was at Mitsubishi's Kobe shipyard in 1972. From there it diffused to other Japanese manufacturers in a variety of industries and eventually to the West. The Ford Taurus, the Cadillac Seville, and the line of Hewlett-Packard Laser Jet printers are among the highly successful American products designed using this tool.

From the development of physical products, the power of Quality Function Deployment has been extended to the development of what QFD expert Bill Barnard has termed the "Management Product." The Management Product consists of the strategies, plans, and directions produced by Top Management for their *internal customers* (other people in the company) and their *external customers* (the outside owners of the business, i.e., the stockholders).

## *The QFD Process*

The QFD process has three main steps:

1. *Capturing the voice of the customer.* This is accomplished through market research and the use of structured processes to develop an array of customer wants. Despite the importance of the customer's voice in the QFD process, few companies listen and heed it to the extent that they should. Most companies are complacent in believing that they know *exactly* what their customers want;

however, this is often not the case. Many companies don't even know who all of their customers are; i.e., they haven't identified all of the individuals who are in the decision-making loop for the purchase of their products.

Traditional market research is increasingly being called into question for failing to generate the customer understandings that are the precursors to breakthrough products.

As important as the "voice of the customer" is to QFD, the "voice of the company" is of equal importance. This voice indicates what the company and its owners want and what they are capable of delivering. Top Management must hear both voices clearly and work to harmonize them.

2. *Translating customer wants into "measures," i.e., how the customer wants to be satisfied.* This step involves defining how a given customer's wants will be satisfied and how the customer will *know* they have been satisfied. This is done via a form of matrix analysis. Since the matrix resembles a house, it is often called the "House of Quality" (see Figure 1).

In addition to the wants and measures, QFD matrices can carry information on the relative importance of the measures, customer perceptions of the company versus its competitors, target values, and trade-offs between measures. (See chapter II–6 for more in-depth information on the the mechanics of QFD.)

3. *Cascading the resulting measures from the first matrix into wants for subsequent matrices.* As Figure 2 shows, the target values from the business unit strategy matrix become "wants" for the matrices of marketing, product design, and manufacturing. This cascading aspect of QFD enables the voice of the customer to be channeled into linked strategies for marketing, product design, and manufacturing. Each of these functions, in turn, develops its own set of strategies with respect to fulfilling customer wants.

## *Benefits*

Quality Function Deployment provides a practical approach to embedding the voice of the customer in the strategic plans of the

**FIGURE 1. THE HOUSE OF QUALITY**

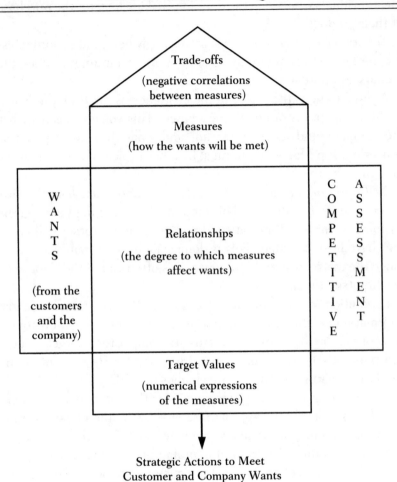

company; it makes it possible to link quantifiable goals to those plans and to build teamwork within the Top Management team and between company functions.

**FIGURE 2. CASCADING QUALITY FUNCTION DEPLOYMENT**

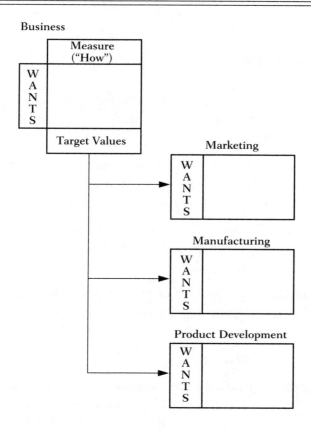

## *Implementation*

To succeed with QFD implementation, the following must be taken into account:

- As with any strategic planning process, QFD must be the responsibility of senior management; it cannot be delegated to a staff group or to line people lower in the organization.
- The organization must have valid customer information. Knowing who they are, what they want, and what will delight them is essential. Few businesses have this kind of information.
- The company should be prepared to spend four to eight months implementing the strategy/QFD process, depending on the amount

of market research to be done. The market research requirement is a function of the usable customer data that exists within the company.

## KEY CONCEPTS

**Business strategy**: The company's overall game plan, spelling out objectives for profitability, market share, growth, and the overall means to achieve them.

**Customer wants**: What customers want, need, desire in a product or service. Customer wants are often unspoken, and customers don't know they want a given feature until they see it.

**Functional strategies**: The specific strategies for marketing, manufacturing. and product development. They are subsets of the overall business strategy.

**House of Quality**: Quality Function Deployment uses a powerful form of matrix analysis. The QFD matrix often peaks at the top, and thus looks like a house.

**"Hows"**: *See* **Measures**.

**Management product**: The strategies, plans, and leadership developed by Top Management. They provide this product to their internal customers (the rest of the company) and their external customers (the outside owners of the business).

**Measures**: How a customer or company want will be satisfied. Measures can be thought of as the "how" plus a target value.

**Top Management team**: The executive group, including the leader of the business unit (e.g., president, CEO, general manager), his or her direct reports, and other key executives.

**Voice of the company**: The wants of the owners of the business, either directly or as established by senior management.

**Voice of the customer**: The customers' communication of their wants.

## ACTION STEPS

All of the steps below need to be carried out by the Top Management team and facilitators, except as noted.

- Learn about the mechanics of QFD and the role of QFD in setting strategies.
  - Select facilitators.
  - Capture the voice of the customer.
    - Identify customers.
    - Determine the amount of market information needed and the research tools to be used.
    - Conduct necessary market research.
    - Using affinity techniques, group the resulting customer wants.
  - Capture the voice of the company.
  - Using a series of QFD "houses," derive measures of customer satisfaction and strategic responses to meet those customer and company wants.
  - Formalize the resulting customer-driven strategies, document them, communicate them to all involved employees throughout the organization, and execute them.

## PROBLEM-SOLVING

"In our industry, we play follow the leader. We have a me-too product line, me-too production processes, and a me-too distribution setup. Can QFD helps us to break out of this rut and start acting like a market leader?"

Using QFD, companies have been able to make breakthrough discoveries about their customers' wants and how to respond most effectively. Done correctly, QFD enables the Top Management team to:

- Listen very closely to the customers, to gain real insight into what will satisfy and delight them
- To develop, with rigor and coherence, what the strategic responses should be
- To identify where trade-offs exist between these responses
- To quantify the competitive impact of these responses in the marketplace

*"Our strategies are focused inward; we concentrate too much on the bottom line."*

The process of linking customer wants to the business strategy is the opposite of the bottom-line myopia that has dominated—and decimated—so many companies. QFD elevates the company's sights to the customer, whose satisfaction should be the first test of any business strategy.

*"Our operating environment is highly political. Also, the person who talks the loudest usually carries the day in our planning sessions."*

The QFD process, because of its intense focus on the customer, can help *depoliticize* the environment and get the Top Management group working as a team. Companies using QFD find that the focus of attention shifts from personal agendas to customer agendas—and it's hard to argue against what customers clearly want. This depoliticizing has been shown to occur in cases involving both development of Management Products (strategies and plans), physical products, and services.

*"We have a difficult time getting the rest of the organization to buy into our strategic plans. Can QFD's customer focus help?"*

Everyone has hands-on experience at being a customer. Therefore, people throughout the company can more readily relate to strategies that focus on customer satisfaction.

## SUMMARY

- Strategic planning is deficient in most companies; it is weakly linked to issues of customer wants and to how the company will provide high-value products and services to meet those wants.
- Quality Function Deployment (QFD) is emerging as an important tool for developing strategies with a high degree of customer focus.
- Using QFD to set strategies enhances the possibility for making breakthrough discoveries that result in decisive market leadership.
- Setting strategies via QFD helps executives and senior managers to focus on customer issues, not internal departmental issues; it enhances teamwork within the Top Management team.

## INFORMATION RESOURCES

*The Customer-Driven Company*, William E. Eureka and Nancy E. Ryan, ASI Press, 1988.

"The House of Quality," John R. Hauser and Don Clausing, *Harvard Business Review*, Reprint No. 88307.

*The Innovation Edge: Creating Strategic Breakthroughs Using the Voice of the Customer*, William Barnard and Thomas F. Wallace, Oliver Wight Publications, 1994.

## INTERNAL CROSS-REFERENCE

Your understanding of this topic may be enhanced by the following chapters:

I–4. Hoshin Planning: Breakthrough Tool for Strategy Deployment

II–2. Understanding the Voice of the Customer

II–6. Quality Function Deployment: Breakthrough Tool for Product Development

## About the Author

Thomas F. Wallace is an independent consultant, author, and educator specializing in strategic planning and resource planning. In addition to editing this book, he is also the author/co-author of a number of books, including *MRP II: Making It Happen* (1990), *Customer-Driven Strategy* (1992), and *The Innovation Edge* (1994). Mr. Wallace is president of T. F. Wallace & Co. of Cincinnati, Ohio, and is a distinguished fellow at the Ohio State University Center for Excellence in Manufacturing Management.

# Hoshin Planning: Breakthrough Tool for Strategy Deployment

*Charles J. Cormier*

## IN A NUTSHELL

Hoshin Planning (HP), also known as Management by Policy or, alternatively, Strategy Deployment, is a means by which goals are established and measures are created to ensure progress toward those goals. HP keeps activities at all levels of a company aligned with its overarching strategic plans. It accomplishes this by:

- Deploying strategic plans through all levels of the organization
- Getting people from all departments to buy into strategic plans
- Avoiding the overloading of personnel with too many tasks
- Facilitating cross-functional cooperation
- Measuring progress toward the achievement of plans

For companies trying to implement breakthrough strategies like Just-in-Time (JIT), or self-managing teams, Hoshin Planning is a means of ensuring successful company-wide adoption.

Hoshin Planning originated in Japan as an adaptation of the American practice of management by objectives. (MBO) Known in Japan as *Hoshin Kanri*, it is widely practiced throughout Japan and has been adopted by a number of world class companies in other nations. Xerox quality executive Gregory Watson has described it as a "planning system with feedback, a review cycle, reward, recognition, and teamwork built in."

Hoshin Planning shares a number of characteristics with management by objectives. Both proceed from Top Management with a set of strategic goals, and both are used to maintain alignment of activities with those goals. Among the fundamental differences, however, are these:

- MBO focuses on results; HP focuses on both results and the means of achieving them.
- MBO cascades from the top to successively lower levels; each lower level determines how it will meet the objective handed down to it. HP, on the other hand, starts at the top, but provides feedback from lower levels.
- MBO measures progress toward stated goals. HP does the same, but diagnoses the causes for variance from goals and seeks the means to correct them.

Hoshin Planning typically begins with the "visioning process," which addresses the key questions, Where do you want to be in the future? How do you want to get there? When do you want to achieve your goal? and Who will be involved in achieving the goals? HP then systematically explodes the whats, whens, whos and hows throughout the entire organization. Figure 1 illustrates how the various initiatives are translated across the organizational levels—in this case from the General Manager to the Director of Operations and down the line.

**FIGURE 1. HOSHIN PLANNING THROUGH ORGANIZATIONAL LEVELS**

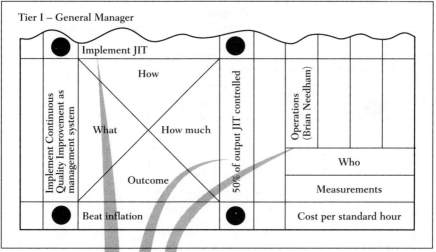

1. The "Who" becomes the owner of the next tier
2. The "How much" becomes the "Outcome" of the next tier.
3. The "How" becomes the "What" of the next tier.

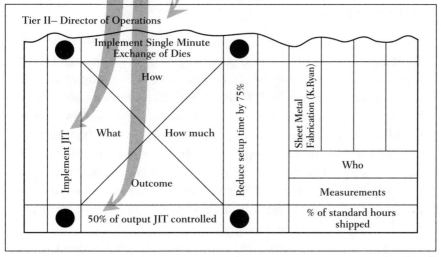

*(continued)*

**FIGURE 1. HOSHIN PLANNING THROUGH ORGANIZATIONAL LEVELS (CONTINUED)**

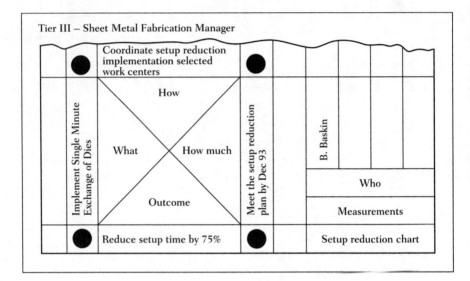

## *HP in Action*

To continue the example of implementing JIT as a breakthrough strategy, consider how a company might go about using HP to translate the larger strategic goals into an effective program. From the decision to implement JIT (the "what"), the company would then focus on the "how." Perhaps the answer to the "how" is allow change to JIT to begin in the machine shop. The question than gets reiterated for the machine shop: How will JIT be implemented in the machine shop? The answer might be, With product line XYZ. Next, the questioning shifts to when and how much. In other words, the questions are run through various layers of management until the breakthrough strategy is deployed.

As the questions raised during the visioning process filter down through the organization, people are expected to engage in process thinking, which focuses on *what* is the problem, not *who* is the problem. For example, if a manager were to say to a person in his department, "I want you to reduce costs by ten percent by April," and the person agrees, the manager would then review *how* the target will be achieved. If, during performance review, the person has not achieved the goal, the manager would focus on whether or not the person carried out the agreed upon action, rather than the absolute result. While the person is still accountable at some point for hitting the goal, the manager would take *corrective*, not punitive, action to make sure that the objective was reached. In this way, process thinking moves quickly to problem resolution.

One way to initiate process thinking is by means of "catch-ball," the term that Japanese managers use for tossing an idea around as children would toss a ball among themselves. In catch-ball, a manager explains the goal he or she wants to achieve and then "tosses" it to the next person down the ladder. That person then says, "I can do this, but not that," and tosses it back to the manager. For example, if you were pursuing JIT, Top Management might say that they wish to achieve an inventory reduction of 75 percent within a year. After assessing this request, the people who would implement the JIT program might establish that the reduction is simply not possible within twelve months, but that a 50 percent reduction *is* possible. The team would present to Top Management an analysis supporting their counter position. Management would then negotiate with the team until a mutually agreeable plan is reached.

Through catch-ball, the breakthrough strategy will eventually be deployed, after which HP triggers review, and where required, diagnosis and correction. This entails management's checking the whole process from the bottom up and comparing it to the original goals. This review might entail a review committee or a set of formal meetings during which observations are recorded and action items are identified.

## *Benefits of HP*

- HP galvanizes and aligns the efforts of the organization. HP provides a rallying point for effectively channeling everyone's energies and efforts. People no longer work counter to each other, but rather, in sync with each other. Often, without HP, when a new initiative is announced at the top level of the organization, people at the lower levels don't know if what they're doing is in step with the overall effort. With HP, all actions can be evaluated against the plans as they filter down from level to level, and are given a reality check through the catch-ball process.

- HP provides a new communication tool for the nonmanagement ranks. Since HP answers the key questions about what everyone is supposed to be doing, it opens a new channel for important feedback.
- HP promotes teamwork. The shift to process thinking can bring about dramatic changes in people's confidence in and the desire to work in teams. Rather than throwing spears at others (and often being rewarded for doing so), the focus shifts to the shared goal of solving problems. This spirit of cooperation can be harnessed and applied to nonbreakthrough strategies as well.
- HP promotes a preventive mentality. Traditionally, management, especially in North American companies, has operated in a reactive mode. If the reject rate is escalating, it reacts to it. If cost targets aren't being met, it reacts to them. HP allows the company to effectively deploy large-scale initiatives that prevent the problems from occurring in the first place. Managers can then do what they're supposed to do—manage people and processes rather than problems.
- HP exposes fat in the organizational structure. As mentioned earlier, the more layers of management, the more iterative the HP process becomes due to the process of catch-ball. A lengthy process of catch-ball can stimulate thinking about whether there are too many layers of management involved.

## *Implementation*

There is an up-front time expenditure associated with implementation of Hoshin Planning. People need some training in problem-solving techniques, group processes, and other Total Quality Management (TQM) skills (see chapters IV–1 and IV–2).

## KEY CONCEPTS

**Catch-ball**: A series of discussions between managers and their employees during which data, ideas, and analysis are thrown like a ball—back, forth, up, down, and horizontally across the organization. This opens a productive dialogue throughout the entire company.

**Customer "in"**: An orientation to the customer involving an acknowledgment of the need to continually meet the customer's specific requirements, expectations, and changing needs. It also reflects a commitment to developing the systems and practices that will provide assurance of quality to the customer.

**Hoshin Planning (HP)**: The process by which managers identify objectives for the organization and explode them at lower levels. It defines the goals, objectives, and hows throughout various tiers of the management structure.

**Organizational priorities**: Priorities that drive strategic initiatives, such as those related to satisfying the customer or improving customer satisfaction.

**Process mentality**: An approach to problem-solving that focuses on what's wrong, not *who* is wrong. For example, a nonprocess mentality applied to quality might entail inspecting the product once it is built and putting aside defective units. The process mentality attempts to correct the process so that defects are eliminated.

## ACTION STEPS

The action steps follow the improvement cycle known as the Deming (or Shewhart) Wheel: Plan, Do, Check, and Act.

- *Plan.* Senior management should use the visioning process in the context of its Business Plan. HP translates the Business Plans to action plans, meaningful to all levels of the organization.

- *Do.* Answer the whats, hows, and whos for the total number of tiers for your organization; remember, the fewer the number of tiers, the better. Also, this is the time to bring management together and provide them with a basic understanding of HP mechanics.
- *Check.* On a periodic basis, review the measurements and note what you've learned that can help in the future.
- *Act.* Make the necessary adjustments to plans and priorities in order to ensure the success of the strategy breakthroughs.

## PROBLEM-SOLVING

*"We don't seem to be focused—we're all going in different directions. What are our priorities?"*

Hoshin Planning forces an alignment of goals and objectives and strategic initiatives. HP helps identify and enumerate the priorities for each level of the organization.

*"Senior management seems concerned only with results and expects middle management to miraculously achieve them."*

Senior management should go through the visioning and catchball processes. This will give executives a better understanding of the realities involved in getting the job done and will give subordinates a chance to voice their opinions and buy into their ideas.

*"People on the front line don't know if their efforts are paying off on the bottom line."*

HP clearly lays out the company's priorities, focus, and alignment. When HP is deployed, everyone understands how all functions and resources in the organization are linked.

## SUMMARY

- Hoshin Planning is a deployment process for achieving breakthroughs in an organization.

- Hoshin Planning creates a sense of focus throughout the organization and is supported by process thinking.
- With Hoshin Planning, everyone is synchronized with top-level plans, so energy and resources are effectively applied to the achievement of shared objectives.

## INFORMATION RESOURCES

*Hoshin Kanri,* Yoji Akao, editor, Productivity Press, 1992.
*The Innovation Edge: Creating Strategic Breakthroughs Using the Voice of the Customer,* William Barnard and Thomas F. Wallace, Oliver Wight Publications, 1994.

## INTERNAL CROSS-REFERENCE

Your understanding of this topic may be enhanced by the following chapters:

I–3. Linking Customers to Strategies via Quality Function Deployment (QFD)

III–3. Energizing Your Workforce with High Performance Teams

IV–1. Total Quality Management (TQM)

### About the Author

Charles J. Cormier is director of operations support at Boeing Canada, Arnprior Division. He leads a number of strategic initiatives, such as the implementation of MRP II, JIT, TQM, and Hoshin Planning. Mr. Cormier is trained as an industrial engineer and has twelve years of experience in the manufacturing field. He was formally the director of the Manufacturing Technology Center of New Brunswick in Canada.

# Sales and Operations Planning: Top Management's Handle on the Business

*Thomas F. Wallace*

### IN A NUTSHELL

Sales and Operations Planning (S&OP) makes it possible for senior managers to proactively manage customer service levels, inventory investment, and lead times for customer order fulfillment. As such, it represents their "handle"—their direct control—over these strategically important aspects of the business.

In most companies, Top Management lacks this handle; customer service levels, inventories, and customer order lead times are neither well planned nor well managed. The result is poor customer service, unnecessarily high inventories, or long order backlogs that drive customers to the competition. Because it prevents these kinds of problems, S&OP is considered by many to be an indispensable tool for Top Management.

## Origins

Sales and Operations Planning was developed as a component of Manufacturing Resource Planning (MRP II) (see chapter I–6). As a result, most companies that currently use S&OP began doing so when they implemented MRP II. A number of these companies have reported that the benefits from S&OP alone more than covered the entire cost of implementing MRP II.

Other companies implement Sales and Operations Planning on a stand-alone basis, not as a subset of a larger initiative. A division of a major chemical manufacturer implemented S&OP on this stand-alone basis. The results were customer service levels improved dramatically and the finished-goods inventory dropped by more than 20 percent. A Midwest container manufacturer took the same approach and experienced similar results on a highly seasonal product line.

## Benefits

Direct benefits from Sales and Operations Planning include improved customer service levels, shorter customer order lead times, more stable production rates, and lower inventories. A significant indirect benefit is that S&OP promotes teamwork among the executive group. The president of Abbott Laboratories' U.S. pharmaceutical division commented that S&OP helped his vice presidents to "see the business through my glasses," i.e., to view the business holistically rather than in terms of marketing, manufacturing, finance, and other individual functions. (For details, please see the first reference in the Information Resources section of this chapter.)

The cost of implementing S&OP typically ranges from $20,000 to $80,000. This cost includes education and training, data acquisition, and consulting/facilitation.

## The Sales and Operations Planning Process

The most important element in this process is the Top Management S&OP meeting, which takes place monthly. In this forum, each major product family is reviewed. The information—displayed in aggregate, not in detail—shows sales performance to forecast, production performance to plan, and the resultant inventory levels and/or customer order backlogs. Figure 1 shows how the information is displayed.

In this example for a make-to-stock product family called Medium Widgets, the demand/supply strategy specifies a target customer service level (shipments on time and complete) of 99 percent. The target finished inventory necessary to support this shipping performance is set at thirty days' (or one month's) supply. (See Area A in Figure 1.)

Let's examine the thirty day-supply inventory target. Why does this company feel it needs thirty days of finished-goods inventory? Answer: Its experience over the recent past has shown that thirty days is a minimum level necessary to provide 99 percent customer service. Should this thirty-day supply target be considered as a constant, fixed far out into the future? Definitely not. The principle of Continuous Improvement should drive this company to improve its sales, production, and logistics processes so that 99 percent customer service is attainable with only, say, a twenty-five-day supply. Then a twenty-day supply. And then fifteen days. But for now, the realities of life are that it takes a month's worth of inventory to provide the 99 percent service level.

In Area B, actual sales are compared to forecast. For the past three months, sales are running ahead of forecast by 22,000 units. Actual production performance to the plan is evaluated in Area C; production performance is close to perfect.

Area D shows inventory performance to plan and actual customer service performance. We can see a serious problem developing here: as the forecast was oversold, the actual inventory dropped below plan. The result: Customer service has dropped to 89 percent for May, far below its 99 percent target.

The new sales forecast is shown in Area E. Toward the right, notice a total for the next twelve months and totals in units and dollars for the fiscal year ending in December. The fiscal year total is made up of both sales history (Jan–May) and sales forecast (June–Dec). To the right are shown the forecasted dollars in the Business Plan. The latter allows for an easy comparison between the Business

## FIGURE 1. SALES AND OPERATIONS PLAN FOR JUNE 1994

Family: Medium Widgets (Make-to-Stock)  
Target customer SVC Level: 99%  
Unit of Measure: 000 Units  
Target INV Level: 10 Days on Hand

|  |  |  |  |  |  |  |  |  |  |  |  | Totals |  |
|---|---|---|---|---|---|---|---|---|---|---|---|---|---|
|  |  |  |  |  |  |  |  |  |  | 3rd | 4th | Next | Fisc | Bus |
| Sales | Mar | Apr | May | Jun | Jul | Aug | Sep | Oct | Nov | 3Mos | 3Mos | 12Mos | Year | Plan |
| Forecast | 100 | 100 | 100 | 105 | 105 | 110 | 110 | 110 | 110 | 345 | 345 | 1335 | $12,770 | $12,700 |
| Actual | 110 | 98 | 114 | | | | | | | | | | | |
| Diff +/−: | | | | | | | | | | | | | | |
| Month | +10 | −2 | +14 | | | | | | | | | | | |
| Cum | +10 | +8 | +22 | | | | | | | | | | | |

| Production | Mar | Apr | May | Jun | Jul | Aug | Sep | Oct | Nov | 3rd 3Mos | 4th 3Mos | Next 12Mos | | |
|---|---|---|---|---|---|---|---|---|---|---|---|---|---|---|
| Plan | 100 | 100 | 100 | 105 | 110 | 115 | 115 | 115 | 115 | 345 | 350 | 1365 | 1272 | 1300 |
| Actual | 100 | 102 | 99 | | | | | | | | | | | |
| Diff +/−: | | | | | | | | | | | | | | |
| Month | 0 | +2 | −1 | | | | | | | | | | | |
| Cum | 0 | +2 | +1 | | | | | | | | | | | |

| Inventory | Mar | Apr | May | Jun | Jul | Aug | Sep | Oct | Nov | 3rd 3Mos | 4th 3Mos | | | |
|---|---|---|---|---|---|---|---|---|---|---|---|---|---|---|
| Plan | 50 | 50 | 50 | 30 | 35 | 45 | 50 | 55 | 45 | 45 | 50 | | | |
| Actual | 40 | 44 | 30 | | | | | | | | | | | |
| Days-on-Hand | 8 | 9 | 6 | 6 | 7 | 9 | 10 | 11 | 9 | 9 | 10 | | | |
| Cust SVC % | 97% | 98% | 89% | | | | | | | | | | | |

*Demand Issues and Assumptions:*

1. Forecast assumes no competitor price changes
2. Accelerated export demand will continue

*Supply Issues:*

1. June & July production plan represents maximum effort due to vacations

Plan and the S&OP forecast for the fiscal year's volume. Based on this comparison, the Top Management team will sometimes elect to change the Business Plan. The assumptions underlying the forecast are listed in Area H.

The future Production Plan, based on the new forecast and other considerations, is shown in Area F, and the relevant supply (production/procurement) issues are listed in Area J.

Area G contains the future inventory projection for finished goods. It shows that the target inventory of ten days on-hand will not be reached until September.

In summary, Figure 1 is an example of a proven and effective format for Sales and Operations Planning. The intent is to have all of the relevant information for a given product family on one piece of paper, making it possible to view each product family's situation in terms of its recent past and its future outlook. For decision-making purposes, this has proven to be far superior to displays of information that focus only on sales or inventory levels or production.

The essence of the S&OP meeting is decision making. For each product family reviewed, a decision is made based on recent history, recommendations from middle management, and the executive team's knowledge of business conditions. The decision can take the form of a change in the sales plan, the Production Plan, or the inventory/backlog plan. Or it may result in no change whatsoever, the current plans being recognized as fundamentally sound.

These decisions represent the agreed-upon plans by the company president and all involved vice presidents, and are documented and disseminated throughout the organization. They form the overall marching orders for marketing, sales, manufacturing, materials, finance, and product development. (New product plans are reviewed within S&OP in terms of their impact on the demand/supply picture.) These groups break down the aggregate plans from S&OP into the necessary level of detail: individual products, customers, regions, plants, and materials.

The total S&OP process, however, is not a point event that occurs in one two-hour, Top Management meeting each month. Rather, preliminary work begins shortly after month's end and continues for some days. This phase, called pre-S&OP, involves middle management and others throughout the company. It includes the following activities:

- Capturing sales history, production data, and inventory/backlog levels from the month just ended
- Updating the sales forecast
- Reviewing the impact of these changes on the Production Plan and determining whether adequate capacity exists to support them
- Identifying alternatives where problems exist
- Formulating agreed-upon recommendations for Top Management regarding overall changes to the plans and identifying areas of disagreement where consensus is not possible.
- Communicating recommendations and problem areas to Top Management with sufficient time for them to review the information prior to the S&OP meeting

The information contained in Figure 1, therefore, would represent the recommendation transmitted from the pre-S&OP team to Top Management regarding Medium Widgets. Top Management must then decide to accept the plan as submitted or change it. In the example in Figure 1, the below-target inventory levels in June through August may be viewed by Top Management as unacceptable, because the company will not be providing good customer service. They may decide to incur the added, and perhaps substantial, costs of either overtime, subcontracting, or temporary help so that the inventories and customer service can get back on target earlier than September.

Thanks to pre-S&OP, the Top Management S&OP meeting should require only two hours or less (the norm in companies that have honed the S&OP process). The net result of S&OP for the Top Management group should be fewer meetings, shorter meetings, a more productive decision-making process, and a higher quality of work life. Most of the middle-management people involved in the pre-S&OP process will experience the same benefits.

## *Implementation*

- S&OP is truly a Top Management function. It balances demand and supply on an aggregate basis and forms the linkage between the company's overall Business Plan and the detailed plans for sales, production, and procurement. As such, the decision-making element of S&OP cannot be delegated to middle management.
- Capturing the necessary data can be a substantial job for middle management. This is particularly true in companies that need to build up aggregate sales forecasts from the detail but lack a robust forecasting process at the detail level.
- Computer software to support S&OP is not a problem. Most companies use PC-based spreadsheet software modified for S&OP.
- It takes most companies between eight to twelve months to become proficient at Sales and Operations Planning. As with virtually any new process, S&OP involves a learning curve. With S&OP, that curve is lengthened because the planning cycle occurs monthly; incremental experience and expertise are gained only once per month.

## KEY CONCEPTS

**Aggregate planning**: Planning at the macro level, by broad product categories or families. This is necessary to set overall rates of activity for sales, production, and purchasing. If the aggregate plans are not valid, managing the detail—the mix—is substantially more difficult.

**Aggregation of the forecast**: Building up the aggregated forecasts for families from the detailed forecasts for individual products.

**Backlog**: All unshipped customer orders, including past due, current, and future. Backlog can be thought of as negative inventory. In many make-to-order businesses, the size of the backlog, expressed in time, is a key competitive variable; it determines how long customers will have to wait to get the product. All other things being equal, competitors with shorter backlogs will get more business.

**Business plan**: The overall company plan covering all aspects of the business and extending three to five years into the future. The first year of the Business Plan typically exists in substantial detail and represents the company's operating budget. The primary unit of measure in the Business Plan is dollars.

**Capacity Planning**: Translates the Production Plan, usually in product families, into terms meaningful to manufacturing, such as plants, departments, people, etc.

**Customer service level**: In a make-to-stock business, the percentage of business shipped off-the-shelf (no backorders). In a make-to-order business, the percentage of business shipped on time (no late shipments).

**Demand/supply balance**: The goal of virtually all logistics planning is to establish balance between demand and supply. Sales and Operations Planning does this at the aggregate level.

**Disaggregation of the forecast**: Generating the forecasts for individual products from the aggregate product family forecasts.

**General manager's meeting**: A term sometimes used for the Top Management S&OP meeting. It connotes that the meeting truly belongs to the general manager (president or CEO).

**Horizon**: The length of time into the future that the S&OP plans extend. A workable minimum here is twelve months of future planning. This enables the Business Plan (typically created once per year) to be updated via the Sales and Operations Plan (recreated monthly). In this context, the S&OP plan becomes a rolling monthly update to the Business Plan and can dramatically enhance its validity.

**Pre-S&OP**: The middle-management portion of the overall Sales and Operations Planning process. It includes all of the activities leading up to the S&OP meeting itself.

**Product families**: Aggregate groupings of products. Typically, these groupings are based largely on marketing and sales considerations, to facilitate forecasting. In many companies, these groupings are not meaningful to manufacturing, and Capacity Planning processes are used to translate them into manufacturing-oriented groupings (e.g., manpower, equipment, key suppliers).

**Production Plan**: The production counterpart of the sales forecast. It is driven by the sales forecast and target inventory/backlog levels; it is constrained by issues of how much (capacity) and how quickly (flexibility) changes can be made.

**Sales and Operations Planning (S&OP)**: The Top Management process of managing aggregate demand and supply for the business.

**Target inventory or backlog levels**: The desired level of inventory or backlog. These should be based on what's necessary to provide superior customer service without adversely affecting inventory investment and/or production efficiencies.

**Unit of measure**: For S&OP, this is typically units, cases, pounds, thousands, etc., but hardly ever dollars. Dollars are the primary unit of measure for the Business Plan; the Sales and Operations Plan is typically expressed in units that the customers buy and the company produces. Good S&OP processes, however, will translate the unit plans from that process into dollar terms to enable a direct comparison with the Business Plan, as shown in Figure 1.

## ACTION STEPS

- Learn about Sales and Operations Planning, its objectives, its processes, and the roles of the pre-S&OP and S&OP participants.
- Select an S&OP-knowledgeable person to facilitate the early meetings and to provide needed advice and other assistance.
- Determine product families, unit of measure, horizon, desired customer service levels, target inventories and/or backlogs, resource groupings, and any other necessary information.
- Modify and enhance sales forecasting processes as required.
- Begin the process with one product family and expand to other families rapidly as the process takes hold.

- Schedule the next twelve months' S&OP meetings in advance. This is vital, because the Top Management group tends to be extremely busy and has extensive travel commitments. Since these are decision-making meetings, attendance is critical. If the president can't be there, reschedule the S&OP meeting. If a vice president can't attend, someone must attend who is empowered to make decisions for him or her.

## PROBLEM-SOLVING

*"We're not consistent. We lurch back and forth between emphasizing customer service, which causes the inventories to go way up, and inventory reduction, which causes customer service to deteriorate. The executive who shouts the loudest determines the marching orders."*

Sales and Operations Planning establishes up front the desired levels of customer service and the inventories and backlog times necessary to meet them. Then Top Management, working as a team led by the president, manages these variables to achieve the company's goals.

*"We need better control over our budget. We set next year's operating budget late in the fiscal year. At that point we have more than twelve months of forward budget, which is our authority to spend. However, as the new year goes on, the amount of forward budget drops to nine months, then six, then three. But often we need to make spending commitments for things with longer lead times. Then we have to work around the system, and we can lose control."*

Sales and Operations Planning is done monthly, extends out for twelve or more months, and can readily be translated into dollars. As such, it can be a rolling monthly update to the Business Plan, hence the budget. These important elements in running a business can be kept far more current with S&OP. Further, S&OP can make creating next year's budget a lot easier.

*"There's a disconnect between our top-level plans and what happens day to day. We in Top Management really have little control over what goes on at the detailed operational level on the plant floor, in sales, and in purchasing."*

An important part of Sales and Operations Planning is to communicate the new plans, which have been tested in pre-S&OP for workability, to the operating-level people. The operating-level people are then held accountable for hitting the plans. Performance against the plans is measured and reported each month.

*"We're in a very seasonal business. Every year during the peak season, we go through the same fire drill: late shipments, lost orders because of our long lead times, enormous amounts of overtime, and heavy training and layoff costs. There's got to be a better way."*

Sales and Operations Planning has helped many companies in seasonal businesses to identify the relevant costs and benefits of more level Production Plans, make decisions on an informed basis, and then manage the business accordingly throughout the year.

*"We've been meeting once per quarter to review the sales forecasts and make changes to the budget. But that hasn't helped to solve our operating problems with demand and supply."*

Sales and Operations Planning is a monthly process. Virtually all manufacturing businesses are too dynamic and fast-paced. Further, Production Plans and inventory/backlog plans also need to be reviewed, not just the sales plan.

## SUMMARY

- Many companies have difficulty establishing a valid high-level game plan for sales, production, and inventory levels. Without valid plans, performance suffers: customer service is poor, production is inefficient, inventories are too high, or all of the above.
- Sales and Operations Planning (S&OP) is a Top Management

tool for establishing desired levels of customer service, inventory investment, and lead time for customer order fulfillment—and then to manage the business proactively to achieve the desired performance.

- The results from the monthly S&OP process are driven downward to impact directly the day-to-day activities in sales, purchasing, and on the plant floor.
- The results from the monthly S&OP process are driven upward, so that the company's overall Business Plan can reflect current realities and future plans. As such, Sales and Operations Planning is a pivotal process that links the top-level Business Plan with the day-to-day activities of running the business.
- Sales and Operations Planning enhances teamwork among the Top Management group. Further, it has helped executives in charge of specific areas of the business—marketing, manufacturing, finance—to see the business holistically, as a unit, rather than a series of discrete functions.

## INFORMATION RESOURCES

"Game Planning," David Rucinski, *Journal of the American Production and Inventory Control Society*, First Quarter 1982.

*Orchestrating Success: Improve Control of the Business with Sales and Operations Planning*, Richard C. Ling and Walter E. Goddard, Oliver Wight Publications, 1988.

## INTERNAL CROSS-REFERENCE

Your understanding of this topic may be enhanced by the following chapters:

I–6. Resource Planning: For Manufacturing, the Business, and the Enterprise

II–4. Forecasting Systems to Support World Class Competitiveness

## About the Author

Thomas F. Wallace is an independent consultant, author, and educator specializing in strategic planning and resource planning. In addition to editing this book, he is also the author/co-author of a number of books, including *MRP II: Making It Happen* (1990), *Customer-Driven Strategy* (1992), and *The Innovation Edge* (1994). Mr. Wallace is president of T. F. Wallace & Co. of Cincinnati, Ohio, and is a distinguished fellow at the Ohio State University Center for Excellence in Manufacturing Management.

# 1-6

# Resource Planning: For Manufacturing, the Business, and the Enterprise

*Darryl V. Landvater*

**IN A NUTSHELL**

Resource planning processes—called variously Manufacturing Resource Planning, Business Resource Planning, and Enterprise Resource Planning—have become the dominant operational/tactical planning tool in industry. Used by manufacturing businesses of all types and sizes, they enable effective planning and control of the sales, production, and logistics resources of the enterprise.

These tools enable people to take the top-level plans of the company, break them down into the specific tasks that must be accomplished on a day-to-day basis, keep the plans up-to-date as conditions change, and monitor performance.

The most widely used term in this field is Manufacturing Resource Planning (MRP II), and we'll use that for the balance of this chapter. MRP II is a blend of business procedures and computer software tools that creates an accurate simulation of the business, one that can be used to make decisions about customer order promising, production levels, purchasing, Capacity Planning, plant scheduling, and other key areas. MRP II–based plans are linked to the company's marketing and financial plans, making it possible for the entire company to operate as a team in which everyone uses a single set of numbers.

The unified plan leads to enhanced ownership and accountability, because each group has agreed to the numbers or has identified problems and had the plan changed to match reality. Finally, the various plans are used to monitor performance against the larger Business Plan.

## *Origins*

The development of what we now refer to as MRP II took approximately two decades. The advent of high-speed computers provided the power capable of carrying out key scheduling calculations in a reasonable period of time—hours or minutes instead of weeks—making it possible to answer the question, When do we need to order?

With this question answered, it became important to answer yet another question: When do we *really* need it? In the constantly changing world of manufacturing, a valid plan today might be worthless tomorrow. The need date is a moving target because of customer changes, engineering changes, inventory adjustments, scrap, overruns, capacity problems, vendor problems, and so forth. As a result, the scheduling problem must be solved again and again.

With the development of up-to-date and accurate schedules for material and capacity, several companies discovered that they had an accurate simulation of their business in the computer. They could link this simulation to their financial systems and accurately project scenarios for the future. This development was given the name MRP II (Manufacturing Resource Planning) to draw attention to the fact that it was a tool that would be used to plan and control *all* resources in a manufacturing company.

## MRP II *in Action*

Companies using MRP II can anticipate problems because their high-level Business Plans are connected in rack-and-pinion style to lower-level detailed plans; when the top-level plans have to be changed to accommodate the realities of the marketplace, the lower-level execution plans change in sync.

The flow of planning information at a company with MRP II is shown in Figure 1. It all starts with the Business Plan, which is usually stated in dollars; the plans for which people are accountable are stated in units or hours. The first step in converting financial plans into operational plans happens in the Sales and Operations Planning process (see chapter I–6). Sales and Operations Planning evaluates anticipated sales and planned production in terms of product families.

One output from this process is the Production Plan, which is typically stated as output by product family; for example, 200,000 small electric motors per month; 400,000 gallons of silicone fluid per week; or 3 steam turbines per quarter. Sales and Operations Planning is the responsibility of the president (or general manager) and staff.

To give the Production Plan a reality check, people use an abbreviated form of Capacity Planning called Rough-Cut Capacity Planning, a technique that looks at the demand on key resources. In most companies, ten or twenty key resources are evaluated before the plan is taken to the next level of detail. If the plan is not achievable, it is changed before proceeding.

The box labeled "Demand Management" refers to forecasting, customer order promising, distribution and interplant demands, and, where they exist, service demands. These activities represent the specific needs of customers within the planning and scheduling system.

The next level of detail is the Master Schedule, or Master Production Schedule (MPS)—a statement of production by item, date, and quantity. Within a family of small electric motors, for example, there may be 200 different types of motors. The Master Schedule shows

**FIGURE 1. MANUFACTURING RESOURCE PLANNING (MRP II)**

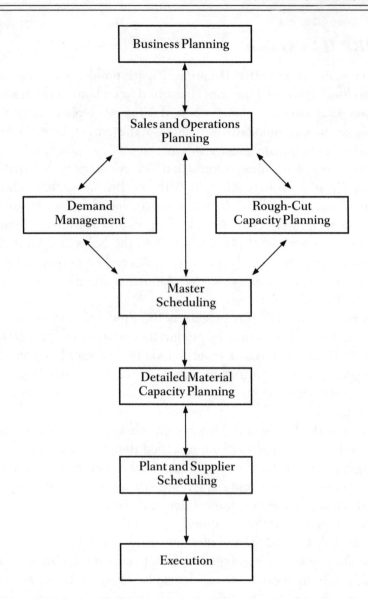

SOURCE: Darryl V. Landvater, *World Class Production and Inventory Management,* Oliver Wight Publications, 1993, p. 42.

how many of a given item are scheduled to be built in a given period for all the types of small electric motors. It reveals the schedule for as far out as the planning system extends (at least a year for most companies). The MPS, when summed up by product family, must equal the Production Plan for that family.

Material planning—often called Material Requirements Planning (MRP)—is also based on the Master Schedule. Material planning describes what material is needed and when. "Material" is a general term that can mean assemblies and subassemblies, fabricated items, purchased items, raw materials, intermediates (solutions, mixtures, formulations), bulk production, etc. Material planning answers the fundamental manufacturing equation (see below) for material needed for each item, and extends as far as the planning horizon.

Once you know what material is needed and when it is required, the next (and sometimes optional) step in the planning process is to determine the necessary capacity and its "need" dates at a more detailed level than what was calculated in rough-cut Capacity Planning. Capacity can be either equipment or manpower. Detailed Capacity Planning answers the fundamental manufacturing equation:

1. What are you going to make?—the material plan
2. What does it take to make it?—the routings
3. What do you have?—the planned capacities
4. What do you have to get?—any additional capacity

When a company using MRP II performs detailed Capacity Planning, it creates a plan for every work center or line and manpower level, and extends across the full planning horizon. In some industries, such as chemical processing, the company may not need detailed Capacity Planning. Chemical processors have a limited number of mixing vats and packaging lines, so rough-cut Capacity Planning may suffice for the company's Capacity Planning needs.

At this point in the planning process, the top-level plans have been broken down into specific tasks. People can evaluate the plans and ask, Where are the problems? What must happen for the plan to succeed? For example, it may be necessary to get 1,000 pounds per week of a particular raw material in order to meet the plan. Or the plan may require that a purchase order be pulled up for delivery four weeks earlier than its current due date. Capacity could also be a problem. The plan may call for 300 standard hours per week from a particular work center or line over the next six weeks.

Is there a way to make these things happen? If there is, the plan is valid, and people's energy can be channeled into execution. The best companies put an enormous effort into executing the plan once they determine that it's valid and achievable. If, however, the plan simply isn't realistic, it's important to face up to this fact. There are a number of reasons why it just may not be possible to make a plan happen, most of which relates to time or money. It may not be possible to increase capacity next week from 200 to 300 standard hours per week at a particular work center. And while it may be theoretically possible to charter a 747 to deliver material in time to meet a delivery, the cost would be prohibitively high. In situations where there is no other course, the plan is changed to accurately reflect what is actually going to happen.

Once the plan has passed the validity test, it must be communicated to the people responsible for making it happen. This is Plant and Supplier Scheduling, as shown in Figure 1. The material plan is communicated to suppliers, and the material and Capacity Plans are communicated to the plant. At this point, the top-level plans of the company have been broken down into the specific tasks for which people can be held accountable.

With the closed-loop plan shown in Figure 1 in place, accountability can be maintained and performance can be measured. Overall management effectiveness goes up dramatically when compared to the situation in which the business is run with an informal system. This is represented by the box labeled "Execution" in Figure 1.

The closed-loop approach has an added advantage in the management of change. Even the best-laid plans must change when unexpected events occur within the company (a strike, equipment breakdown, etc.), in the marketplace (a competitor goes out of business, a new technology makes your product obsolete, etc.), or within the political/economic arena (currency rates change, new regulations affect your product, etc.) As thousands of companies have learned, an effective closed-loop system makes it possible to see the impact of change at all levels, and to reposition the company to meet increased or decreased customer demand.

## *Benefits*

Surveys have shown consistent benefits across a broad range of companies that implement MRP II. Companies that use MRP II will experience more than a 200 percent return on investment (ROI). These companies also rate as Class A on the *Oliver Wight ABCD Checklist for Operational Excellence*. Companies that use MRP II poorly experience a 33 percent ROI, and score at the Class D level using the checklist. Companies in the middle, at the Class B and Class C levels, report more than 100 percent ROIs and 60 percent ROIs respectively. Benefits manifest themselves in the areas of improved customer service (resulting in greater sales), improved productivity, reduced purchase costs, and reduced inventories.

For a $60 million company or division, the costs to implement MRP II typically total $1 million. A smaller company will spend less, and a larger company will spend more. Interestingly, the costs are about the same for Class A companies and Class D companies. There is, however, a difference in how the companies spend their money; Class A companies spend more on education and data integrity, while Class D companies spend more on computer software.

## *Implementation*

MRP II can be implemented using what is called the Proven Path. The sixteen steps of the Proven Path are based on the accumulated experience of thousands of manufacturing companies over nearly twenty years.

Figure 2 is a graphic representation of the Proven Path. At zero, the starting point, a formal commitment is made to proceed with the implementation. Notice the number of activities to the left of this commitment; they're designed to ensure that a company makes an

## FIGURE 2. THE PROVEN PATH

[Figure 2: The Proven Path — a timeline diagram showing phases including Audit/Assessment #1, First-Cut Education, Vision Statement, Cost/Benefit Analysis, Project Organization, Performance Goals, Sales/Logistics/Manufacturing Process (Planning and Control, Data Management, Process Improvement, Software), Initial Education, Pilot and Cutover, Performance Measurements, Ongoing Education, and Audit/Assessment #2, plotted against Time (Weeks or Months).]

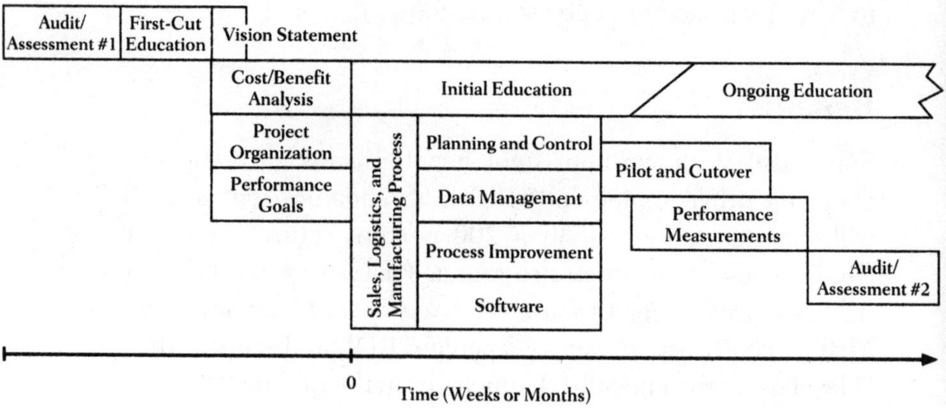

SOURCE: Darryl V. Landvater, *World Class Production and Inventory Management,* Oliver Wight Publications, 1993, p. 221.

informed decision, with a clear understanding of the efforts and resources involved.

The time frame for implementation will vary depending on the approach: company-wide or slice. Company-wide is implementation across an entire plant or division; the typical company-wide implementation may take twelve months to have all products on MRP, and eighteen months to MRP II, including the financial integration. Slice is an implementation for only a small segment of the business—a test to demonstrate success in a short period of time; a typical time frame for a slice would be three to four months.

## KEY CONCEPTS

**Business Resource Planning (BRP):** An approximate synonym for MRP II. It has the advantage of more clearly communicating the fact that resource planning applies to most of the entire *business*, not just the manufacturing department. MRP II does all of this, but the use of the term "manufacturing" sometimes leads people to mistakenly conclude otherwise.

**Class A**: A company scoring at the top level using the *Oliver Wight ABCD Checklist for Operational Excellence*. The checklist also contains thresholds for Class B, C, and D levels of performance.

**Closed-loop MRP**: A system in which MRP II is primarily a manufacturing system rather than a company-wide system. Because of the financial linkages, companies can use closed-loop MRP II as a means of managing the entire business.

**Enterprise Resource Planning (ERP)**: An approximate synonym for MRP II. It has the advantage of more clearly communicating the fact that resource planning applies to most of the entire *enterprise*, not just the manufacturing department, and that it can span a wide variety of locations. MRP II does all of this, but the use of the term "manufacturing" sometimes leads people to mistakenly conclude otherwise.

**Informal system**: A state that arises when the planning and control system (the formal system) cannot answer the question, What do I need and when do I need it? in sufficient detail and in a timely manner. Since decisions must be made, people go outside the planning and control system to get information that helps them decide what to do first, second, and so on.

**Integration**: MRP II works with other advanced manufacturing management approaches, not against them. Many companies have implemented one or several of the following: MRP II, Just-in-Time (Continuous Improvement), Total Quality, Employee Empowerment, supplier and customer partnerships, Design for Manufacturability, and business process redesign.

**Material Requirements Planning (MRP)**: The material planning part of MRP II.

**Manufacturing Resource Planning (MRP II)**: A far-reaching business process, consisting of a series of procedures and practices along with computer software, that allows effective planning and control in a manufacturing business.

**People are the "A" item**: The most successful companies using MRP II have put their focus on their employees—educating them, providing them with appropriate tools, and holding them accountable. They have not allowed themselves to be distracted by the computer and computer software aspects of MRP II.

**Proven Path**: A tested and proven approach for implementing MRP II.

**Silence is approval**: An approach to consensus that says, If the plan is not valid, it's your responsibility to feed back the information and get the plan changed. If we don't hear from you on why the plan is not achievable, then you are accountable for hitting it.

## ACTION STEPS

- Use the *Oliver Wight ABCD Checklist for Operational Excellence* to identify areas of strength and weakness in your organization.
- Based on ABCD assessment, begin implementing activities that will provide the greatest benefit. It's better to start with one area, successfully implement improvements, and then move on to another area than to attempt to change more than you can handle and have the implementation fail. No one tires of success, but nearly everyone is beaten down by repeated failure.
- Demonstrate consistency and dedication through your actions. Jumping from one initiative to another without completing the first generally ensures that none will be completed. Picking your implementation initiatives well, staying the course, and holding people accountable generate results.

## PROBLEM-SOLVING

*"We can't deliver on-time to our customers."*

Through the use of MRP II, you can gain control of the elements that result in on-time deliveries (matching production to customer needs, making and buying the right items at the right time, having the right capacity at the right time, having sales, manufacturing, finance, and new product development working as a team).

*"Competitors are able to deliver to customers in shorter lead times and/or reduced costs. We don't seem to be able to compete."*

Use MRP II to reduce the lead times to customers, to improve productivity, and reduce purchase costs.

*"We are not effective in implementing our top-level plans. When we try to determine where the problem is, it ends up with everyone pointing fingers at each other."*

Use MRP II to provide a single set of numbers that are based on the top-level plans. Everyone has an opportunity to identify where the numbers in the plan are not valid and have the plan changed. But then people are accountable for completing their tasks, and it will be clear where things are getting done and where they are not.

## *SUMMARY*

Resource planning processes—called variously Manufacturing Resource Planning (MRP II), Business Resource Planning, and Enterprise Resource Planning—have become the dominant operational/tactical planning tool in industry.

- MRP II takes the top-level plans of the company, breaks them down into the specific tasks that people must accomplish on a day-to-day basis, keeps the plans up-to-date as things change, and monitors people's performance against these plans.
- The MRP II process works as follows: Financial plans are translated into operational plans in the Sales and Operations Planning process. A rough-cut Capacity Plan is done to verify the validity of the plans. The plans are then broken down into the Master Production Schedule, which is further broken down into detailed material and Capacity Plans. These are checked for validity (at the detailed level), and if so, form the basis for measuring performance. If they are not valid, the plans are changed to reflect reality. These detailed plans are used in the financial system.

- There is a tested and proven approach for implementing MRP II, called the Proven Path. This series of sixteen steps focuses on business and people issues (such as data integrity and education) but also includes a step for installing the software.

## INFORMATION RESOURCES

*Manufacturing Resource Planning: MRP II Unlocking America's Productivity Potential*, revised edition, Oliver W. Wight, Oliver Wight Publications, 1984.

*World Class Production and Inventory Management*, Darryl V. Landvater, Oliver Wight Publications, 1993.

*MRP II: Making It Happen—The Implementers' Guide to Success with Manufacturing Resource Planning*, 2nd edition, Thomas F. Wallace, Oliver Wight Publications, 1990.

## INTERNAL CROSS-REFERENCE

Your understanding of this topic may be enhanced by the following chapters:

    I–5. Sales and Operations Planning: Top Management's Handle on the Business

    II–3. Efficient Consumer Response (ECR)

    VI–1. Enterprise Logistics Management (ELM)

---

### About the Author

Darryl V. Landvater is president of Oliver Wight Video Productions, chairman of Oliver Wight Publications, and an Oliver Wight consultant. He is the author of *World Class Production and Inventory Management* and *The Standard System*. He also authored a number of the Oliver Wight video library modules. Mr. Landvater holds a B.S. in engineering physics from Cornell University and is a former teacher-trainer in the Peace Corps.

# PART II
# CUSTOMERS AND PRODUCTS

1. **Being a World Class Customer**
   *Patricia E. Moody*

2. **Understanding the Voice of the Customer**
   *William Barnard*

3. **Efficient Consumer Response (ECR)**
   *André J. Martin*

4. **Forecasting Systems to Support World Class Competitiveness**
   *Stephen A. DeLurgio, Sr.*

5. **New Approaches to New Product Development**
   *Douglas Daetz*

6. **Quality Function Deployment: Breakthrough Tool for Product Development**
   *William Barnard*

**W**ORLD CLASS MANUFACTURING begins and ends with the customer. Acquiring and maintaining a customer-centered focus throughout the organization can be considered a prerequisite for true success in a manufacturing enterprise. A variation of the Golden Rule applies here: Treat your customers as you want your suppliers to treat you.

Part II begins, therefore, with a discussion of how to enable your suppliers to provide you with superior performance in **Being a World Class Customer** by Trish Moody, editor of *Target* magazine. Next we move into a discussion of powerful techniques to learn what the customers really want in **Understanding the Voice of the Customer** by Bill Barnard from the University of Dayton.

André Martin, CEO of LogicNet, then explores new developments in linking together manufacturers, distributors, and retailers in **Efficient Consumer Response (ECR)**. This is followed by a discussion of effective forecasting techniques in **Forecasting Systems to Support World Class Competitiveness** by Steve DeLurgio from the University of Missouri at Kansas City.

Part II concludes with two chapters on developing—quickly and effectively—new products that delight the customers. These are **New Approaches to New Product Development** by Doug Daetz from Hewlett-Packard and **Quality Function Deployment: Breakthrough Tool for Product Development**, also by Bill Barnard.

# Being a World Class Customer
## Patricia E. Moody

**IN A NUTSHELL**

The concept of world class producer is now familiar to most manufacturers. It conjures up the image of a company that produces high-quality goods, operates with a minimum of inventory or waste, moves new products to market quickly, and so forth. The concept of world class customer is less well understood, yet it goes hand-in-hand with the first. In fact, in their relationship with supplier companies, producers need to be world class customers if they want to attract and maintain the best sources of supply. The number of first-rate suppliers is limited—particularly in industries like electronics—and their output is finite. Ensuring a share of that supply output requires more than simply paying supplier invoices.

Simply stated, if you want to be a *world class company*, if you want to maintain access to the best of the supply base and to the technical expertise of that supply base, then you must be a *world class customer*. The best suppliers hire and fire their customers. From their viewpoint, dealing with second-rate customers is costly and disruptive to their own finely tuned operations. They want to deal only with the best.

The importance of being a world class customer is illustrated in the case of one of the best U.S. printed circuit board suppliers, which set out to reduce its scrap and rework expense. Of its pool of established customers, many forced this supplier to deal with inconsistent specifications, their own unstable schedules, multiple quality requirements, and other special needs, all of which contributed to costs, longer lead times, and occasional errors for the supplier. Motorola, one of the supplier's customers, on the other hand, had its own house in order and offered valuable engineering and training assistance to this supplier. Motorola and two other firms were the type of customers that the circuit board supplier needed to work "smart" and to improve its own skills. The supplier's conclusion? Since it could sell all of its output to just the best customers, why bother with those that were the sources of its added costs and errors? This supplier needed customers that listened to its production and design issues, respected schedule stability, communicated its specifications and schedules with clarity, and reinforced its willingness to be a long-term partner with accessibility and commitment.

The circuit board supplier fired its less desirable customers and expanded its business with Motorola and its other world class customers.

The importance of the customer-supplier relationship has been understood for some time. Major manufacturers have recognized the need for programs to strengthen supplier performance and have responded with quality audits, certification, testing, visiting, training, and threats. These programs have been single-mindedly directed toward the supplier, saying, in effect: This is what you must do to sell to us.

Some companies, however, have discovered that this focus on the supplier represents only *half* of the equation, and that if they want their suppliers to do the best job for them, they must look at their own operations and how they deal with suppliers.

An early example of this discovery was Motorola's Six Sigma

quality standard. Motorola came to understand that its suppliers would not deliver Six Sigma quality without very specific information, assistance, and process instruction shared early in the design cycle; Motorola would need to create a relationship with its suppliers based upon communication and trust.

## *Characteristics of World Class Customers*

World class customers are characterized by their adoption of what have come to be recognized as the Seven Drivers of Breakthrough Partnering® with suppliers. These drivers are:

1. Excellent quality
2. Timeliness
3. Flexibility
4. Superior communication
5. The attitude of Continuous Improvement
6. A habit of collaboration
7. Trust

The supply management processes of world class customers are as important as their products. In a 1993 survey conducted by six large customers, suppliers agreed that critical success factors include management behavior and communication; suppliers mention honesty, ethics, and responsiveness as key. World class customers invite suppliers to supplier advisory councils, where common product and process problems can be addressed; they also share scheduling and new product information, and monitor their suppliers' situations through confidential surveys.

Good customers have a number of characteristics that are genuinely beneficial to both partners. These include:

- Awareness of and attentiveness to their suppliers' needs
- A record of keeping promises made to suppliers
- A willingness to share plans and information with suppliers

- A willingness to explore process and product improvement with suppliers
- A pattern of providing quick responses to problems raised by suppliers
- An active hunger for feedback from key suppliers on all functions that touch the supplier, and corrective action when required

Supplier companies are measurably aided when their customers have these characteristics. Jim Schwarz, president of OMNI-Circuits, a Motorola supplier, credits his customer with much of his company's exponential growth. Without Motorola's dedication to quality and engineering help, this supplier would have experienced lower growth.

Honda's 256 suppliers are held to tough quality and delivery standards, but they receive as much help from Honda as they can absorb. Its supplier development program, BP (Best Product, Best Partner, Best Position), allows Honda procurement professionals, including engineers, to spend up to thirteen weeks on-site, helping suppliers solve their productivity and quality challenges. Honda's BP program, representing more than sixty suppliers, is a systematic approach to supplier development from which only two suppliers have withdrawn. In exchange for supplier resources, time, effort, and commitment, Honda, as a model customer, dedicates one or two of its professionals to working with suppliers that sign on for the program. For example, Honda once sent its own people to help a small electronics assembly facility that had at several times been a problem supplier. The first activity of the Honda team—picking up a broom to sweep the area—surprised everyone, but set an important example.

The BP program continued at this facility for thirteen weeks, costing Honda about $100,000 in meals, travel, and missed time for the two Honda professionals. Investments of this type are small, however, relative to the payback. The *smallest* productivity gain experienced among sixty suppliers that have experienced the program has been 21 percent.

## *"Same Face"*

Another characteristic of world class customers is "same face"—i.e., no matter where the supplier touches the customer's organization, whether it is engineering, accounts payable, materials, or production, the supplier always receives the same message. Suppliers are put off by the run-around or different stories from different customer functions. They need to hear a *consistent* message repeated in the same language. A customer's stated policies and day-to-day activities should be consistent, with no gaps between what the procedures manual proscribes for supplier selection, for example, and the way buyers narrow down the supply base. When a supplier representative talks with purchasing buyers, the specifications and manufacturing tolerances required for new products should be no different from what engineering asks for.

Honda personnel refer to this "same face" concept as *kintori amay* (samuri warrior candy), the name of a traditional confection; no matter where this spaghetti-like candy is cut in cross-section, the same samurai warrior face appears!

## *Benefits*

1. *Cost savings.* World class customers lower their administrative costs by communicating better with suppliers. They remove administrative and management layers that interfere with good communication. EMC Corporation's in-plant purchasing scheme, in which supplier representatives operate *inside* its plant, exemplifies this cost-saving approach. Two electronics distributors have each agreed to dedicate one professional to working inside EMC, replacing sales personnel. These individuals access EMC's planning systems, chase down requirement questions, and resolve delivery problems—saving the suppliers and EMC time and money. Under a traditional buyer/salesperson approach, the intervening layers would add time and expense to the procurement cycle.

2. *Time savings.* World class customers cut lead times by giving suppliers as much information as they can early in the process. Time

accumulates in the most expensive phase of a product cycle—the design phase—when sourcing, design, and manufacturing process decisions add up to total cycle time. SUN Microsystems, Picturetel, Solectron, Motorola, and many other companies have found ways to leverage supplier expertise in product designs that incorporate their ideas sooner and more frequently through closer linkages—electronic data interface, schedule sharing, in-plant supplier representative schemes, and supplier advisory councils.

3. *Better products and processes.* In a June 1993 article in the *Boston Globe*, Michael Schrage, an MIT researcher and industry analyst, recounts a highly instructive story about Procter & Gamble's chief executive E. L. Artzt. The consumer products giant had a terrible problem producing the thin rubber leggings that stop leaks in its Pampers disposable diapers. According to Artzt, the thinness of the rubber caused it to "creep" and made high-speed production of the diapers virtually impossible.

In desperation Procter & Gamble invited a supplier into the plant to help solve the problem. The supplier's people looked at the problem and said two words, "Golf balls." The supplier happened to be the leading manufacturer of the ultra-thin, tightly wound rubber filaments in golf ball cores. Based on its filaments experience, the supplier was able to solve P&G's production problem with a minimum of fuss and expense.

4. *Improved customer organization and professional skills.* Suppliers benefit from the pressure that world class customers apply to their quality and delivery systems. But customers also benefit. Customer personnel learn new communication skills when they spend time with suppliers (the best way to learn new techniques is to teach them to someone else). And in explaining to suppliers how their organization works, customers are, in effect, forced to map their own processes.

## KEY CONCEPTS

**BP (Best Product, Best Partner, Best Position)**: A thirteen-week supplier development program of Honda in which the automaker and the supplier work together in a team environment to improve supplier performance.

**"Same face"**: A term that derives from the spaghetti-like Japanese candy called *kintori amay*; no matter how you cut the candy in cross-section, the image of a samuri warrior is seen. The parallel for the supplier is that no matter which customer function the supplier deals with, the same consistent message comes through.

**Supplier (advisory) councils**: Meetings convened by a customer that bring together a number of supplier to work on product and process problems.

**Supplier surveys**: The documents that customers send out to evaluate supplier performance.

**World class customer**: An enterprise that manifests the Seven Drivers of Breakthrough Partnering®.

**World class customer surveys**: Specific surveys that customers use with their supplier to elicit feedback.

## ACTION STEPS

- Eliminate "trust destroyers." A survey by the Association for Manufacturing Excellence indicates strong feelings among suppliers on the subject of "trust destroyers." A steel industry customer talks quality and service, but buys on price alone. Another expects a formal presentation on the supplier's quality system, then makes the purchase decision on price alone. Sealed bid quotes, price-only meritability, and leveraging one supplier against another rank at the top of the list of "trust destroyers."
- Listen for clear signals. Establish a regular, consistent, and formal feedback mechanism to your suppliers. Supplier surveys and supplier councils are among the mechanisms that work.
- Share important information. Honda of America shares designs, schedules, cost data, and special topic information with suppliers. Remember that all communication instruments need review;

evaluate for usefulness all paperwork routinely initiated or processed by purchasing customers, such as purchase orders, blanket orders, weekly schedules, invoices, and shipping reports.

- Invest in relationships. Supplier councils, supplier recognition days, joint benchmarking forums, and other open-door activities characterize world class customers.
- Eliminate the boundaries between you and your suppliers. When the distinctions between customer and supplier partners begin to blur, customer/supplier partnership teams take on the appearance of a virtual company, a new organization formed with elements of all contributing partners.

## *PROBLEM-SOLVING*

*"We are a small plastic component supplier. Our customers talk quality and delivery, but in the end they hammer us on price alone. What can we do?"*

This is a difficult challenge for smaller suppliers. The good news is that companies have become sensitized to suppliers who want customers for life. Nypro, a Massachusetts custom plastic injection molding company, has reduced its customer base to concentrate on high-quality, world class customers like Gillette and Johnson & Johnson. The challenge of partnering and becoming a world class customer is communication and trust—the first steps are regular feedback, and specific recommendations about products that show your knowledge and understanding of the customer's market challenges.

*"Our customers hound us with a wide assortment of supplier certification audits and plant visits."*

Some of these audits draw on the same resource material, and world class customers recognize that certification takes time from building product. A number of companies use ISO 9000 registration as a substitute for some on-site customer visits. Leading companies like Hewlett-Packard, Motorola, and AT&T are pioneering standardization and consolidation of audits.

*"Our buyers complain that suppliers don't give us engineering data in time to make changes for current deliveries."*

Cross-functional customer/supplier teams solve many integration problems before they happen. Buyers and planners need access to engineering and production personnel. Other benefits accrue from teams—new manufacturing ideas, as well as training opportunities for both sides.

*"We ask our suppliers how we are doing with our annual scorecard, but they always say we are four stars! We need feedback that will truly help us improve our processes, but they always say we are four stars! We know that we're not that good."*

Third-party customer/supplier surveys protect supplier confidentiality and build trust in the partnership. Try developing your own survey; have a neutral third party handle the mailing, compilation, analysis, and feedback. Make the responses easy to complete (no more than fifteen minutes' time is reasonable), and do not require the respondents to reveal their names. Response rates are higher when 1) questionnaire results are shared with the respondents, and 2) when actions result from the questionnaire.

## SUMMARY

- World class suppliers in a number of industries can pick and choose whom they will do business with; they generally find it cost ineffective to deal with non–world class customers.
- Companies need to form strong partnerships with suppliers to build competitive advantage. These partnerships are mutually advantageous.
- Traditional purchasing practices such as bid-and-quote, leveraging suppliers, and maintaining multiple suppliers are barriers to the close relationship upon which customer/supplier partnerships are based.

## INFORMATION RESOURCES

*Breakthrough Partnering: Creating a Collective Enterprise Advantage*, Patricia E. Moody, Oliver Wight Publications, 1993.

"Take Down the Walls," Patricia E. Moody, *Target* magazine, September–October 1992, vol. 8, no. 5.

## INTERNAL CROSS-REFERENCE

Your understanding of this topic may be enhanced by the following chapters:

III–4. Crossing Boundaries with Teamnets

VI–2. Supplier Quality Management (SQM)

VI–3. Supplier Scheduling: Linking Suppliers with Customers

### About the Author

Patricia E. Moody is a manufacturing management consultant certified by the Institute of Management Consultants. She has more than twenty years' experience in the industry as a practitioner and a consultant, including seven years with Rath and Strong, and as president of her own management training and development firm, Patricia E. Moody, Inc. She is the author of *Breakthrough Partnering*, and co-author of *Strategic Manufacturing* (Business One Irwin, 1990). She is editor of *Target* magazine and is on the board of the Northeast Region of the Association for Manufacturing Excellence.

# 11-2

# Understanding the Voice of the Customer
## William Barnard

**IN A NUTSHELL**

The 1990s will go down in business history as the decade of the customer. Understanding customers—identifying who they are and knowing what delights them—is a primary survival issue in this decade and will remain so in the years to come.

Most companies are *convinced* that they understand their customers intimately, and that the voice of these customers finds its way directly into their product development and other important business functions. Given their market research budgets, many companies have every right to be so convinced. But the facts indicate otherwise: traditional market research techniques support the status quo and rarely lead to innovative discoveries regarding what customers want. Many companies have no clear idea as to *who their customers are*, and *what influences customer purchasing decisions*.

Understanding customers and their wants has always been a troublesome process. As early as 1954, Peter Drucker underscored this difficulty when he wrote in *The Practice of Management*: "What the customer considers value is so complicated that it can only be answered by the customer himself. Management should not even try to guess at it—it should always go to the customer in a systematic quest for the answer."

The chronic failure of companies to "go to the customer in a systematic quest" for what they *value* is plainly seen in the failure rate of new products. Estimates of new product failure rates range from 80 to 95 percent. Some companies, however, appear to do much better than others. Hewlett-Packard, for example, is reported to have a very high success rate with its new personal computer products. Integration of customer values into its products has brought it tremendous market success. Other U.S. companies such as Ford, Motorola, and Chrysler also have achieved success by listening to and heeding the voice of the customer.

## *The Whole Product Package*

The idea of the voice of the customer and its integration into the product planning process reflects today's more holistic definition of a product. Traditionally, a product was articulated in terms of physical specifications and functions; but product planners today understand product in a broader sense—as a combination of all "values" wanted by a customer. To be successful in the marketplace, new products must be planned with these broad-ranging, customer-articulated values as a starting point, and the details of specifications and functions derived from those values.

Adopting this comprehensive product definition requires a shift in the way companies identify markets and understand the needs and wants of customers. The voice of the customer is essential in all phases of the product or service definition. Including the voice of the customer in product development efforts has provided the following positive results:

- A more complete product picture, including "value" targets for the customer segment
- A greater awareness of the components of the overall product

picture, making it easier to analyze by a multifunctional company team
- A clearer understanding of customer expectations by product development teams, especially those that use planning tools such as Quality Function Deployment (QFD)
- A source of knowledge that can be used to clarify product development issues

## *What Is the Voice of the Customer?*

The voice of the customer is what the customer communicates—through words, writing, and action—as needs and wants. In *Hearing the Voice of the Market*, authors Vincent Barabba and Gerald Zaltman extend this definition slightly to include what the customer "is willing to pay for." To truly hear this voice, it is essential to focus on these questions:

- How do customers buy?
- On what basis will customers differentiate our products from those of our competitors?
- How will customers determine if our products are worth the price we charge?
- How can customers be reached?
- Which of our product development activities will indicate that we are listening to customer needs?

## *Benefits*

Heeding the voice of the customer in the development of products and services produces both external and internal benefits. External benefits are observed in terms of unit sales and profits that conform to product development plans; internal benefits are experienced in product development time and cost reductions.

Like many improvement initiatives, programs that attempt to bring the customer voice into the product development process may create an additional expense at the beginning of the paradigm shift in the way we develop products—principally for market research; but from the perspective of total product expense, this expense is minimal and pays for itself many times over.

## *The Voice of the Customer Process*

Six steps are involved in identifying the voice of the customer:

1. Identify market, segments, and customers
2. Select a method to gather the "voice"
3. Extract and reduce the data gathered
4. Analyze the data gathered
5. Make and test decisions
6. Communicate the knowledge gained

For purposes of this chapter we will focus on describing the first two in detail; the other four activities are unique to each company.

*Identify market, segments, and customers* Market segmentation is one of the fundamental principles of modern marketing and, according to Northwestern University's Phillip Kotler, means: "Subdividing the market into understandable parts, any one of which can be selected as a target segment to be reached with a distinct marketing mix." Except for staple, commodity-type items, new products have discrete and identifiable classes of potential buyers. Market segmentation helps us identify these potential buyers, and through this identification, determine their needs and wants and create products for them in ways that make the most of limited company resources.

*Select a method to gather the "voice"* Market research provides many tools for acquiring the voice of the customer. Two powerful tools for modern-day product development are In-context Customer Visits and Choice Modeling. Both provide a clear understanding of the benefits that customers desire and the criteria customers use for making decisions.

- In-context Customer Visits have the objective of determining customer needs from direct observation of customers as they go through daily routines and use certain products and services in their own environment.
- In-context Customer Visits help create a rapport between company and customer and help align the company's understanding of wants and needs with the customer's own understanding. They also indicate the extent to which current product technologies are capable of fulfilling those wants and needs. The activities of these visits—observing, learning, and dialoguing—have much in common with good sales calls. But in-context visits have a much different objective; they do not bring the customer and company together to make a sale, but to help the company learn the customer's needs.

In-context visits also contradict one of business's most cherished myths—the idea that customers don't know what they want today, much less in the future. The fact is that customers always know what they want, but they cannot always verbalize it. In-context visits give the customer—speaking in his own voice—every opportunity to express his wants, or for company team members to observe and experience the "need" or "want."

- Choice Modeling (sometimes called "predictive modeling") is a research method for determining which attributes, or characteristics, of a product or service will increase the probability that the customer will buy. The term "attribute" is used broadly, encompassing product features, how well the product works, how it's wrapped, priced, etc. The objective of Choice Modeling research is to predict the set of product characteristics with the greatest potential for meeting customer expectations and generating customer delight.

Using questionnaires that ask customers to assign importance weights to various product characteristics, researchers can create a profile of the product and the extent to which each characteristic is viewed favorably by customers. The importance of each product characteristic as it relates to winning or losing customers can also be determined.

## KEY CONCEPTS

**Choice Modeling**: A research method for determining which attributes, or characteristics, of a product or service will increase the probability that the customer will buy.

**In-context Customer Visit**: A market research method whose objective is to determine customer needs from direct observation of customers as they go through daily routines and use certain products and services. Emphasis is placed on understanding the context in which products are used.

**Market segmentation**: The process of subdividing a market into understandable parts, any one of which can be selected as a target segment to be reached with a distinct marketing mix.

**Quality Function Deployment (QFD)**: A systematic process for planning products and services. QFD helps managers bring together all the elements needed to define the product requirements that will satisfy and delight the customer, and to develop the means to provide that satisfaction.

**Voice of the customer**: What the customer communicates—through words, writing, and action—as needs and wants and what the customer is "willing to pay for."

**Wants and needs**: The wants and needs of customers for products and services, expressed in their own words. A product development team must determine wants and needs in order to make market-based decisions on product characteristics, pricing, etc.

## PROBLEM-SOLVING

*"Our products don't meet profit and/or volume projections. We're always reducing our prices to get the deal."*

The company should evaluate the segments for which it is designing products. It may be competing in a segment that has a position leader or many other competitors. If there is a position leader then the company should conduct research to determine the product function/feature set that will satisfy customer wants and needs more completely than do competitors. Also, the company may use research to uncover other product possibilities for this or other market segments.

*"We compete in markets that are technology-driven and fast-changing. How can we keep up with customer wants and needs?"*

The use of In-context Customer Visits, QFD, and, potentially, choice models that have the ability to include large (60 to 100) topics and carry out simulations that predict customer choice behavior, will support your understanding of customer (and competitor) potential reactions to your product decisions. Simulations done prior to product definition and during development, when the competition releases product before you do, can help predict customer reactions to product decisions made by you and your competitors.

## SUMMARY

- The voice of the customer is a critical ingredient in any product or service development effort.
- Integration of the customer's voice into the product planning process creates a holistic definition of a product that extends beyond physical specifications, colors, and functions to all "value" wanted by a customer.
- The voice of the customer is systematically revealed through the use of market research, including In-context Customer Visits, QFD, and Choice Modeling.

## INFORMATION RESOURCES

*Competitive Advantage, Creating and Sustaining Superior Performance,* Michael Porter, The Free Press, 1985.
*Fast Cycle Time: How to Align Purpose, Strategy, and Structure for Speed,* Christopher Meyer, The Free Press, 1993.

*Hearing the Voice of the Market,* Vincent Barabba and Gerald Zaltman, Harvard Business School Press, 1990.

*The Battle for Your Mind,* Al Ries and Jack Trout, Warner Books, 1981.

*The Practice of Management,* Peter F. Drucker, Harper and Row, 1954.

## INTERNAL CROSS-REFERENCE

Your understanding of this topic may be enhanced by the following chapters:

I–3. Linking Customers to Strategies via Quality Function Deployment (QFD)

II–6. Quality Function Deployment: Breakthrough Tool for Product Development

---

### About the Author

William Barnard is a practitioner, educator, and author who works in customer-integrated strategy and product development with companies such as Motorola, Hewlett-Packard, NCR, AT&T, and numerous small businesses. He is currently a senior fellow at the University of Dayton's Center for Competitive Change. He is co-author of *The Innovation Edge: Creating Strategic Breakthroughs Using the Voice of the Customer.*

# Efficient Consumer Response (ECR)

*André J. Martin*

**IN A NUTSHELL**

Efficient Consumer Response (ECR) refers to the control of information and product from point of manufacturing to the point of sale, with the intent of eliminating waste and reducing cost across an entire distribution pipeline. ECR is also known as quick response; Just-in-Time distribution; continuous replenishment; partners in merchandise flow; and stockless materials management.

With ECR, the entire pipeline is driven by scanned data at the point of sale. Replenishment orders are communicated via electronic data interchange (EDI) to direct store delivery (DSD), to retail distribution centers (DCs), to wholesaler/distributors, and to manufacturers. This ensures that the right amount of product is delivered in a timely fashion, eliminating unnecessary inventory in the pipeline, eliminating stockouts, and eliminating the need for each pipeline participant to conduct its own forecast. In essence, ECR makes it possible for participants in a distribution pipeline to substitute information for inventory. The benefits to them are increased product velocity and the competitive benefits of significantly lower costs.

## *Origins*

ECR evolved during the early 1990s. Grocery retailers, distributors, suppliers, and brokers began looking for new ways to regain the competitive edge they had lost to mass merchandisers and other retail channels that had refined their pipeline logistics since the mid-1980s. Wal-Mart was a pioneer in this field, having achieved as much as a 5 percent cost advantage over competitors by using information to streamline its distribution pipelines; that translated into enormous profit improvements.

Wal-Mart's early success with ECR (called quick response at the time), painted a clear picture of the future for others in the retail world: ECR was going to become an essential ingredient for success. In 1990 a study by several major grocery chains and five industry associations revealed that the grocery industry could 1) cut $30 billion of waste from its distribution pipelines, and 2) cut inventory across the pipelines from 104 days to 61 days. Together, these represented 11 percent of consumer prices. According to the study, which was conducted by Kurt Salmon Associates, Inc., the industry would need to improve in four areas if these stunning reductions were to be realized: efficient store assortment; efficient replenishment; efficient promotion; and efficient product development. A number of grocery chains, Giant Foods being one, and companies in other industries are now implementing these ECR initiatives and are poised to reap significant rewards in the years ahead.

## *ECR in Action*

The underlying concept of ECR is "natural pull"—i.e., replace the product across the entire pipeline as it sells. Scanned data drives the entire "pull" process. Consider what happens when a consumer makes a purchase in a retail setting. First, the inventory is automatically updated. Rules within the inventory management system trigger a replenishment order when the inventory drops to a certain level. Replenishment information is communicated electronically, and generates a further set of activities at the retail DC and wholesaler/distributor level, such as preparing orders, loading trucks with product identified by shelf, and deploying the trucks to the stores. Replenishment information also enables buyers at retail DCs and wholesaler/distributor organizations to better manage their own inventory and procurement requirements.

Information flows effectively through an ECR pipeline because the various pipeline organizations use well-established and accepted EDI standards established by the Uniform Code Council and other organizations. That underscores the ability of ECR to use readily available and proven tools such as EDI, bar-coding, and Distribution Resource Planning (DRP).

## *Benefits*

Companies that participate in ECR-based distribution pipelines realize a number of significant benefits, all of which lead to a competitive advantage. The major benefits include:

- Greatly improved inventory management. Because replenishment is driven by actual sales, practices such as forward buying and diverting, which tend to clog the pipeline with excess inventory that diminishes profits, can be reduced or eliminated.
- Reduced forecasting requirements. Ideally, forecasting needs to be done only at the point of uncertainty: the retail shelf. Traditionally, each pipeline organization created its own forecast. ECR makes it possible to forecast *independent* demand at the point of final sale, then drive the rest of the pipeline with demand that is calculated (often called *dependent* demand). The ability to work with calculated demand gives pipeline partners a tremendous advantage over competitors. By no longer having to forecast independently, they no longer have to guess. They can accurately produce and ship product based on actual sales, and they can shift the resources formerly used for forecasting to other business activities. In 1994, Nabisco and Kellogg will no longer have to forecast one of their key accounts, Giant Foods; Giant will electronically share its

time-phased requirements with both suppliers. By eliminating the need to forecast this large account, Nabisco and Kellogg can eliminate a great deal of uncertainty about Giant and greatly improve their ability to synchronize logistic and manufacturing resources.

- Better service to the consumer. Companies that participate in ECR pipelines experience fewer stockouts because product is replaced as it is sold. Moreover, automated replenishment eliminates the need for store employees to walk the aisles and determine what needs to be ordered (a job often relegated to part-timers and students with insufficient expertise to make informed reordering decisions).
- More attractive pricing. Eliminating hidden logistics costs makes lower prices possible. As surprising as it may be, logistics can account for as much as one third of the total cost of producing products and getting them to the store shelves.
- More efficient execution of manufacturing and distribution functions. ECR pipeline information is communicated electronically and fed directly into the logistics and manufacturing systems of suppliers. This enables suppliers to better synchronize their resources to the needs of their retail partners.

## *Distribution Resource Planning (DRP): The "Heart and Soul" of ECR*

Successful ECR required proficiency in resource planning and scheduling. This means implementing and refining the proven concepts of Distribution Resource Planning (DRP)—from the end of the production line to the retail store shelves. At the plant level, DRP is often integrated with Manufacturing Resource Planning (MRP II) and Just-in-Time/TQC.

Distribution Resource Planning is a management process designed to ensure that supply sources are able to meet demand. This is accomplished through three phases:

*Phase 1* DRP receives input from:

- Sales forecasts by stock-keeping-units (SKUs) by distribution location

- Customer orders for current and future delivery
- Available inventory for sale by stock-keeping-unit (SKU) by distribution location
- Outstanding purchase orders and manufacturing orders by product purchased and/or manufactured
- Distribution and manufacturing and purchasing lead times
- Modes of transport used as well as deployment frequency
- Safety stock policies by SKU by distribution location

*Phase 2* DRP generates a time-phased model of resource requirements necessary to support the company's logistics strategy. The requirements include:

- Which product is needed and where and when it is needed
- Transportation capacity needed by mode of transport by distribution location
- Required space, manpower, and equipment capacity
- Required inventory investment
- Required level of production and/or purchases by product and by supply source

*Phase 3* DRP compares the required resources to what is currently available and what will be available in the future. It then recommends what actions must be taken to expedite or delay production and/or purchases, thereby synchronizing supply and demand. This third phase forces integration and feedback into the system, thus closing the loop between manufacturing, purchasing, distribution, and the customers.

The primary benefits of DRP extend to five areas:

*Marketing* DRP improves customer service through on-time deliveries; more effective promotion planning; advance visibility of product availability; better working relationships with distribution, manufacturing, and the rest of the company; and the ability to help the customer improve inventory management.

*Physical distribution* Reduced freight costs as a result of fewer rushed shipments and improved scheduling of regular shipments; lower inventories; reduced warehouse space; better obsolescence control; reduced distribution costs from the DCs to the customers; better coordination between the distribution operation, manufacturing, and purchasing; and improved budgeting.

*Manufacturing* Significantly more accurate information for Master Scheduling; showing true, up-to-date needs of the distribution network; better working relationship with the distribution organization; lower costs due to fewer surprises and sudden disruption of manufacturing schedules.

*Finance* Better cash flow projections; better prediction of inventory levels; more accurate budgets; the ability to carry out financial planning when unexpected changes within the company or marketplace occur.

*Purchasing* Better information about what to buy, when to buy it, and in what quantities to order; better indication of which POs need to be expedited or unexpedited; elimination of paperwork through the enhanced use of EDI to communicate time-phased future requirements; improved service to internal customers.

While the savings that DRP offers will differ in each area of a distribution business, experience reveals that more than 90 percent of the typical costs of distribution can be reduced by using the DRP management process.

## KEY CONCEPTS

**Dependent demand**: Demand that can be calculated based on scanned data from actual sales, existing inventory positions, lead times, etc.

**Distribution Resource Planning (DRP)**: A resource planning and scheduling approach to distribution management that ensures the right product is available at the right place at the right time. Unlike traditional approaches to logistics management, DRP enables its users to plan both materials and capacity.

**Distribution pipeline**: A chain of linked organizations that includes the factory, warehouses, distribution centers, and retail stores.

**Efficient Consumer Response (ECR)**: An approach that substitutes information for inventory to reduce cost and improve service for all trading partners. Also known as quick response; Just-in-Time distribution; continuous replenishment; partners in merchandise flow; and stockless material's management.

**Independent demand**: Demand that must be forecasted. In reality, independent demand occurs only at the end of the pipeline—the point of final sale.

**Manufacturing pipeline**: A chain of suppliers of raw materials and packaging linked to their customers—manufacturers that produce semifinished and finished products.

**Natural pull**: The concept of replacing what is sold on a real-time basis, as opposed to "pushing" products in anticipation of a sale. Basing business on pull eliminates uncertainty across the distribution pipeline and enables the trading partners to align their resources so as to smooth the flow of product from manufacturer to retail shelf.

**Product velocity**: The speed at which product moves through a manufacturing and/or distribution pipeline. The greater the velocity, the less inventory required and the lower the operating costs.

**SKU**: Stock-keeping-unit, a specific product in a specific inventory location.

## ACTION STEPS

- Commit the total company to change to ECR. This can be done only by Top Management.
- Determine the extent to which the company currently has control of information and product from point of manufacturing to the point of sale.
- Analyze the distribution pipeline for opportunities to substitute information for inventory.
- See to it that key participants in the pipeline are proficient in resource planning and scheduling. This means implementing and refining the proven concepts of Distribution Resource Planning from the end of the production line to the retail store shelves.
- At the factory level, integrate DRP with MRP II and Just-in-Time/TQC.

## PROBLEM-SOLVING

*"After a major promotion, some of our retail stores are swimming in inventory, while others have run out well before the sale was over. How can we eliminate this situation?"*

Implement DRP at the store level so that actual scanned sales in retail stores drive the entire distribution pipeline. By electronically linking with your distribution and manufacturing partners, you set the stage for rapidly communicating changes in consumer demand patterns, thus enabling the partners to respond faster, eliminate a great deal of uncertainty, increase product velocity, and lower their operating costs—all while maintaining exceptionally high levels of service. Applying the concept of DRP enables all pipeline participants to answer the two most critical questions in managing a distribution pipeline: What will I need on the shelf? and What will I need to produce?

*"Product flows too slowly through our pipeline even though we seem to work an excess amount of overtime at our distribution center."*

There are many hidden capacity constraints in logistics, such as: How many trucks do I need to ship product from point A to point B? How much receiving capacity do I need to unload dozens if not hundreds of trucks arriving at my dock? How much manpower do I need to put product away, take orders, and ultimately ship product to my retail stores? How much space capacity do I need to hold the inventory?

DRP makes it possible to plan not only what products are needed, but how much capacity is needed to transport, receive, hold, and ship product across the entire distribution pipeline. To solve your problem completely, however, DRP must become a standard method of operating your business.

*"There's a 'disconnect' between the needs of our logistics operation and the capabilities of our factories."*

DRP will generate the proper demand pull information to drive Master Production Schedules in your factory; it will also provide the manufacturing people with a window into the needs of logistics. This will eliminate a great deal of the surprise and uncertainty that add costs to manufacturing.

*"All of our partners are excellent at their own niches, but they don't do a good job communicating their business needs with one another."*

Create a formal ECR arrangement in which Top Management agrees to link people, information, and systems across the pipeline. By agreeing to share information by EDI and by agreeing to work with cross-company, cross-functional teams to manage the flow of information and product, you will achieve a high degree of integration. Partners will enjoy inventory and cost reductions far beyond any they could achieve on their own.

## SUMMARY

- Most manufacturing companies exist in a distribution pipeline and are connected by natural linkages. When these linkages are exploited through the process outlined here, the pipeline can be positioned to replace what it is selling on a real-time basis.

- When information is timely and accurate, it becomes a substitute for inventory, dramatically reducing logistics and manufacturing costs.
- When ECR is driven by Distribution Resource Planning, trading partners can eliminate the need for sales forecasting across the distribution pipeline, except for the area of final point of sale. This has a profound impact on the way businesses are managed, since forecasting uncertainty is one of the greatest stumbling blocks to efficient management of resources.
- ECR, based on natural pull and currently available technology, can dramatically change the way business is done across distribution channels, be they mass merchandising, consumer electronics, grocery, or health and beauty care.

## INFORMATION RESOURCES

*DRP: Distribution Resource Planning,* André J. Martin, Revised Edition, Oliver Wight Publications, 1990.

*Infopartnering: The Ultimate Strategy for Achieving Consumer Response,* André J. Martin, Oliver Wight Publications, 1994.

"Efficient Consumer Response: Enhancing Consumer Value in the Grocery Industry," Kurt Salmon Associates, Inc., 1993.

"Wholesale Food Distribution Today and Tomorrow," Anderson Consulting, 1993.

"New Ways to Take Costs Out of the Retail Food Pipeline," Mercer Management Consulting Group, 1993.

## INTERNAL CROSS-REFERENCE

Your understanding of this topic may be enhanced by the following chapters:

I–2. Time-Based Competition

I–6. Resource Planning: For Manufacturing, the Business, and the Enterprise

IV–4. Just-in-Time: Driver for Continuous Improvement

### About the Author

André J. Martin is president and CEO of LogicNet, which assists retailers, wholesaler/distributors, and manufacturers in the integration of their distribution systems from retail point of sale terminals to the supplier's manufacturing facilities. The former director of manufacturing and materials manufacturing for Abbott, Canada, André has more than twenty-five years of experience in distribution and manufacturing. He is the author of *DRP: Distribution Resource Planning* and *Infopartnering: The Ultimate Strategy for Achieving Consumer Response.*

## 11-4

# Forecasting Systems to Support World Class Competitiveness

*Stephen A. DeLurgio, Sr.*

**IN A NUTSHELL**

World class competitiveness is achieved by having the right product or service, in the right quantity, at the right time, in the right location—this is possible only through excellence in forecasting.

There are forecasting *methods* and forecasting *systems*. And it's important to understand the difference. A forecasting method is a statistical or subjective technique for generating a forecast; linear regression, moving averages, etc., are among them. Most statistical forecasting software programs advertised in the popular literature are simply implementations of these and other forecasting methods. A forecasting system, on the other hand, has a broader definition, extending to data collection, storage, presentation, and use. An effective forecasting system is one that:

- Automatically selects the correct forecasting model—seasonal, trend, linear, or nonlinear forecasting models—for thousands of items
- Provides a graphic user interface to ease use by a variety of managers
- Processes thousands of records accurately and quickly
- Captures and maintains at least thirty-six months of demand data
- Provides monthly forecasts for one to three years ahead for all stock-keeping-units (SKUs)
- Groups items with low demand to achieve good group forecasts
- Generates hierarchical reports for several levels of management
- Integrates information for operations, marketing, and finance
- Highlights exceptions when they occur

### *Basic Elements of Forecasting*

Forecasts are necessary because it takes time to implement decisions; decisions have lead times. If a decision has a long lead time (e.g., the decision to build a new plant), then long-term forecasts are necessary. In contrast, if a decision takes only one week to implement, then we need to forecast only one week into the future. One of the most popular forecast periods is twenty-four months into the future using monthly data. With the advent of JIT and Quick Response, however, more firms are becoming interested in weekly forecasting.

The basis of almost all statistical methods of forecasting is that the past repeats itself, not perfectly, but within some bounds (e.g., +/− 200 units). For example, let's say that for the past five years, demand has averaged 1,000 units and has been between 800 and 1,200 for the month of June. Assuming there is no increase or decrease this year over previous years (i.e., no trend), then June's demand is expected to be from 800 to 1,200 units, with a best single estimate of 1,000. Unfortunately, we don't know what will happen next June; there is always the risk that the past will not be repeated in the future. We forecast on the basis of the probability rather than on the certainty that next June will be like previous Junes.

A forecast, then, is a probabilistic estimate of a future value or condition that includes an average, a range, and a probability estimate of that range. For example, a forecast statement might say "expected demand next month is 1,000 with a 70 percent chance that sales will be 800 to 1,200 units" (i.e., a 35 percent chance of demand from 800 to 1,000 and a 35 percent chance of demand from 1,000 to 1,200). The difference of 1,000 minus 800 (200 units) is approximately equal to one standard deviation or 1.25 MADs (mean absolute deviation; see Key Concepts). By measuring the standard deviation or MAD, we can assess some of the risks or uncertainty in the forecast. When forecasting future events, uncertainty can be assessed, but never eliminated.

## *Benefits*

Well-designed and executed forecasting leads to a number of beneficial business outcomes:

- Better marketing, financial, and operations information
- Increased customer service
- Increased manufacturing and operating efficiency
- Better allocation of scarce resources
- Elimination of wasted finished goods, work-in-process, and raw materials
- More flexibility to respond to customer preferences
- Increased profitability and return on investment

The cost of implementing a new forecasting system is a function of its complexity. Off-the-shelf systems cost anywhere from $2,000 to several hundred thousand dollars. Inexpensive systems (less than $10,000) are normally just the forecasting modules depicted in Figure 1. They generate the necessary forecasting numbers but do not represent an entire system. The most inexpensive forecasting systems that purport to have all of the modules shown in Figure 1 cost about $10,000. As with all information system implementations, however, software costs are only a fraction of the total system costs. Typical forecasting system costs are in the $50,000 to $2 million range when user education and customization are accounted for in the price.

## *The Forecasting Process*

Table 1 and Figure 1 illustrate the modules and summary functions of a forecasting system. The demand data module captures and processes demand before it becomes part of the demand database. It automatically verifies that the data has not been entered incorrectly or affected by unusual events. The demand data module highlights unusual demand and reports exceptions.

The forecasting module selects a good forecasting model for each item or group that the company manages. In addition, it should generate group forecasts for product lines and low-demand items. The forecasting modules of most, if not all systems, use "univariate methods," sometimes called intrinsic methods, to generate forecasts. Univariate methods use only past demand for products to forecast future demand. Consequently, no external variable such as GNP, income, or competitor prices is used in most forecasting systems. These external variables require the use of "multivariate models" such as regression analysis; at this time, no fully integrated forecasting systems routinely use multivariate methods in forecasting.

The managerial interface and interaction module is the user interface to the forecasting system. It should provide a user-friendly graphic interface, screen displays, and navigational aids, thereby facilitating manager interaction with the forecasting system.

The output module generates routine periodic batch reports and output files, including exception reports. These exception reports are important because they identify situations requiring human intervention in the forecasting process.

The database module holds actual demands, adjusted demands, seasonal information, and special-event data for each item and group forecast. This database can be very large because it contains this information for the previous thirty-six months or longer. The

**TABLE 1. THE MODULES AND DATABASE OF A FORECASTING SYSTEM**

I. Demand Data Module
    Input of local and remote demand data
    Demand capturing
    Logical filtering (demand versus supply or shipments)
    Special-event filtering (promotions, price changes, product introductions)
    Initial outlier detection, adjustment, classification

II. Forecasting Module
    System forecast selection
    Outlier detection, adjustment, classification
    Reasonableness test
    Final forecast
    Error measures
    Tracking-signal control

III. Managerial Interface and Interaction Module
    Graphical user interface
    Screen displays
    Management forecasts
    User help
    Management feedback
    User notepad
    Expert advisory menu

IV. Output Module
    File generation
    Routine reports
    Ad hoc reports
    Exception reports

V. System Control and Maintenance Module
    Module and navigation control
    Simulation control
    Database updating and maintenance
    Detection of system malfunctions and bugs

VI. Database
    Actual demand history
    Adjusted demand history
    Promotional profiles
    Seasonal profiles
    Item and group relationships structure
    Performance measures
    Item relationships
    Item descriptions
    Demand forecasts

**FIGURE 1. THE MODULES OF A FORECASTING SYSTEM**

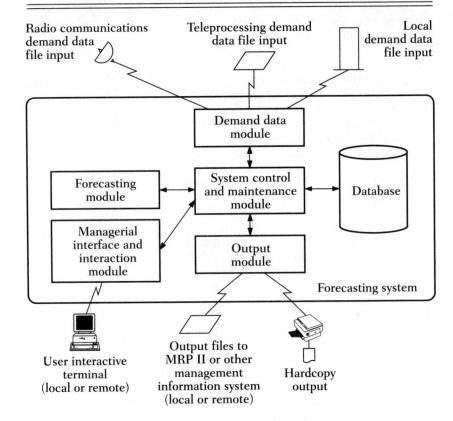

SOURCE: Reprinted from Stephen A. DeLurgio, Sr., and Carl D. Bhame, *Forecasting Systems for Operations Management*, Irwin Professional Publications, 1991.

database also stores additional data, such as twenty-four monthly forecasts and the past performance of item and group forecasts. This database is updated periodically, typically every week or month.

## *Implementation*

Many important implementation issues in forecasting systems have been mentioned above. In addition, the system should:

- Maintain at least three and preferably five years of demand data
- Be able to forecast daily, weekly, four-week, monthly, quarterly, and annual data
- Allow subjective and objective user overrides of forecasts and past demands
- Capture and model past and future marketing promotions
- Detect out-of-control situations through the use of tracking signals and demand filters
- Derive seasonal factors for groups
- Facilitate the combining of low-volume items into meaningful groups
- Forecast accurately

Surprisingly, the last characteristic is often overlooked. When buying or developing a system, benchmark the forecasting accuracy of its statistical methodologies; don't rely on the developer's generalized statements concerning system accuracy. A system should have significant intelligence built into the forecasting methodologies so that the correct demand patterns (e.g., trends and seasonality) and outliers are identified. Do not rely on one-period-ahead forecast accuracy; instead, one-seasonal-cycle forecast accuracy should be used in judging system accuracy.

## KEY CONCEPTS

**Bias**: A systematic (i.e., consistent) over- or underforecasting that yields increasing errors over time. A good forecast has zero bias; positive errors are offset by negative errors. A good forecasting system generates forecasts that have low bias and low standard deviations.

**Cyclical**: Variations caused by business, demographic, and long cycles. Cyclical influences recur, but with no known or predictable period. Business cycles have historically lasted for three to five years.

**Demand filter**: A statistical limit that checks whether a recent demand is statistically different than expected. When an actual demand is recorded, the system should check whether this value is an outlier. If the demand is an outlier relative to the forecast, then an exception report is generated.

**Forecast error**: The numerical difference between actual and forecast.

**MAD (mean absolute deviation)**: MAD is approximately equal to 1.25 standard deviations. As a measure of scatter, the MAD is inferior to the standard deviation, because the standard deviation provides more accurate probability statements.

**Outlier**: An unusually large, nontypical demand or forecast that should be investigated and adjusted. In statistical terms, an outlier is more than two or three standard deviations from its expected value.

**Seasonality**: Recurrent and periodic movement in demand caused by climatic and human conventions (e.g., holidays). Seasonal demands have a known period (e.g., every twelve months or seven days).

**Standard deviation**: A measure of the scatter of actual demands or forecast errors. For an in-control forecasting system, about 70 percent of the errors will be within plus and minus one standard deviation, 95 percent of the errors within two standard deviations, and 99.73 percent of the errors within three standard deviations.

**Tracking signals**: A control device that checks for biased errors. When bias is detected, an exception report is generated.

**Trend**: Long-term, general movement in demand caused by long-term demographic, technological, and economic movements. A trend is normally assumed to be seven periods or longer.

## ACTION STEPS

When improving or selecting a forecasting system, it is important to consider the following important steps:

- Have the implementation team learn about the principles of forecasting and forecasting systems.
- Apply the principles and procedures of good system development.
- Create a system specification committee to oversee the development or selection process. Identify all users and select a well-respected user as a project team leader.
- If purchasing a system, benchmark the system's accuracy, flexibility for expansion, and compatibility with existing systems.
- Prudently use outside or inside consultants in the system design process.
- Don't overlook the importance of a user-friendly database system to support effective use of forecasts and demand information.
- Don't be seduced into buying a low-cost unsophisticated forecasting system. The return on investment from a good, higher-cost system may be extraordinary, while the return on investment from a mediocre, lower-cost system may be negative.

## PROBLEM-SOLVING

*"The demand for many of our products is seasonal. But when we graph and analyze past sales data, there is no seasonality in sales. What's the problem?"*

The majority of firms, small and large, do not capture actual demands for their products. Sales figures rarely reflect demand. In fact, at best, sales reflect the minimum of demand or supply. At worst, sales figures bear little resemblance to actual demands for products. The solution is to record customer request dates and quantities for products, whether products are shipped on time or not. If shortages have occurred in the past, or shipments are late, then sales do not equal demand. Also, in many cases, actual demand data does not exist in the system because people do not recognize the differences between independent and dependent demand (see the next problem-solving solution).

*"We have constant debates on what should be forecast in our company. Just what should we forecast?"*

The concepts of dependent and independent demands determine what should be forecast. Forecast independent demand as close to the ultimate consumer as possible. Then calculate the resulting dependent demands. For example, a manufacturer-distributor with six regional distribution centers supplied by twenty-four factories should forecast demand for each product at each of the six regional distribution centers. Then, using Distribution Requirements Planning (see chapter II–3), the manufacturer-distributor can calculate dependent demand back to each supplying factory. Normally, demand at each factory does not have to be, and should not be, forecasted; rather it should be calculated.

Ideally, the manufacturer-distributor should forecast demand at each of the retail outlets supplied by each regional distribution center. As customers, however, the retailers may or may not provide this information to their supplier, the manufacturer-distributor.

*"Our demand database is a mess; there are so many exceptional demands (i.e., outliers), how can we possibly use it to forecast the future if it doesn't even reflect the past?"*

Unplanned events such as strikes and wars are very unusual events. Consequently, when they occur, extremely high errors may occur. It is important to have contingency plans when these extraordinary events occur. It is also important that when these events affect demand greatly, and you do not expect these events to occur again in the future, that you adjust past sales to reflect normal demand. This is why you should maintain actual *and* adjusted past demand databases.

*"Marketing is always running promotions that result in forecasting problems. The promotions also wreak havoc on our past demand database. What can we do about them?"*

Past promotions affect sales projections in abnormal ways. For example, if a promotion during the month of May increases the demand in May by 4,000 units and decreases the demand in June by 1,000 units, then this information should be captured and used in predicting the effects of future promotions. The past demand database used to make forecasts of months in which there are no promotions, however, should not include the inflated May promotion values or the deflated June demands. The past adjusted demand database should be adjusted in those months. You will still need to keep a separate history file of past promotional effects so that they can be used to predict future promotional effects.

*"The life cycles of our products are very short. How do we detect demand shifts as our products evolve from one phase of their life cycle to another?"*

A good forecasting system will detect when the forecasting process is out of control. The tools to do this are based on statistical process control methods. Tracking signals and demand filters are statistical tools that are an essential part of a good forecasting system.

## SUMMARY

- Measuring customer demand as quickly as possible is an essential part of achieving world class competitiveness. Only by measuring demand of customers as close as possible to the ultimate consumers of products or services can we achieve the highest levels of customer service.
- JIT, Quick Response, EDI, and Time-Based Competition have not reduced the need for better forecasting information. Rather, they have increased the need for more timely information.
- The attention to data processing and statistical details in forecasting systems must be extraordinary. Many firms fail in achieving good forecasting systems because of this.

## INFORMATION RESOURCES

*Forecasting Systems for Operations Management,* by Stephen A. DeLurgio, Sr., and Carl D. Bhame, Irwin Professional Publications, 1991.

*Advanced Service Parts Inventory Control*, 2nd edition, by R. G. Brown, Materials Management Systems, 1982.

"Master Planning Module," *CPIM Certification Study Guides*, American Production and Inventory Control Society, 1994.

## INTERNAL CROSS-REFERENCE

Your understanding of this topic may be enhanced by the following chapters:

- I–5. Sales and Operations Planning: Top Management's Handle on the Business
- I–6. Resource Planning: For Manufacturing, the Business, and the Enterprise
- II–3. Efficient Consumer Response (ECR)

---

### About the Author

Stephen A. DeLurgio, Sr., CFPIM, Ph.D., is an associate professor of operations management at the Henry W. Bloch School of Business of the University of Missouri, Kansas City. He is the co-author of a number of books, including *Forecasting Systems for Operations Management*. Dr. DeLurgio is currently a member of the Logistic CIRM committee and was chairman of the Inventory Management CPIM committee of APICS. He also serves on the editorial review board of the *Journal of Production and Inventory Management*.

# New Approaches to New Product Development
## Douglas Daetz

**IN A NUTSHELL**

The survival and growth of most companies depend on their ability to identify new product opportunities and develop new products. Today, with increasing worldwide competition, an effective and continuously improving New Product Development (NPD) process is essential for success. Leading organizations actively manage new product development as a key cross-functional process, their goal being faster, more predictable, and less costly development of products that delight customers.

Companies in the United States have been taking steps to make their NPD process more effective. Some of the major efforts have sought to:

- Eliminate the lengthy, problem-prone "throw it over the wall" (from marketing to R&D to manufacturing) approach to product development

- Reduce the frequency of market failures by changing product development from technology-driven to market-driven
- Clearly define and measure the NPD process in order to actively manage and improve it

Concurrent Engineering (also called simultaneous engineering) was developed in response to the first issue above. Several variants of Concurrent Engineering are in use today, but all entail the use of cross-functional teams formed at the start of an NPD project. These teams usually involve members from marketing, R&D, and manufacturing, at the very least, and have the goal of reducing time-to-market and development cost by concurrently developing the product and the manufacturing processes so that both are ready at the same time.

A methodology called Quality Function Deployment (QFD) has increasingly been used by U.S. companies in the shift from technology-driven to market-driven product development (see chapter II–6 for more information on QFD). Since QFD also relies on cross-functional teams, it fits nicely within the Concurrent Engineering paradigm.

## *Measuring the Process*

Stimulated by the increased attention to new approaches like Concurrent Engineering and QFD, there has been a growing focus on product development as a process that should be formally defined, with process performance measures (process metrics) and an identifiable "process owner."

Process performance measures (PPMs) are monitored as part of the process management task and fall into two categories: output PPMs and internal PPMs. The former address externally observable effects of the process while the latter indicate the health of the process itself. For the NPD process, two (of several possible) output PPMs may be used:

- *Cycle time,* or the time from the start of a new product development project (generally, the initial concept phase) to the start of production of customer units

- *Product success rate,* the fraction of new product introductions that are successful (e.g., in terms of return on investment, capture of targeted level of market share, or recognition as a serious contender in a new market area)

An internal performance measure of the effectiveness of the NPD process is the project *slip rate,* the ratio of the actual time to complete the project (or a phase of the project) compared to the forecasted time.

## Benefits

The benefits of a streamlined, market-driven, well-managed, continuously improving new product development process include:

- Lower per-product development costs due to shorter development cycle time
- The ability to develop more products with the same size staff (a consequence of the shorter cycle time)
- Increased revenues due to faster time to market, a higher percentage of new product success, and more new products developed by the same number of staff

In their book *Product Development: Success Through Product and Cycle-Time Excellence,* Michael McGrath, Michael Anthony, and Amram Shapiro state: "We have found that a 50 percent reduction in product development cycle time typically leads to direct reduction of development costs of between 30 percent and 35 percent." The cost of achieving these results is more a matter of policy and process discipline than capital investment. In some cases, additional investments in computers, networks, database software, or design tools are required to improve communication among team members, provide them with real-time access to project information, and increase designers' modeling and simulation capabilities. Even so, the costs are relatively small (perhaps $10,000 to $50,000 per team member) in comparison to the benefits of improved results with the NPD process.

## The NPD Process

The new product development process may be defined in different ways and different terms, but ideally it should include the following steps:

1. Form an appropriately cross-functional project team with a defined charter and objectives.
2. Develop an understanding of the market and specific customer needs.
3. Define the product requirements and the marketing channel requirements.
4a. Design a product that meets the requirements. This step, which many divide into two separate steps—concept development and detailed design—has many activities, among which might be:

- Concept development, concept evaluation, and concept selection
- Design for "x" implementation (especially Design for Manufacturability, testability)
- Design simulation and computer-aided design
- Rapid prototyping (with mock-up prototypes shown to key customers)
- Functional testing (including testing under various environmental conditions)
- Reliability testing
- Alpha site testing (evaluation of early working models by selected customers)
- Beta site testing (evaluation of near-final product by selected customers)

4b. Design and establish the manufacturing and production processes. Activities frequently included in this step are:

- Development and qualification of suppliers for purchased parts
- Prototype production runs
- Pilot production runs

4c. Prepare the marketing materials and channels of distribution for the product.*

5. Release the product to manufacturing for volume production.

6. Conduct a project post-mortem, i.e., a retrospective look at the project and resulting product to determine what went well, what went poorly, and what needs to be done to improve the NPD process. While a post-mortem is most commonly conducted just after the product is released to manufacturing (or at some specified number of months after the product has been on the market), some organizations conduct post-mortems after each major phase of the project to obtain earlier feedback on the product development process.

Though not explicitly indicated among the above six steps, checkpoint reviews are typically held after steps 2, 3, and 4.

Many companies define their product development process in terms of a phase-review process and/or a product life cycle that may have four to six phases (from concept or investigation phase through design and production to obsolescence).

## *Implementation*

The key to a successful NPD process is the vision of the Top Management team. Whether the process is market-driven or technology-driven is ultimately determined by Top Management, as is the degree of cross-functional teaming that takes place during NPD. The naming of an appropriate owner of the NPD process, and support for that person, depends also on the Top Management team.

The actual time required to define and develop a product—NPD process cycle time—depends to a significant extent on the complexity of the product and on whether the project involves a completely new design or a redesign/updating of an existing product. In any case, with today's worldwide competition, most companies see a need to reduce their traditional cycle times by 50 percent or more.

---

* Note: Step 4 is shown as steps 4a, 4b, and 4c because, with Concurrent Engineering, these substeps are done in parallel with much interaction among the team members from the different functional areas.

## KEY CONCEPTS

**Checkpoint review**: Management review at a key phase transition point of a project. The review of the project's accomplishments and prospects for meeting objectives determines the future course of the project (e.g., approval to continue, conditional approval, or termination).

**Concurrent Engineering**: An approach to product development that uses cross-functional teams from the early stages of a project in order to achieve a more well-considered, well-balanced product (i.e., one that incorporates the ideas and concerns of marketing, R&D, and manufacturing), to eliminate errors and time-extending handoffs, and to concurrently develop the product and the processes needed to produce it.

**Design for Manufacturabilty (DFM)**: Consideration of the ease, consistency, and cost of manufacture or assembly of a product.

**Design for "x" (DFx)**: Indicates that there are many "design for" dimensions. Besides manufacturability, "x" may stand for testability, usability, serviceability, reliability, and environmental friendliness.

**Market-driven product development**: Product development guided by an understanding of the market situation and trends, customer needs, and competitive environment. Contrast with technology-driven product development.

**Process management**: The active management of a process, starting with its documentation, including specification of process performance measures (process metrics), the regular monitoring and maintenance of the process, restoration of the process if it goes out of control, and Continuous Improvement of the process.

**Process owner**: The person responsible for managing a process.

**Process Performance Measures (PPMs)**: Key variables that indicate the performance of the process under consideration. These may describe the output of the process (output PPMs) or give an indication of the internal functioning of the process (internal PPMs).

**Product definition**: An early stage in the product development cycle during which the project team, using customer input about customer needs, establishes the requirements for the product (what it will be, might be, won't be). In this stage, the viability of the project should also be confirmed (e.g., by considering its strategic fit, level of organizational support, availability of necessary resources, the likely return on investment and profitability).

**Product life cycle (PLC)**: The series of stages or phases of a product's life from conception of the idea for the product until the discontinuation of the product. A PLC document defines the activities that must be undertaken in each phase or stage of the life cycle. This document usually includes checklists and/or sign-off sheets that must be completed before continuing to the next phase or stage.

**Project retrospective (post-mortem)**: Discussion of what went well in a project, what did not go well, and what needs to be done to improve the process for future projects.

**Quality Function Deployment (QFD)**: A cross-functional, team-based approach that starts with the gathering of information about customer needs and then translates those needs into technical requirements for a product (and, if carried all the way through, the requirements for the product's parts and production process).

**Rapid prototyping**: The creation of mock-up models of a product—which may be functional or only partially functional—in order to elicit the reaction of key customers to the design options under consideration.

**Simultaneous engineering**: *See* **Concurrent Engineering**.

**Technology-driven product development**: Product development that is driven primarily by what engineers can develop using available or developable technology, without particular regard to market conditions or existing customer needs. Contrast with market-driven product development.

## ACTION STEPS

- Assess your current new product development process. In this assessment, which you may want to have conducted by a third party, consider the current scope of the process, its ownership, cross-functionality, the presence or absence of the voice of the customer, defining documentation, measurement of the process, performance, process management and improvement.
- Compare the performance of your NPD process to that of key competitors and other successful firms that make products of a generally similar nature.
- Based on the assessment and comparative benchmarking data, develop a plan of action. This plan should be clear in who "owns" the NPD process. Improvement goals should be specified. The people and other resources needed for the NPD process should be identified, as should the linkages and coordination with other cross-functional processes of the organization.
- Charge the NPD process owner with responsibility for developing, in concert with appropriate colleagues from other functions, a detailed implementation plan to achieve the established improvement milestones. Have the organization's highest-level management team review the plan, endorse it, and commit the required resources.
- Implement the plan.
- Review progress on a regular basis, making adjustments as needed. Recognize and celebrate achievement of milestones.
- Retrospectively review the process, documenting what went well, what did not go well, and the participants' recommendations for improving the organization's key cross-functional processes.
- Conduct another assessment of the NPD process and start the cycle again.

## *PROBLEM-SOLVING*

*"All kinds of ills—misunderstood or lost product requirements and design details, design and manufacturing rework, non-manufacturability of designs—plague our NPD process, making it costly, long, and unpredictable."*

At the start of a new product project, adopt a Concurrent Engineering approach: form an appropriately cross-functional team, co-locating them as much as possible, and charter them with the task of concurrently developing the product and the processes to build it. Develop the means for them to communicate clearly, completely, and accurately.

*"Too many of our products are 'market misses.' We think they're really good products, but economically they are failures because too few customers buy them."*

Within the framework of Concurrent Engineering use an approach like Quality Function Deployment that starts with identification of the target market segment(s) and the collection of customer data. If necessary, do original market research to get a clear idea of what customers need the product and your organization to provide.

*"No matter how hard we try, we don't seem to be able to gain ground on our competitors. They get their products to market faster than we do, and they appear to spend less money to develop each product than we do."*

Assuming your managers and engineers are as talented as those of your competitors, a likely cause of this problem is failure to see new product development as a process that can be defined, measured, and regularly improved. Therefore, identify the NPD process as one of your organization's key cross-functional processes, assign a high-level and respected person as NPD process owner, and support that person and all NPD participants in their efforts to define, measure, and improve the process.

If the NPD process has not been thoroughly examined (or not within recent years), then large opportunities for reducing the cost and time to develop products by streamlining or reengineering the NPD process are sure to exist.

## SUMMARY

- An effective and continuously improving new product development (NPD) process is critical to a technology company's survival and growth in today's environment.
- Concurrent Engineering, Quality Function Deployment, and active management of NPD as a cross-functional process are some of the approaches being used to make the new product development process faster, less costly, more predictable, and capable of producing products that delight customers.
- Cross-functional, multidisciplinary teams and effective teamwork are an essential part of these newer approaches to new product development. Incorporating the voice of the customer into the definition and development of products is also critical.
- The key to improving the NPD process is the Top Management team's vision for the process.
- Significant improvements in the cycle time and cost of the NPD process (often on the order of 50 percent reductions) have been made by organizations adopting the approaches described.

## INFORMATION RESOURCES

Boothroyd Dewhurst Inc. (BDI), 138 Main Street, Wakefield, RI 02879. This firm specializes in Design for Manufacture and Assembly (DFMA) and has expanded its activities to include Concurrent Engineering. BDI has developed and markets software for doing DFMA analyses.

Concurrent Engineering Resource Center, West Virginia University, Drawer 2000, Morgantown, WV 26506. This center has many publications in its CERC Technical Report Series. For example,

*Proceedings of CERC's Second Workshop on Product Development Process Capture and Characterization,* May 1992 (CERC-TR-RN-92-014).

*Concurrent Engineering: The Product Development Environment for the 1990s,* Donald E. Carter and Barbara Stilwell Baker, Addison-Wesley, 1992.

"Timed to Perfection," *Manufacturing Breakthrough,* Don Clausing, January–February 1992, vol. 1, no. 1. [Covers Concurrent Engineering.]

*Product Development: Success Through Product and Cycle-Time Excellence,* Michael E. McGrath, Michael T. Anthony, and Amram R. Shapiro, Butterworth-Heinemann, 1992.

*Accelerating Innovation: Improving the Process of Product Development,* Marvin L. Patterson (with Sam Lightman), Van Nostrand Reinhold, 1993.

*Total Design: Integrated Methods for Successful Product Engineering,* Stuart Pugh, Addison-Wesley, 1991.

*Improving Performance: How to Manage the White Space on the Organization Chart,* Geary A. Rummler and Alan P. Brache, Jossey-Bass Publishers, 1990. [Covers process mapping, metrics, process owner, process management, and improvement.]

*Concurrent Engineering and Design for Manufacture of Electronic Products,* Sammy G. Shina, Van Nostrand Reinhold, 1991.

*Developing Products in Half the Time,* Preston G. Smith and Donald G. Reinertsen, Van Nostrand Reinhold, 1991.

*Revolutionizing Product Development: Quantum Leaps in Speed, Efficiency, and Quality,* Steven C. Wheelright and Kim B. Clark, The Free Press, 1992.

## INTERNAL CROSS-REFERENCE

Your understanding of this topic may be enhanced by the following chapters:

I–2. Time-Based Competition

II–6. Quality Function Deployment: Breakthrough Tool for Product Development

## *About the Author*

Douglas Daetz is a senior member of Hewlett-Packard's Corporate Quality Department in Palo Alto, California. Since 1985 he has played a significant role in promotion of Design for Manufacturability, Quality Function Deployment, and Total Quality Management at HP. Mr. Daetz holds a Ph.D. in electrical engineering and has served as an assistant professor of industrial engineering at Stanford University.

# II-6

# Quality Function Deployment: Breakthrough Tool for Product Development

*William Barnard*

## IN A NUTSHELL

Quality Function Deployment (QFD) is a systematic process for planning strategies (see chapter I–3), products, and services. QFD helps managers bring together all the elements needed to define the product requirements that will satisfy and delight the customer, and to develop the means to provide that satisfaction. QFD is a disciplined methodology that ensures that customer wants are understood, documented, and converted into appropriate product and service requirements as well as the company's strategic plans.

Part of the power of QFD is its ability to integrate core teams, linking management, engineering, manufacturing, and marketing in the development of breakthrough products. It provides support for initiatives to reduce time-to-market, to attain high-quality levels, and to link manufacturing process and product design.

## *QFD and the Perilous New Product Game*

As generally practiced, new product development is riskier than a trip to Las Vegas; few initial product concepts pay off. A 1992 study of consumer goods product success revealed the following results: Of the product concepts developed, only 8 percent actually reached the marketplace. Of those, only 17 percent met their business objectives—that's an 83 percent failure rate for those products lucky enough to make it to the marketplace. The cumulative rate of success, therefore, would be a paltry 1.4 percent!

A first step in beating those dreadful odds, and in using QFD, is to understand that a product is more than just a physical object. It is a combination of *many customer values*: ease of acquisition, ease of use, technical support, after-sale service, visual appeal, functionality, and much more. Defining the product in terms of this comprehensive set of customer values requires a change in the way most companies identify markets and integrate the wants of customers. QFD supports this change.

## *Product Planning with the QFD Matrix*

Product planning, the first step of the QFD process, uses a matrix as a systematic approach to analyzing the voice of the customer and responding with a valid set of technical requirements, or "quality characteristics." Completing the matrix requires the following activities:

1. Acquire, organize, and enter the customer wants via:
   - Research into customer requirements
   - Analysis and organization of these requirements
   - Understanding the importance of these requirements

A QFD matrix takes the shape of a house, suggesting the popular term the "House of Quality." In this matrix (see Figure 1) customer wants are listed in the section identified as section A[1]. The example in Figure 1 involves the development of a pen; variety of purpose, ease of use, etc., are determined through research methods such as In-context Customer Visits. The matrix also supports the understanding gained from market research as to the importance of those wants (identified in section A[2]); this data can be acquired from surveys or in critical product development efforts from choice models (see chapter II–2).

The QFD process requires an understanding of the competitor's ability to satisfy these wants as perceived by the customer; this is identified in section A[3]. Again, surveys are used to develop this data.

2. Translate the voice of the customer into quality characteristics. These are sometimes called measures or hows. For example, the voice of the automobile buyer may say "I want to be able to merge with traffic and pass safely." The technical requirements, or quality characteristics, for this want might take the form of 0 to 60 miles-per-hour acceleration specifications.

These quality characteristics are developed through analysis, brainstorming, and consensus by cross-functional teams representing a variety of viewpoints found both inside and outside the company. In the pen example of Figure 1, these measures include requirements aimed at number of colors, size, shape, weight, and so forth, and are shown in section B.

3. The product development (or QFD) team will analyze the relationships between the wants and measures (where wants and hows intersect) and characterize each relationship as either strong, moderate, or weak. (See section C of the matrix.) By QFD convention, a moderate relationship is weighted at three times that of a weak relationship, and a strong relationship at three times the weight of a moderate relationship.

4. Evaluate trade-offs (negative correlations) using the information in section D. The next step is to develop the various target values (section E). For each measure, the team would consider technical benchmarking information and market researched values that define quality standards.

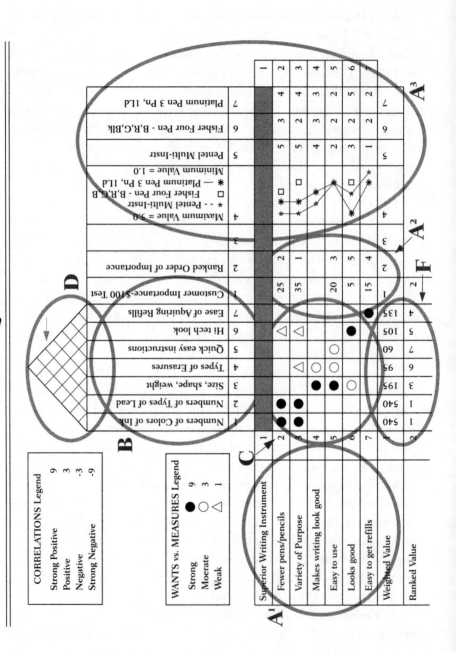

FIGURE 1. THE QFD MATRIX

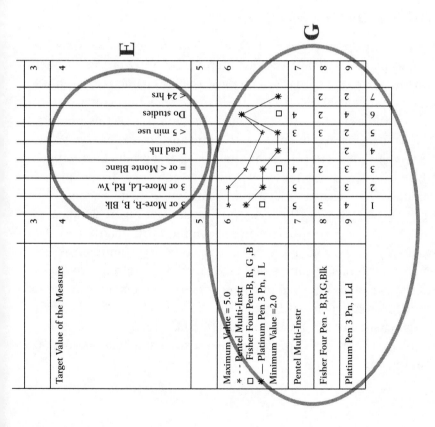

The outcome of this work is found in section F of Figure 1 and takes the form of weighted values and rankings. In the pen example, the number of colors and types of leads are shown to have high weighted and ranked values, while quick and easy instructions are of minimal relative importance.

The team will use competitive benchmarking, advertising and product data sheets, and/or reverse engineering to evaluate—in its own judgment and experience—the competition's apparent ability to meet the customer's measures of satisfaction as described in section B. This data is found in section G of Figure 1.

## *Linking the Houses Of Quality*

Expressing customer wants in terms of quality characteristics, or product planning, is just the first step in the QFD process. Other activities are required to translate those quality characteristics into a physical product of high value. Design, manufacturing, marketing, and other functions of the company are each part of this process. QFD is instrumental in ensuring that the customer view is not lost, but remains the focus of all subsequent stages of product realization.

QFD preserves the customer view at each stage by linking all activities. The measures determined in one activity become the wants in the House of Quality of the next activity. Figure 2 indicates the linkages between the product planning QFD matrix and the matrices for subsequent activities. In product planning, as we learned, customer requirements are transformed into quality characteristics. In design planning, technical requirements are converted to part characteristics. In process planning, the part characteristics create process characteristics. Finally, process control planning converts process characteristics to actual production requirements.

**FIGURE 2. THE QFD LINKING PROCESS**

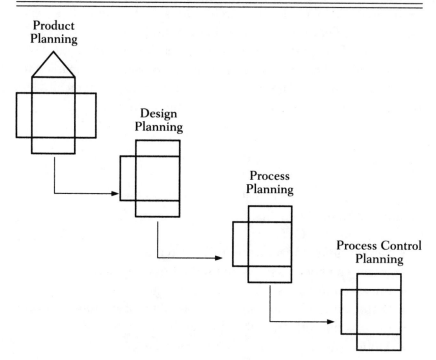

## Implementation and Time Issues

The following issues, listed in order of importance, influence the successful implementation of QFD:

- Management must understand the need for properly focused and structured customer research and be prepared to provide the support required to acquire it for QFD.
- Marketing must become a strong contributor to the team. Their contribution includes development of the segmentation strategy. Segmentation refers to the understanding of how customers subdivide themselves into understandable groups.
- Marketing must acquire advanced research capabilities such as In-context Customer Visits and Choice Modeling. (See chapter II–2.)

Companies new to Quality Function Deployment typically take four to five months to complete the QFD process, owing largely to up-front work in market research. Firms with world class capabilities in market research and team skills find that the matrices can be developed in as little as one month after the research data exists. As companies become more skilled and proactive in market research, the time for the product definition phase is typically less than that of traditional product development efforts.

## *Benefits*

The integration of QFD with the product development process creates substantial benefits:

- Design time reductions up to 50 percent
- Fewer engineers needed for product development
- Improved market share and profit margins
- Better internalization and understanding of customers' needs
- Improved information flow for better decision making
- More awareness of market segmentation
- Better understanding of the competition

While well-executed QFD leads to tremendous cost savings and fewer failed new products, implementation can create added expense, especially if the company is not presently allocating the proper funds for market research to support product development. Other costs of QFD involve education, facilitation, travel (for customer visits), and PC-based software.

## **KEY CONCEPTS**

**House of Quality**: *See* **Relationship Matrix**.

**Marketing and competitive data**: Provides analysis of customer wants and of the competitive situation.

**Measures (also called "hows")**: The product characteristics measures, the requirements that must be supplied to be able to provide "delight" in a solution. The translation from the voice of the customer to product characteristics occurs through the efforts of the multifunction team.

**Relationship Matrix**: The point at which the impact of each *how* (the product characteristic measures) upon each *want* is evaluated by the cross-functional team. This process leads to a weighted prioritizing of the hows in terms of their ability to satisfy customer wants. This matrix is sometimes called the House of Quality because of its shape.

**Technical target values**: The values of the measures that must be achieved in order to supply the product/service in a quality manner to the customer. This data can also be used to do competitive analysis of the company's product with other products in the market.

**Wants**: The voice of the customer. These wants represent the attributes and capabilities that the company must provide for in its design efforts.

## ACTION STEPS

- Train personnel in the integration of the marketing research and the QFD processes.
- Create a full-time position of QFD facilitator. This is a key role in leading the company in its journey to become truly integrated with its customers.
- Acquire outside QFD facilitation support. This will allow for success in the development of the matrix and the data acquisition critical to the process.

## *PROBLEM-SOLVING*

*"My products most often are competing on price only."*

Few companies compete in truly commodity-type businesses where price is all that matters. And even there, customer values exist that can differentiate one producer from another—delivery reliability, packaging, service, and so forth. If the only customer value you know about is price, get closer to the customer to determine if there are other customer voices. If others exist, use QFD to transform those customer values into the products or services that will make you a price setter instead of a price taker.

*"My after-sale costs for providing wanted customer satisfaction are seriously cutting into my profit and my image as a quality supplier."*

Provide a structured methodology that allows your team to come to agreement on the product that meets the customer's needs. QFD provides this needed structured methodology.

*"Our product development teams and marketing teams seem to be working with two different customers—neither of which is the one management thinks we are selling to."*

Management needs to direct more resources to understanding the customer and the market segments that have profit potential. That understanding will provide direction for the teams responsible for developing products and services. QFD will focus the customer definition process.

*"We spend heavily on customer interaction and on market research that no one believes is helping in the design of innovative and profitable products."*

Customer visits help company engineers and marketers understand how products are actually used and the context of that use. Such visits provide more qualitatively valuable customer information than do other forms of research. The use of the QFD matrix tools provides the structure for incorporating this information in products and services.

## SUMMARY

- Quality Function Deployment is a disciplined methodology that ensures that customer wants are understood, documented, and converted into appropriate strategy, product, and service requirements.
- QFD pinpoints customer wants, the priority of customer wants, and helps companies develop the solutions that will delight those customers.
- QFD helps companies cut costs and development times and increases the efficiency of new product development.
- By linking the many activities and business functions involved with product development, QFD preserves the voice of the customer throughout the entire process.

## INFORMATION RESOURCES

*Integrating Customer Requirements into Product Design,* Yoji Akoa, Productivity Press, 1990.
*Quality Function Deployment: A Practitioner's Approach,* James Bossart, ASQC Press, 1991
*Building Competitive Advantage Using QFD: A Comprehensive Guide for Leaders,* Douglas Daetz and William Barnard, Oliver Wight Publications, 1994.
*The Innovation Edge: Creating Strategic Breakthroughs Using the Voice of the Customer,* William Barnard and Thomas F. Wallace, Oliver Wight Publications, 1994.

## INTERNAL CROSS-REFERENCE

Your understanding of this topic may be enhanced by the following chapters:

I–3. Linking Customers to Strategies via Quality Function Deployment (QFD)

II–2. Understanding the Voice of the Customer

II–5. New Approaches to New Product Development

### About the Author

William Barnard is a practitioner, educator, and author who works in customer-integrated strategy and product development with companies such as Motorola, Hewlett-Packard, NCR, AT&T, and numerous small businesses. He is also a senior fellow at the University of Dayton's Center for Competitive Change. He is co-author of *The Innovation Edge: Creating Strategic Breakthroughs Using the Voice of the Customer*.

# PART III
# PEOPLE

**1. Building a Learning Organization**
   *Daniel R. Tobin*

**2. Making Employee Empowerment Work**
   *Steven R. Rayner*

**3. Energizing Your Workforce with High Performance Teams**
   *Grace L. Pastiak*

**4. Crossing Boundaries with Teamnets**
   *Jessica Lipnack and Jeffrey Stamps*

**5. Organizational Communication**
   *Eric K. Hatch*

**6. Compensation for the High Performance Enterprise**
   *Donna R. Neusch and Alan F. Siebenaler*

It's HARD TO write about the topic of people without reverting to what sounds like clichés: "People are our most important asset," "our people are our strength," etc. That's because these truisms are true; people really are the heart of a manufacturing enterprise. Over the long run, the prosperity of the organization will hinge heavily on how well the talents of its people are developed and utilized.

Part III opens with Dan Tobin's chapter, **Building a Learning Organization**, a call for companies to recognize the value of knowledge and the need for it to be constantly replenished. The importance of empowering people, and how to do it, is addressed in **Making Employee Empowerment Work** by Steve Rayner. In the next chapter, **Energizing Your Workforce With High Performance Teams**, Grace Pastiak from Tellabs focuses on teaming within the company, and this is followed by a discussion of "external" teaming in **Crossing Boundaries with Teamnets** by Jessica Lipnack and Jeffrey Stamps. The final chapters in Part III deal with how to communicate well and how to compensate effectively: **Organizational Communication** by Eric Hatch and **Compensation for the High Performance Enterprise** by Donna Neusch and Alan Siebenaler.

# III-1

# Building a Learning Organization
*Daniel R. Tobin*

## IN A NUTSHELL

Knowledge is a key competitive advantage for the modern enterprise, and most companies have all the knowledge they need to be successful. Unfortunately, most don't know how to identify the knowledge that exists within their own boundaries, nor do they know how to capture and disseminate it to the people who need it for decision making and action. The learning organization understands the power of knowledge; it knows how to seek it out, capture it, and apply it to the solution of current problems and the creation of new opportunities.

In today's competitive marketplace, knowledge assets provide as much or more value than physical assets. Since key technologies can be purchased and installed virtually anywhere in the world, a company's unique added value derives from the knowledge of its employees and the ways that knowledge is put to use. North American industry cannot compete for "busy fingers work" with less-developed countries whose wage rates are dramatically lower—it must compete on the basis of innovation and the application of knowledge.

The learning organization lays the foundation for innovation, efficiency, and competitiveness in the world economy of today and of tomorrow. Whether a company is using Total Quality Management, Concurrent Engineering, Business Process Reengineering, or any of the other "hot" transformation initiatives in vogue today, the following three characteristics of the learning organization must be present if the company is to succeed in its transformation efforts:

- An openness to new ideas
- A culture that encourages and facilitates learning and innovation
- Widespread understanding of the organization's overall goals and how each person's work contributes to them

Becoming a learning organization requires a basic change in a company's culture, in the way people at all levels relate to their jobs and to each other, and in the methods by which people and the business are managed. But, as in the case of any major change effort, there is apt to be greater agreement on the goals than on how to achieve them. Few companies argue with goals such as improving quality, reducing time-to-market, and improving customer satisfaction, but even fewer have been successful in transforming themselves into learning organizations.

## *Origins*

The term "learning organization" has been used by a number of prominent authors to explain how companies can harvest their knowledge assets. Charles Handy, for example, states in *The Age of Unreason* that: "The learning organization can mean two things, it can mean an organization which learns and/or an organization which encourages learning in its people. It should mean both." Peter Senge of MIT is credited with popularizing the term with his book *The Fifth Discipline: The Art and Practice of the Learning Organization*, which focuses on a set of five high-level disciplines and methodologies for the learning organization, primarily focusing on systems thinking, the "fifth discipline."

## Benefits

- Efficiency and effectiveness in the solution of business problems through the application of relevant knowledge and capability from throughout the company.
- Greater levels of innovation and new ideas for improving company performance coming from all employees in all parts of the organization.
- The ability for the company to create its own future, rather than passively reacting to changing market conditions.
- Greater satisfaction for employees whose ideas are heard and who have greater opportunities for personal learning and growth.

## Learning in the Learning Organization

When most people think about learning in company settings, they think of formal education and training programs. In the learning organization, learning takes place both inside and outside of the classroom; it is part of each person's daily job responsibility. The open sharing of ideas is encouraged through a variety of formal and informal, structured and unstructured methods.

The learning organization views expenditures on learning activities as an investment in human capital, not as an expense. Shared knowledge is a peculiar type of economic good; you can give it away many times without ever losing it.

## Implementation

To create a learning organization, a company must establish a set of five foundations:

1. *Visible Leadership.* Without strong, visible leadership from the top down and throughout a company, the learning organization

cannot be achieved. Leaders must be committed to change and must be constant in their insistence on and encouragement of new ways of working.

2. *Basic Skills.* The standard definition of "functional literacy" is much too narrow for the twenty-first-century enterprise. Employees need higher levels of achievement in the three R's, but they must also master a broad range of technical and nontechnical skills to be effective. These include communications, teamwork, and business skills, as well as knowledge of one's self, one's job, and how one's work fits into the overall business.

3. *Overcoming Functional Myopia.* Employees at all levels and in all functions must remove their functional blinders and keep the larger goals of the corporation in sight. Too often local or functional goals subvert larger company goals.

4. *Effective Teamwork.* Effective teamwork is a requirement for the learning organization as well as for most other transformation programs. But working as part of a team goes against the way most Americans are raised and trained. Creating effective teamwork requires more than throwing people into a room and telling them to work together—it requires training, coaching, and constant reinforcement.

5. *Managers as Resources.* American industry is on a campaign to strip out levels of middle management. While industry does not need as many levels of management as it once did, middle managers are valuable resources who should not be lightly tossed aside. There are new, important roles for middle managers—as teachers, coaches, and "intrapreneurs." Middle managers are key knowledge assets that should be utilized to help companies achieve their goals.

Putting these five foundations in place makes it possible for a company to succeed as a learning organization or with any of the other transformation initiatives they may have in mind: TQM, Concurrent Engineering, Business Process Redesign, etc. Without solid foundations, none of these programs can succeed.

## KEY CONCEPTS

**Education and training**: Formal education and training programs, while important for specific purposes, are only a small part of the learning organization's methods for encouraging learning. Rather, all employees must participate in continuous learning, using both formal and informal learning methods.

**Functional myopia**: The constant focus on local or functional goals and standards often results in a company's not achieving its overall goals. Functional myopia must be overcome to maximize organizational performance.

**Human capital**: Companies must invest in their employees (human capital), for the companies' stock of human capital will prove just as (or more) valuable than their stock of physical capital (plant and equipment).

**Knowledge assets**: The knowledge of a company's employees is fast becoming its most valuable asset. Physical assets can be replicated easily, and almost instantaneously anywhere in the world; knowledge assets are unique.

## ACTION STEPS

- Learn about learning organizations and decide if they represent the direction your company wants to take.
- Assess the current status of the five foundations for the learning organization within your company.
- Develop and implement plans to build, or shore up, the five foundations.
- Provide constant reinforcement of new practices.
- Be constantly open to the new ideas that will emerge as employees are freed to learn and share their ideas.

## *PROBLEM-SOLVING*

*"Every group in our company has so many set procedures and standards that it takes forever to get anything done."*

Getting people from different groups to work together and to understand how their jobs relate to each other can overcome the functional myopia that pervades your company. This will get everyone working together toward overall company goals, instead of focusing on local measurements. The key is to get people to understand how their work fits into the overall business and to get them to work toward optimizing overall company results. Overcoming functional myopia also requires that the company:

- Remove structural barriers to cross-functional communication and work
- Align pay and other incentives to support the new goals
- Provide tools and training so that employees can see the larger business picture and understand how their work fits into it

*"We've spent a lot of money on new technology to improve our work processes, but we aren't getting any return on our investment."*

Technology can facilitate and enable new ways of working, but it doesn't cause them to happen. In some cases, workers may lack the basic skills to learn to use the new technologies. Assess your workers' levels of basic skills and work with local educational institutions to bring skills up to par. In other cases, there is so much rivalry among various groups that no technology will get them to work together. These cases require training and development of new, cross-functional work methods as well as constant reinforcement and coaching.

*"Our company has suffered from a 'program of the week' plague—TQM last week, JIT this week, CIM next week. How do we convince our employees that the learning organization is real and important?"*

Leaders must not only tell employees that the program is important, but must be exemplars of the new program, first making their own learning very visible to employees. Leaders should also do the initial training—employees will immediately recognize that the topic is important and that their leaders are serious if they take the time to train their own employees.

## SUMMARY

- In the learning organization, both the organization and its employees constantly learn, constantly replenish their own and their company's store of knowledge assets.
- To achieve the learning organization or any other type of major company transformation, companies must build a set of solid foundations: leadership, basic skills, overcoming functional myopia, effective teamwork, and transforming managers into enablers.
- The methods of the learning organization are not limited to formal education and training programs, but include constant formal and informal learning opportunities.

## INFORMATION RESOURCES

*Re-Educating the Corporation: Foundations for the Learning Organization*, Daniel R. Tobin, Oliver Wight Publications, 1994.
*The Age of Unreason*, Charles Handy, Harvard Business School Press, 1989.
*The Fifth Discipline: The Art and Practice of the Learning Organization*, Peter M. Senge, Doubleday Currency, 1990.

## INTERNAL CROSS-REFERENCE

Your understanding of this topic may be enhanced by the following chapter:

III–2. Making Employee Empowerment Work

IV–1. Total Quality Management (TQM)

## About the Author

Daniel R. Tobin is an independent consultant on corporate change and learning strategies, located in Framingham, Massachusetts, and author of *Re-Educating the Corporation: Foundations for the Learning Organization*. With more than two decades of experience in the training and development field, he has spoken at a variety of university and industry symposia on managing major change initiatives. His paper "Managing Concurrent Engineering: A Full-Spectrum Approach" will appear in *Concurrent Engineering/Integrated Product Development: Handbook to Understanding and Implementation*, a forthcoming U.S. Department of Defense publication.

# III-2

# Making Employee Empowerment Work

*Steven R. Rayner*

## IN A NUTSHELL

Many major U.S. corporations are exploring ways to increase their level of workforce participation and involvement. The names used to describe their efforts include: high-performance work systems, socio-technical systems, high involvement, employee involvement, bossless systems, self-directed work teams, self-management, and participative management. Underlying these differing names is a common theme: The greatest long-term competitive advantage resides in the human resources of the organization. Ultimately, all companies have access to the same pool of technology, machinery, and information. Their only unique assets are the intellectual, creative, and innovative powers of their employees.

While this may seem like common sense, few organizations truly operate as if their employees are their most valuable asset. Historically, corporations have limited employee involvement by narrowly defining jobs; filtering information; maintaining tight spans of control; and concentrating decision making, responsibility, and authority in the upper echelons of management. This approach to controlling the work behavior of employees is so pervasive that some experts have come to see it as a dominant management paradigm, one that directly affects how managers interact with members of the workforce.

## *Benefits*

Employee Empowerment efforts directly oppose these traditional management approaches. Their intent is to develop the capability of the workforce so that the organization can more effectively adapt to change, increase its productivity and quality performance, more creatively solve problems, and react quickly to market opportunities. Where the approach has been effectively deployed, at companies such as AT&T, Corning, Hewlett-Packard, Procter & Gamble, Martin Marietta, Monsanto, and Motorola, results have been dramatic: productivity and quality improvement in the 20 to 40 percent range; 50 to 60 percent reduction in time-to-market; 15 to 20 percent improvement in safety; 20 to 30 percent lower costs; and 15 to 40 percent improvement in quality of work-life measures.

## *Characteristics of Employee Empowerment*

Employee Empowerment has six major characteristics:

1. *Leadership that empowers others.* The leadership removes barriers that limit individual and team contributions.
2. *A relentless focus on strategy and results.* There is a clear connection between business strategy, team structure, work design, and individual work roles. The utilization of Employee Empowerment is recognized as a technique for achieving superior results.
3. *Sharing of relevant information.* Virtually all relevant business information is shared. Teams use the information to help in solving problems, developing innovations, and making decisions.
4. *Borderless sharing of power.* Authority and responsibility are based on the issue being addressed, not on one's position or status. Those most directly affected by an issue, problem, or strategy are given responsibility for it.

5. *Team-based design.* Teams are the primary work unit and are responsible for the design of their work, including the determination of the required technology and individual work roles.

6. *Teamwork reinforced through rewards.* Formal and informal rewards reinforce the overall team-based design. There are clear links between improvements made by the team and the rewards received by team members.

## *Implementation*

Creating a work culture characterized by these six elements is difficult. In fact, attempts to implement Employee Empowerment fail more than 50 percent of the time, according to some estimates. The reason for the high failure rate is that most change efforts are approached in a piecemeal fashion—only a small piece of the total system is actually changed. To effectively implement Employee Empowerment, the organization must be viewed as a whole—as an integrated system; virtually everything about the organization will be affected by the change including leadership, core work processes, employee development, work roles, organization structure, and work design. For this reason, employee-empowerment efforts should be undertaken only by organizations that are willing to allocate significant budget and resources to the effort.

While there is no step-by-step recipe for implementing Employee Empowerment, a six-phase process called the Transformation Pathway can greatly increase the likelihood of success (see Figure 1). Each phase helps build momentum and strength for the phase that immediately follows, creating a natural pull for the desired changes.

*Phase 1—Leadership* The first phase of the transition focuses on securing a champion who will support the change. The champion must be someone who can articulate why the change is important and who can provide a vision of the organization's new direction. The champion also needs a working knowledge of empowered organizations, the clout to make a change take place, and a clear sense of the concerns and aspirations of the people in the organization.

**FIGURE 1. THE TRANSFORMATION PATHWAY**

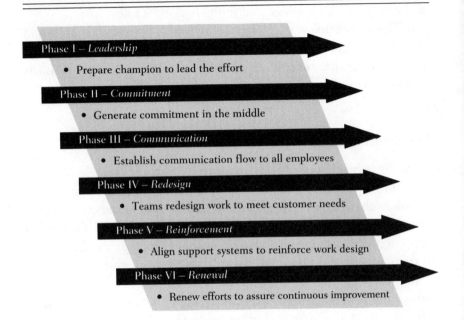

*Phase 2—Commitment* In this phase, the effort is expanded to include key opinion leaders within the organization. Initially, their efforts focus on clarifying the linkage between Employee Empowerment and overall business strategy. The opinion leaders then become actively involved in planning the change process and recognizing how roles, including their own, will be affected by the transition.

*Phase 3—Communication* The third phase stresses altering the flow of information in order to expand its accessibility to nearly everyone in the organization. Often this means dismantling the hierarchical information pathway, restructuring reports, and reassessing what information should be considered confidential. As teams begin using the expanded flow of information, problem-solving expands.

*Phase 4—Redesign* During this phase, the focus shifts to improving the design of the entire organization. Teams take an active role in the redesign effort and address such issues as streamlining processes, improving quality, lessening functional barriers, and expanding roles. At this point in the transition, the organization has begun to alter the way it operates—many procedures, work-flow processes, and roles have dramatically changed.

*Phase 5—Reinforcement* Next, support systems (such as the compensation system and other internal, corporate systems) are the focus of reform. The intent is to change the support systems so that they reinforce and strengthen the emerging design.

*Phase 6—Renewal* The emphasis in this final phase is on sustaining energy and enthusiasm at a level that ensures continuous performance improvement.

## KEY CONCEPTS

**Champion of change**: Typically a single individual who wants to increase his or her organization's performance through Employee Empowerment. Effective champions have three characteristics:
- Ability to influence others by gaining their trust and acceptance
- Contact with the daily realities of the organization
- Knowledge of Employee Empowerment and its organizational implications

**Empowerment**: Providing employees with greater decision-making, problem-solving, and administrative responsibility and authority.

**Organization as ecosystem**: Concept that sustainable organizational change requires a fundamental alteration and reconfiguration of lasting improvement on a variety of systems and processes. In this view, the organization must be thought of as a kind of ecosystem with highly complex and interrelated subsystems. Virtually all systems, structures, processes, and roles will be affected if sustainable change is to take place.

**Redesign**: Consists of two steps—analysis and implementation. During the analysis phase, a work team examines its core work processes and develops an improved design. The analysis includes an assessment of business factors affecting the team, how technology is used, and the roles that members of the team play in performing work and making decisions. In the second step, the team takes responsibility for implementing the new design.

**Team**: While teams can be structured in many different ways, they share certain core characteristics:

- Purpose
- Understanding of how the activities of the team link to the company
- Awareness of the customer needs that the team's efforts are addressing
- Understanding of team member roles
- Information-sharing, problem-solving, and decision-making mechanisms
- Set of operating guidelines or norms of acceptable behavior

**Transformation Pathway**: The sequence or pathway for implementing Employee Empowerment to ensure sustainable change. The pathway consists of six phases of progression: Leadership, Commitment, Communication, Redesign, Reinforcement, and Renewal.

## ACTION STEPS

- Establish a champion who will lead the effort and articulate a case for change.
- Develop an implementation strategy that, among other things, addresses the doubts and possible resistance of middle management. Encourage a climate of experimentation.
- Move from a "need to know" to "right to know" mode of dealing with information. Give people access to as much information as they think they need.
- Expand training efforts to include technical, interpersonal, and business skills.

- Involve work teams in redesign of work systems and processes.
- See that the rewards system of the organization reinforces teamwork.
- Work at continual renewal and revitalization of the empowerment system.

## PROBLEM-SOLVING

*"We are overly bureaucratic and slow to adapt to change—we lack flexibility."*

By empowering those at lower levels in the organization to make decisions relevant to their work processes, issues are addressed far more quickly. In addition, as the effectiveness of teams increases, it typically becomes evident that the organization can operate with fewer levels of management, less departmentalization, and fewer discrete, highly specialized roles.

*"Morale and job satisfaction are low, turnover is creeping up, and labor relations are tense."*

Employees in empowered organizations generally report higher levels of job satisfaction than their counterparts in traditional work settings. Some experts even have argued that higher levels of job satisfaction and the corresponding reduction in levels of worker alienation make Employee Empowerment an ethical imperative. But Employee Empowerment cannot be created without support from the top. To gain management support, companies commonly benchmark facilities where Employee Empowerment is already well established. Once managers see empowerment in action, they are far more likely to appreciate its potential.

*"Initial efforts at introducing a team-based work system have failed to produce any tangible results."*

Review the phases of the Transformation Pathway as a way of diagnosing what may have gone wrong in the implementation effort. It often becomes obvious that there was an initial lack of upper-management sponsorship or that the flow of information was not effectively expanded. Based on this diagnosis, develop action plans to correct the problems and get the empowerment effort back on track.

## SUMMARY

- Employee Empowerment is a fundamental approach to effectively manage modern organizations.
- Employee Empowerment is characterized by work teams, open access to information, coaches instead of bosses, and business systems that support teamwork.
- Employee Empowerment has been shown to increase job satisfaction, improve quality and time-to-market measures, and lower cost.
- Attempts to implement Employee Empowerment have failed as often as they have succeeded. The direct support of Top Management for implementation is critical in improving the odds.
- The Transformation Pathway provides a systematic approach to implementation.

## INFORMATION RESOURCES

*Recreating the Workplace: The Pathway to High Performance Work Systems,* Steven R. Rayner, Oliver Wight Publications, 1993.

*Leading Self-Directed Work Teams: A Guide to Developing New Team Leadership Skills,* Kimball Fisher, McGraw-Hill, 1993.

*The High Performance Enterprise: Reinventing the People Side of Your Business,* Donna R. Neusch and Alan F. Siebenaler, Oliver Wight Publications, 1993.

## INTERNAL CROSS-REFERENCE

Your understanding of this topic may be enhanced by the following chapters:

   I–1. Hallmarks of Excellence

   III–1. Building a Learning Organization

### About the Author

Steven R. Rayner is co-founder of the consulting and training firm Belgard-Fisher-Rayner, Inc. He is author of *Recreating the Workplace: The Pathway to High Performance Work Systems* and numerous articles on the topic of creating a team-based organization. Steve is a regular speaker at professional societies, including the American Society of Training and Development, the Association of Quality and Participation, and the Ecology of Work Conference.

# Energizing Your Workforce with High Performance Teams

*Grace L. Pastiak*

### IN A NUTSHELL

High Performance Teams (HPTs, also known as High Performance Work Teams) bring people together to solve the complex problems faced daily in the workplace. These teams encourage people to take ownership of their work and to feel that they have a hand in running the business. This is accomplished by allowing people to share in the development of a common team focus that is aligned with the corporate mission, and by giving them training in teamwork and problem-solving.

In the HPT environment, people pull together to maximize customer satisfaction and minimize waste. Teams are given problem-solving tools such as root cause analysis, anticipating problem techniques, and force field analysis. The multiple perspectives, commitments to improvements, and individual knowledge bases that characterize team environments give these tools added power.

When a single person is involved in problem-solving, a one-dimensional view prevails. With two people involved, there are two dimensions. A cross-functional group has an opportunity to create a "hologrammatic" perspective. That hologram comes into focus when the group is honed into a High Performance Work Team. Hidden agendas and individual prejudices naturally wither when they no longer serve a purpose. The power base of the individual becomes the power base of the team, especially when it is used to solve problems and improve the company's competitive position.

## *Origins*

Historically, manufacturing workers were organized into groups with a supervisor and a specific work area. Their role in making changes or improvements was constricted. The responsibility of employees was simple—keep things moving without hassles and look busy when the supervisor walks by. Of course, no one would inform the quality department if they had any problems.

This began to change as businesses began to pass on the responsibility for solving problems and delighting customers to the people closest to the opportunities for improvement. This led to community-focused cultures in which people felt a sense of pride in being involved in making improvements to the business.

## *The Nature of HPT Environments*

The High Performance Team requires supervisors to adopt new roles. Rather than serving as bosses, supervisors in HPT environments become coaches with responsibility for working with multiple teams. Figure 1 shows the interactions between people on the path to participating in High Performance Teams, as outlined by Wilson Learning Corporation.

In the figure, the lowest level of interaction is that of a collection of individuals. People interacting at this level typically lack a common understanding of the organization's short- and long-term objectives. They usually see their role as coming to work to get a job done and earning a paycheck, feeling little or no responsibility for the final

**FIGURE 1. STAGES OF HIGH PERFORMANCE TEAM**

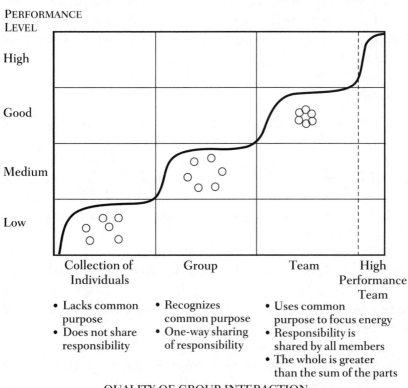

SOURCE: Adapted from *Creating High Performance Teams,* Wilson Learning Corporation, 1985. Reprinted by permission.

output of the company. The next level is that of a group. Here many people begin to see a common objective; however, the responsibility for successfully achieving the goal remains on the supervisor's shoulders. At the next level, the team phase, energy is focused on a common objective, responsibility is shared by all members, and people are able to sustain a synergistic process in which the whole is greater than the sum of the parts. This is where the greatest rewards start to appear; people in the team phase begin to feel that they can run the business. From this foundation comes the ability to creatively solve problems by drawing on the collective imagination of all team members.

At the team level, the group develops a life of its own; it is able to take on problems, resolve internal and external conflicts, and focus on activities that add value. Focus allows the team to get more done with less, communicate more effectively, and refine ideas quickly. All these attributes contribute to a significant competitive edge for the company.

## *Benefits*

The HPT approach offers numerous benefits, the primary one being that it gives people the opportunity to make a difference and to feel connected with their stakeholders. As Tellabs Manufacturing puts it, "HPT allows all of us to share ownership and be involved in the business." At first blush, this sounds simplistic, but it does in fact get at the heart of the issue: HPT enables people to make decisions and act as if they owned the business.

A key side benefit of team-focused companies is a higher level of employee and customer loyalty. Employees feel that they are making a difference, and the customers feel that people inside the company are motivated to do whatever it takes to solve their problems and provide them with excellent service.

The investment needed to initiate the HPT concept varies, depending on the approach and the size of the company. A department of, say, 250 people, just starting with a pilot HPT program, might spend between $4,000 and $8,000 on training materials, travel, and consultants. Travel associated with attendance at local conferences, such as those sponsored by the Association for Manufacturing Excellence, may also add to the HPT startup costs.

## *Implementation*

Before beginning actual HPT implementation, it is important to understand a number of key issues, including:

- The first place to look for improvement is in the mirror! If you, as the leader, are not sold on the value of energizing all of your workforce, your people simply will not be motivated to become problem solvers.

- Co-location speeds the process of teaming because everyone can experience the same problem at the same time. This eliminates the need to pass messages "over the wall," shortening the time it takes to process an idea or receive feedback.
- Basic and ongoing communication training will help to bring out the best skills in team members.
- People must understand that it is a "new day and a new way." Self-managing teams need less supervision. Some supervisors find this threatening, and it's important to be ready to deal with the consequences of such fear. It is not uncommon for as much as 50 percent of the management team to fight the transition to HPT. Eventually, these people will shift to single contributor roles.
- Diverse teams tend to come up with the stronger "holograms."

Implementation of High Performance Teams generally entails the following five steps:

1. HPT should start with an "as is" analysis. Ask your team members to answer the following six questions, developed by Kathleen H. Goeppinger of Chicago's Loyola University:

- What are the positive values the organization needs to maintain?
- What roadblocks stand between us and successful implementation of higher performance teams?
- Do we have a shared definition of a High Performance Team?
- For which responsibilities should the team be held accountable?
- What training do employees need in order to be able to participate?
- Should we begin with pilots or implement HPT's universality at the same time?

Tools such as the Empowerment Profile, a questionnaire developed by Drs. John E. Jones and William L. Bearley, can also assist in the "as is" analysis. The Empowerment Profile helps identify the gap between the level of empowerment the team feels it has and the level of responsibility that management perceives it has given the team.

2. Identify the key leverage points. By using a structured methodology, you can determine the key drivers in your organization and their effect on your teams. One useful methodology is called the Seven Management and Planning Tools, a set of problem-solving tools described in *Memory Jogger Plus+*.

3. Initiate small work teams with key players assigned to work cells. Whether the team is assembling products or developing ideas for new businesses, this arrangement will help players feel a mutual responsibility for the quality of the collective output. Also, seeing each other every day begins the process of forging a strong team spirit.

4. Focus on activities that will make the team most productive. A weekly reality check that tests the team's output and interactions will encourage the team to resolve conflicts. Typical yes/no questions in this reality check are:

- Do I believe the team's direction will increase our competitive advantage?
- Am I a valuable member of the team?
- Do I have any unresolved work issues?
- Have we the tools to accomplish the tasks at hand?
- Do our customers benefit from our efforts?
- Did we have a good week?

5. Once the first pilot is on solid footing, begin planning for the next one. Speed, rather than perfection, is important at this stage; if you spend too much time dotting the i's and crossing the t's, you'll lose momentum and have little chance of making a real change in your corporate culture.

## KEY CONCEPTS

**Co-location**: Physically placing people together in the work areas of those people accountable for the success of their teams.

**Communications training**: Basic training in both positive interventions and conflict interventions, as well as how to run meetings.

**Cross-functional**: Setting up a diverse group of people in order to see many sides of a problem to detect defects in thought quickly.

**High Performance Team**: People focused on a common objective, sharing responsibility and ownership for results. The combined energy of a team is greater and of higher quality than a mere collection of individuals.

## ACTION STEPS

- Identify a pilot group.
- Select a leader.
- Set up joint learning opportunities for the leader, the pilot support staff, and management.
- Get started with a co-located team.
- Work with the results of an "as is" analysis to implement improvements.
- Encourage the team to experiment.
- Protect the team in the beginning from those who believe that everything should stay the same.
- Have the pilot team help with the process for the next team.
- Celebrate the results.
- Continue to educate and train members of all teams in order to keep the teams excited and results-oriented.

## PROBLEM-SOLVING

*"In our company we have many people, but never enough qualified people when we need them."*

Begin the process of developing cross-functionally trained members of High Performance Teams who will be ready when new opportunities arise, such as the expansion of a business. We began a small cross-functional pilot to investigate leveraging one product's technology into other products. Upon completion of the pilot, the team members were in a perfect position to take on three new projects because the breadth of their skills had increased so much as a result of the cross-functional training and team experience.

*"Our order information takes too long to process."*

Combine a sales administration representative with a production scheduler and materials coordinator in U-shaped work areas. Cross-train staff in each function as well as in the benefits of processing information quickly and correctly. Let staff tear down the old processes that supported a slower paper transfer of information.

## SUMMARY

High Performance Teams contribute to the following positive developments:

- Encourage people to take ownership of their work.
- Get people to work together to maximize customer satisfaction and minimize waste.
- Eliminate many supervisory requirements. This is often a source of resistance.
- Bring a multidimensional perspective to problem-solving.

## INFORMATION RESOURCES

*The High Performance Enterprise: Reinventing the People Side of Your Business,* Donna R. Neusch, and Alan F. Siebenaler, Oliver Wight Publications, 1993.

*The TeamNet Factor,* Jessica Lipnack and Jeffrey Stamps, Oliver Wight Publications, 1993.

*Memory Jogger Plus+,* Michael Brassard, Goal/QPC, 1989.

*What a Great Idea: Key Steps Creative People Take,* Charles Thompson, HarperCollins Publishers, 1992.

## INTERNAL CROSS-REFERENCE

Your understanding of this topic may be enhanced by the following chapters:

III–2. Making Employee Empowerment Work

IV–1. Total Quality Management (TQM)

IV–4. Just-in-Time: Driver for Continuous Improvement

### About the Author

Grace L. Pastiak is director of new business development at Tellabs Operations, Inc. She has been at Tellabs since 1979 and has served as the company's manufacturing operations manager, materials manager, director of manufacturing, and JIT project leader. Grace is certified as a practitioner in production and inventory management by APICS and was featured in a recent Sunday *New York Times* article on work teams.

# Crossing Boundaries with Teamnets

*Jessica Lipnack and Jeffrey Stamps*

### IN A NUTSHELL

Teamnets are the new way of organizing companies. Whether your firm works regularly with other companies or your internal departments need to work together more closely, teamnets can be the organization of choice.

Teamnets bring together two powerful organizational ideas: *Teams*, where small groups of people work with focus, motivation, and skill to achieve shared goals; and *Networks*, where disparate groups of people and groups link to work together based on common purpose. Thus, teamnets are networks of teams that cross boundaries.

If you're involved with outsourcing, partnering, or if you consider your firm a "virtual" corporation, the old forms of hierarchy and bureaucracy can stand in the way of getting things done. If you're working in a joint venture with another company, you cannot fire the people on the other team if you don't like what they are doing. Nor can you force people in another organization to fill out forms or follow procedures just because "it's the way we do things." The top-down orders of hierarchies and the endless rules of bureaucracies have little meaning when you work in organizations that span traditional boundaries.

Most people already participate in cross-boundary teamnets, perhaps without realizing it: quality circles, self-managed work groups, cross-functional teams, high performance work systems, joint ventures, alliances, consortia, and flexible manufacturing networks. Reengineering and total quality efforts both involve teamnets. Whenever you work with people outside your own organization—whether suppliers, customers, or people in other departments—you are working in a teamnet.

Why is this happening? Why have we gone from the situation of a single boss and strict allegiance to one chain of command to the challenge of working in many places across traditional boundaries? Because things are getting faster, more complex, and more global. No matter how big we are, we can't do it all by ourselves.

## *Benefits*

Survival in today's dynamic business environment requires more than new technology. It requires new organizations. Teamnets are the organizational form for the twenty-first century, making it possible for companies to link internal and external activities in powerful ways. They make it possible for people to get the job done efficiently and with low overhead. Teamnets offer three competitive benefits:

*Power* With more than one organization on board, teamnets benefit from shared knowledge, learning, skill, and resources.

*Speed* Teamnets streamline decision making. With many people able to act in parallel on different aspects of the same problem, decision making is rapid. A few phone calls replace fifteen levels of signatures.

*Flexibility* Unlike their rigid bureaucratic relatives—organizational "silos"—that prevent creative response to opportunities, teamnets are highly plastic. They bend, conform, and configure themselves to the challenges they face.

Time represents the major cost of developing teamnets. Planning time, and the time required to involve all concerned parties, is a requirement of effective teamnets. Planning time varies with the complexity of the project. A two-week effort to put out a joint-venture marketing brochure requires much less planning than does a five-year effort to build a new jumbo jet. But teamnets are used for both.

The biggest impediment to teamnet success is fear of change. Working with people from other functional areas can, at first, seem strange; they usually bring a different outlook and different set of abiding interests. And it takes courage to believe that working with competitors in joint ventures can be good for your own business.

Many successful companies today practice "co-opetition," a combination of cooperation and competition. The combination of cooperative power and competitive zeal offers companies organizational advantages. When employees can accomplish more together than they can apart, they cooperate; when they can succeed independently, they compete. Part of the art of teamnet work is knowing how to move between cooperation and competition.

## The Five Principles of Teamnets

1. *Unifying purpose.* Successful teamnets begin with a unifying purpose. There is no reason to form a teamnet unless you have something vital to accomplish together. In the face of rapid change, traditional control mechanisms fail, but a unifying purpose provides a context for action.

2. *Independent members.* Every teamnet has a unique set of members, each of whom has something different to contribute to the group. Paradoxically, it is the independence of these members that gives the teamnet its power. The objection that "Teamnets won't work here because we don't want to give up our independence" is contradictory. Without independence, there are no teamnets.

3. *Linkages.* Because teamnets are usually dispersed geographically, the water cooler or cafeteria cannot serve its traditional function as informal gathering place and information exchange.

Thus, teamnets require very different work processes than those used by people located in the same place or in the same organization or department.

Many believe that technology will ensure linkage between teamnet members. Sophisticated computer and communications systems can help; however, they cannot guarantee the linkages teams need to function. Technology can help, but links between teamnet members rely more on trust and sharing than on physical linkages.

4. *Multiple leaders.* Vibrant teamnets have many leaders. This fact arises from the multiple roles, skills, and knowledge required to address the complex tasks taken on by the group. The style of teamnet leadership is different than that found in hierarchical organizations. There is very little crack-the-whip leadership, but much more quiet leadership by people leading by example or through collaboration among peers.

5. *Integrated levels.* Teamnet leaders interact intensively with traditional management. Because teamnet leaders must manage relationships among different levels of the hierarchy, one of the worse mistakes they can make is to ignore existing management. It's just as important to interact with the "lower-archy" as with the "hierarchy." When setting up a teamnet, include people from *all* levels, not just the middle.

Many people think of networks as flat, two-dimensional planes of horizontally connected members. Appealing as this image of flatness is, it is plain wrong. Teamnets are lumpy, clustered, and multileveled organizations.

## *Implementation*

Most teamnets fail because they fail to observe one or another of the five principles just mentioned. The following spells out how those failures occur.

1. *Purpose.* Unless there is a clear purpose, teamnets collapse. Most don't spend nearly enough time talking about purpose. On the other hand, too much uncritical agreement leads to "groupthink." If everyone must agree on everything in order to work together, the

teamnet is headed for trouble. SUGGESTION: Create a statement of purpose and test its currency with members regularly.

2. *Members.* The most difficult thing for many people is to give up control in favor of influence. The higher you go in the organization, the more difficult this becomes. Executive teams often have the most trouble relinquishing direct control. A teamnet cannot function with substantive autonomy. Both the teamnet and its members must be able to stand on their own. SUGGESTION: Maintain a directory of current members; keep it current and circulating.

3. *Links.* When the hierarchy appoints all members of the team, relationships and commitment are involuntary. Lacking the voluntary spirit, trust and share of information are difficult to establish and maintain. Communication is the key to success, and information sharing is critical to meaningful communication. Teamnets also fail from information overload and too much communication. SUGGESTION: Invest in communication, both personal relationships and physical systems.

4. *Leaders.* Teamnets succeed when they have more than one leader. But there can be too much leadership—"too many cooks spoil the broth." Multiple leaders can create confusion if they lead in different directions. SUGGESTION: Reward people who step into the breach to provide leadership; also reward people who are good followers. Every organization needs both.

5. *Levels.* Many internal teams fail to cut across levels in the organization. One way to succeed is to use the buddy system. At an international airline, each person on the teamnet was paired with a senior executive. Likewise, failure to manage down creates the risk of losing touch with the organization as a whole. SUGGESTION: Keep the teamnet plugged into all levels of the organization.

## KEY CONCEPTS

**Boundary crossing**: By reaching across the traditional organizational, corporate, and geographic boundaries that can hinder rapid response in a volatile climate, teamnets allow enterprises, large and small, to achieve global competitiveness.

**Co-opetition**: Teamnets allow companies of all sizes to learn to cooperate and compete at the same time.

**Fewer bosses, more leaders**: Teamnets provide the opportunity for multiple leadership within a hierarchy—unlike bureaucracies, which simply create more boxes.

**More change means more teamnets**: Hierarchies and bureaucracies will be with us for the foreseeable future, but the accelerating pace of change means that organizations will become more networked.

**Those that do, plan**: Teamnets use participatory planning in anticipating the future. Shared planning is essential for all boundary-crossing groups.

## ACTION STEPS

- Clarify purpose by agreeing on mission and goals.
- Identify members of the teamnet.
- Link people to one another in as many ways as possible.
- Multiply leadership to the maximum.
- Integrate levels of the organization.

## PROBLEM-SOLVING

*"Costs are going up while our ability to reach new markets is shrinking."*

Setting up a teamnet with other companies may make it possible to reduce costs while increasing market share. One network of sixteen small manufacturing firms has seen revenues increase fourfold among its core firms. Together, companies can purchase cooperatively, market jointly, combine R&D, cosponsor training, and set up quality programs.

*"In my large company, internal competition is even more difficult to overcome than winning new customers. Internal groups wage war on projects that stray across functional borders, and key projects that require multigroup collaboration are stymied by the central group's slowness and unwillingness to change."*

Call a teamnet meeting, inviting key people from each of the internal organizations. Explain that this is a company-wide effort and that individual group allegiances need to be put on hold for the duration of the project. Engage everyone in planning the project and reward them for being excellent teamnet members. This will ensure buy-in and pride in the project's outcome.

*"My organization needs to become a teamnet, but my boss is against it."*

Education is the first step. Many people are reluctant to try something new unless they are convinced that other companies have used it successfully. So begin with information that makes the case. At the same time, figure out whom your boss turns to for advice. Educate and convince them. Most people come around when evidence is convincing and the people they respect advocate the idea.

## SUMMARY

- Most companies already have teamnets but they don't realize it. By learning the key principles, you can ensure that your teamnets are successful.
- "Co-opertition" enables companies to balance cooperation and competition.
- Companies can do things together that they cannot do alone. Consider developing teamnets if costs are too high to expand your business.
- Bosses are out; leaders are in.

## INFORMATION RESOURCES

*The Age of the Network: Organizing Principles for the 21st Century*, Jessica Lipnack and Jeffrey Stamps, Oliver Wight Publications, 1994.

*The TeamNet Factor: Bringing the Power of Boundary Crossing into the Heart of Your Business*, Jessica Lipnack and Jeffrey Stamps, Oliver Wight Publications, 1993.

*A Catalog of U.S. Manufacturing Networks*, Gregg A. Lichtenstein, National Institute of Standards and Technology, 1992.

*TeamNet Tools*, software and "User Process Guide," Jessica Lipnack and Jeffrey Stamps, Oliver Wight Publications, 1993.

## INTERNAL CROSS-REFERENCE

Your understanding of this topic may be enhanced by the following chapters:

    II–1. Being a World Class Customer

    III–3. Energizing Your Workforce with High Performance Teams

    VI–1. Enterprise Logistics Management (ELM)

    VI–2. Supplier Quality Management (SQM)

### About the Authors

Jessica Lipnack and Jeffrey Stamps are founders and principals of The Networking Institute, Inc., a consulting company in West Newton, Massachusetts, specializing in teamnets—a term they coined for networked organizations. They are co-authors of four books, including *The TeamNet Factor* and *The Age of the Network*, and many articles appearing in publications such as the *Boston Globe*, the *New York Times*, and the *Christian Science Monitor*. They are frequent speakers at conferences and seminars in the United States and abroad.

# III-5

# Organizational Communication

*Eric K. Hatch*

## IN A NUTSHELL

The purpose of organizational communication is to provide—and obtain—information critical to the success of the venture. In the broadest sense, Hoshin Planning (see chapter I–4) is an example of organizational communication. So are product catalogues, annual shareholders' meetings, and employee-attitude surveys.

Organizational communication falls into two categories, with substantial overlap. These categories are Functional Communication and Strategic Communication. Functional communication is the exchange of information vital to the performance of one's immediate task. Telephone books, lab-test results, and Statistical Process Control (SPC) charts are all examples of functional communication.

Strategic communication is defined as information necessary to understand the context into which the task fits. Mission statements, economic news, information about competitive developments or charts on the costs of environmental compliance are all strategic communication. This chapter emphasizes strategic communication in the manufacturing enterprise.

## Benefits

From the organization's point of view, the real purpose of strategic communication is to align all audiences with the company's values, direction, strategies, ethics, and needs. In other words, the value of strategic communication is to:

- Increase congruence—help the organization "walk the talk"
- Sharpen the organization's focus and thereby heighten its productivity
- Meet the psychological needs of the audience *and* the needs of the organization

Costs to acquire an effective communication process vary with the size of the organization and with the media used. All organizations need to have someone who makes communication his or her special task; this approaches a full-time duty as a company reaches 400 to 500 people. In addition, a basic materials and media budget would be about $40,000 and would cover a newsletter and miscellaneous services.

## What People Want to Know

In general, employees want to know the answers to four questions that strategic communication should provide:

- What's in it for me? (How does this affect me?)
- How are we, and how am I, doing?
- How does my work fit in?
- What's going to happen to me tomorrow?

These questions are driven by universal psychological needs. Employees need to feel empowered, in control, valued, and secure. They feel that knowledge is power and "forewarned is forearmed." Communications that address these needs are perceived as more relevant—and hence will have more impact—than communications that do not.

## Plan the Strategy

Planning is an essential part of effective strategic communication. "What should we say" is the *output* of the planning process, not the starting point. Planning answers five questions:

1. What do we want people to do or feel as a result of our communication? For instance, "We want people to accept the introduction of drug testing next month." "We want to make people aware that our customers think our quality is slipping lately, and we want to reinforce our commitment to quality."
2. What is the voice of the customers (audience)? What are their values? What are their wants?
3. What are the constraints governing the communication?
4. How will we know if the communication process is working?
5. What do we want to say or hear?

## Plan the Implementation

These are the elements to plan for:

*The message* What is it? How is it developed? Who writes it? Who is ultimately responsible for the content?

*The audience* Who sees it?

*The media* What are the available media? Which ones are appropriate for this message and this audience? Table 1 compares the uses and limitations of various media. All these media boil down to face-to-face, print, or film/TV. Face-to-face works best for most business communication.

*The spokesperson* Who delivers the message?

*Timing* When will the message go out? What is the production cycle? What is the approval cycle? How long do we have?

**TABLE 1. COMPARISON OF MEDIA**

| Medium | Purpose | Strengths | Problems | Timing | Costs | Comments |
|---|---|---|---|---|---|---|
| Stand-up meetings | quick communications | fast, informal, timely | may underinform or mislead; may get out of hand | daily, weekly, monthly; 10–15 minutes | minimal | supervisors may need training and support materials |
| All-hands meetings | Issues oriented | large groups get identical information | logistics; requires preparation | 2–3 times/year 45–60 minutes | low to moderate | great for sharing visions, company strategy |
| Dialogue meetings | share view; listen to employees | high credibility; top managers get unfiltered information | selecting people may be a problem; not for problem-solving | biweekly or monthly; 1–2 hours | low to moderate | may need facilitation; need a recorder |
| Work-unit staff meetings | info-sharing; problem-solving | credibility and high participation | may be viewed as "here's the party line" | 1–2 weeks; 45 minutes–2 hrs | low | must be planned |
| Stand-alone videotapes | top-level communiqués; training | opportunity to use graphics well | one-way communications; bad for detailed material | do not exceed 20 minutes | high for production, moderate for distribution | always provide a discussion guide. DO NOT USE ALONE |
| Live video town meeting | 2-way communications on important issues | spontaneous; establishes credibility; unifies sites | leader must be good on his feet; risky; logistic problems | 2–3 per year | expensive | success depends on speaker skills, quality of panel and questions |
| In-House TV network | fast-breaking info; training | can be timely | bad production values kill this; endless demands for material | daily | very expensive | |

| | | | | | |
|---|---|---|---|---|---|
| Video staff meeting and teleconferencing | info-sharing or problem-solving | ties in distant sites or customers; cheaper than airfare | need professional setup; security issues | as needed | expensive | graphics need special design because of low resolution |
| Electronic mail | info-sharing | fast | limited graphics | as needed | moderate if everyone has a terminal | |
| Newsletters | business news and issues | fairly quick; good for detailed info, graphics, and tables | easily turns into propaganda or trivia | weekly, monthly, bimonthly | low to moderate | should focus on legitimate news and issues; avoid management preaching |
| Magazines | business news and issues | slow, but permit extended discussion | hard to maintain credibility; lead time | quarterly | expensive | needs high standards for content and graphics; no fluff |
| Bulletin boards | business news; functional news | quick and simple | hit-or-miss readership; hard to stand out from the clutter | daily | low | requires ongoing maintenance |
| Attitude surveys | listening to voice of customers (internal and external) | can tell much and guide policy; quantifiable results | tells little if badly designed | 2–3 years; single issue surveys more often | high | best when combined with focus group data; must act on information |
| Focus groups | listening | good for testing ideas and getting specific info | not quantifiable; need careful selection and faciliation | as needed | low to moderate | excellent if group is carefully selected |
| Electronic bulletin boards | listening | terrific listening tool; gets unfiltered input | may become dominated by cranks | ongoing | moderate to high | some risks; very candid |

*The delivery* When does the message have to be there? How is it distributed?

*The budget* How much will we spend to get the results we want?

*Measurement* How will we determine whether we succeeded?

For very small businesses (1–100 people): use staff meetings, frequent all-hands meetings, and "brown bag lunches" hosted by the CEO. Use bulletin boards or E-mail for print materials.

For medium businesses (100–500 people): stand-up meetings, staff meetings, dialogue meetings, a semiannual all-hands meeting, and a newsletter are probably enough to make sure everybody is hearing the critical messages and that management is able to listen.

Table 1 provides a list of the most workable media for providing organization communications, along with their associated strengths, weaknesses, costs, and optimal timing.

## *Two Formats That Work*

For dealing with day-to-day issues, most of which relate to functional communication, the stand-up meeting for employees is hard to beat. Keys to success: keep them short, deal with only two or three points, and make sure the speaker is prepared. These meetings can be held daily, or two or three times a week. If the gap between meetings expands, the length expands, and then the character of the meetings changes.

"Huddle" meetings for management make sure everybody on the management team has critical information about the customer and major operational issues. A further purpose is to make decisions quickly so that the business can respond to customer needs more quickly. Huddles have only key players, no stand-ins. Multiple sites can be represented by phone or video link. No presentations are allowed (one chart only, and then only if vital), and a maximum of two minutes per speaker are given. Huddles last one hour and are held weekly. Ground rules: no trivia, little debate, fast pace, fast decision making. If an item cannot be resolved, it is handed to the individuals concerned to be settled that day. Notes of decisions are taken, and all attendees are to brief their people that same day.

## *Implementation*

Rule of thumb: For maximum credibility and minimum dilution, the person with the most ownership of the event or issue should do the communicating—unless that person is disastrous for other reasons!

Other keys to successful communicating: good listening, good preparation, good feedback, and good follow-through. Active listening tells your audience you really do hear their concerns and allows you to plan and respond more effectively.

Good preparation means anticipating questions for any issue and preparing sensible answers. Good preparation means making sure supervisors understand the issues they are expected to communicate. Good preparation means making sure that if a video is to be shown, discussion questions that relate the video to major concerns of management are at hand. Good preparation means, above all, knowing what you want to happen when you've let the genie out of the lamp!

Good feedback means closing the loop with your audience so they know you've heard and understood them. It's closely related to the last item, good follow-through.

In one corporation, management preached for years about open communications. Yet the plant news carried ten opinion pieces (usually featuring top managers whom most workers had never met) to every event or news-related piece. The paper had no credibility; workers said "save the trees" when questioned about its value to them.

Management conducted a detailed communication audit and surfaced many problems, of which the newsletter was just one. Management prepared both an overview and a detailed presentation on the audit findings. Each middle-level manager went through the entire presentation with all his or her people, then asked "Does this apply to us?" "What can we do right now to improve?"

This feedback convinced employees that management was serious about improving. Later, minutes of all these feedback sessions were correlated and organization-wide action plans derived from them. These were announced by the relevant vice president, in person, along with a personal phone number to track results. For the first time, people in that organization thought management was serious. Morale improved greatly, and actual changes were made and maintained.

## *Measure Effectiveness*

It is hard to measure the effectiveness of organizational communication. Even though the outcome may be what you want, there are so many influences on what people do that you can't prove your communication was the sole (or even primary) cause. Nonetheless, there are some ways to measure what you're doing. Here are some key questions to ask when assessing effectiveness:

- Did the message reach its destination on time?
- Did the intended audience get exposed to the message?
- Did the receiver believe the message?
- Did the receiver understand the information?
- Did the receiver believe the communication?
- Did the communication get and keep the receiver's attention?
- Did you get the feedback/results you expected when you planned the communication?

## *Measure Frequently*

A couple of open-ended questions at the end of a staff meeting, a feedback sheet attached to every videotape you distribute, even a brief phone survey asking Did you see the newsletter on drug testing? What did you think of it? will help. Ask open-ended questions like these: What do you think is the main point of this communication? What do you think are the reasons we're eliminating the cafeteria subsidy?

## Accountability

Organizational communication works best when each manager (up to and including the CEO) is held accountable for communication. At Federal Express, renowned for the effectiveness of its organizational communication, part of each manager's appraisal is an evaluation by his or her workers of the manager's practices as communicator.

Making individual managers accountable is the only way to prevent "concrete layers" from building up in an organization. In traditional, hierarchical organizations, middle managers often cling to knowledge and dole information out grudgingly to the chosen few. Only if managers are rewarded for communicating will they do so freely and effectively.

## KEY CONCEPTS

**Credible communication**: Communication that respects the needs and values of the audience. People have great built-in BS-detectors. They know when they're being manipulated. Behavior communicates more loudly than anything else and has the greatest credibility.

**Open communication**: Communication that is two-way, candid, based in trust, and relevant. It includes actions, words, tone, and body language.

**Relevant communication**: Communication that the receiver perceives as important to him or her personally or professionally. Since receivers, not senders, control the meaning of a communication, relevance is determined by the audience, not the sender. Communication that speaks to the audience's values has the most impact.

**Timely communication**: Communication is timely when it meets the timing needs of both audience and sender. In general, strategic communication should be delivered as close to a major event as possible and before it is released to the external press. Hierarchy slows communication, and time is of the essence.

## ACTION STEPS

- Begin by answering the basic questions: Where are we going? What's in it for me? How are we doing?
- Face-to-face communication is far more valuable than written communiqués. Institute regular sessions to provide feedback to employees and to learn what is on their minds.
- Pick a few (three to five) main themes and keep pushing them. If you try to communicate fifty things at once, all you'll do is clutter people's desks.
- Get the CEO and his staff involved as communicators. They have (and need) credibility with all the company's audiences.
- Get out of your office and talk to people in the cafeteria, on the assembly line, in the parking lot, or wherever they congregate.
- Expect some rough-and-tumble. If you're not being questioned, you're not getting through to people.

## PROBLEM-SOLVING

*"We have to downsize and restructure. How can we keep productivity loss to a minimum and get people refocused on their work?"*

The objective is to get your audience to accept the changes. You want to reassure them that the business will turn around and that their future will be more secure, rather than less, as a result of these changes. Communicate quickly and clearly both the actions to be taken and the reasons for the actions. Do this in person, rather than in print, if at all possible. Stress the positive results that these changes will make possible, and give concrete examples. Do your best to make your audience feel that their skills and motivation will turn the situation around. Then make sure your managers hold meetings with the survivors to communicate what work is no longer required, what work is now required that wasn't theirs before, and what your expectations are for the future.

> *"We have to communicate a new, and complicated, set of government regulations to our hourly workforce. We need to build understanding and compliance."*

Establish the relevance of the regulations to the workers' daily jobs and to the business as a whole. Do this on an ongoing basis. Embed the relevance into the factual training and information you communicate. If the relevance isn't obvious, encourage work teams to discuss the topic—and communicate their findings to other teams.

If you don't establish relevance, all the words you speak or print will go to waste. Adults simply will not learn unless they see the impact on them.

> *"Our company has just acquired a new CEO, a woman from a different industry. We need to make her a known commodity as quickly as possible."*

Begin with a new manager assimilation for her and her direct reports. This event encourages open communication and demystifies the new person. Then get her out to meet as many people as possible. Have her develop a state of the business address within the first two months. Deliver it in person, and distribute a videotape for wider distribution. Have her tour the various plants and facilities. Schedule dialogue meetings with people from various levels and locations.

## **SUMMARY**

- Organizations cannot keep information from flowing any more than lava will stop flowing on command.
- It is impossible to control communication because it is impossible to control how people react to things.
- It is possible and desirable to *influence* communication, using

the techniques presented here. The benefits are greater productivity, increased loyalty, and frequently better market share.

## INFORMATION RESOURCES

International Association of Business Communicators (IABC), 1 Hallidie Plaza, Suite 600, San Francisco, CA 94102 (415/433-3400). The IABC offers a number of valuable materials for improving organizational communications. They publish a bibliography of all current writings in the field, and they produce The Communications Bank—material on subjects such as doing a communications audit, producing a company newsletter, creating health awareness, and so forth.

## INTERNAL CROSS-REFERENCE

Your understanding of this topic may be enhanced by the following chapters:

   III-1. Building a Learning Organization

   III-2. Making Employee Empowerment Work

   IV-1. Total Quality Management (TQM)

---

### About the Author

Eric K. Hatch, Ph.D., has worked in, managed, and taught organizational communication for more than fifteen years. For eight years he managed communications for a division of GE Aircraft Engines. His publications include more than sixty articles, speeches, monographs, and film scripts. He is president of Hatch Organizational Consulting based in Cincinnati, which provides training and consultation in the communication aspects of Total Quality, culture change, and team building.

# Compensation for the High Performance Enterprise

*Donna R. Neusch and
Alan F. Siebenaler*

## IN A NUTSHELL

The traditional pay and rewards systems of most companies were originally designed to control their most significant cost—payroll. And they do a satisfactory job of control. These traditional compensation systems, however, are seldom linked to the business objectives and strategies of the company and, as a result, do little to improve company performance. Too often, traditional pay and rewards systems are a function of "time spent at work" and merely encourage a pervasive sense of entitlement. Even newer pay-for-performance programs have been largely ineffective for many of the same reasons.

There is an alternative to traditional compensation systems: *NewComp*®, a new compensation approach for companies seeking to become high performance enterprises. *NewComp*® is not a type of pay or rewards. It is not skill-based pay, broad-banding, or gain sharing; rather, it is a process for designing compensation systems that align pay and rewards with the business objectives and strategic direction of the company.

Changing compensation schemes is a daunting step for any company, which partially explains why so many are loath to take on the task, and why so many traditional compensation systems remain in effect. Even when companies move from individual to team-oriented work—a move that significantly changes the way work is done—they often leave their old compensation systems in place. The result is that the new team initiative is unsupported by an appropriate compensation plan and company performance continues as in the past. (See chapter III–4). Team initiatives and other Employee Empowerment programs require new compensation approaches.

## NewComp® *and the High Performance Enterprise*

*NewComp®* is one step in the larger process of creating a high performance enterprise. Figure 1 describes this larger process, one part of which is concerned with strategy and the other part with people systems. *NewComp®* is step 7 of the people process. It builds on the output of the six process steps that precede it and is eventually integrated with the strategic process steps shown on the left side of the model.

Once an organization has completed People Systems Process steps 1 through 6, it will have:

- Changed the way work is done in the company
- Defined flexibility and designed new, broader jobs that create flexibility in the workplace; this does away with the narrow mind-set expressed as "but that's not my job"
- Defined teams and their evolution, and matched the evolution of supervision to that of teams and the empowerment of teams
- Designed a skills and competency development process to guarantee quality and ensure flexibility
- Created a feedback system focused at the job performance level of both teams and individuals

**FIGURE 1. PROCESS FOR THE HIGH PERFORMANCE ENTERPRISE**

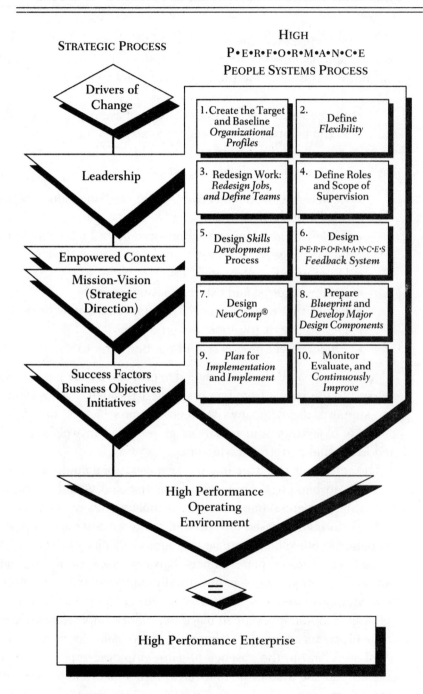

© 1994 Millennium Management Tools, Inc. All rights reserved.

Process step 7, *NewComp®*, builds on this base and employs two specific approaches for turning the output of the first six steps into pay and rewards suited to the high performance enterprise:

1. Strategy-based Pay®. This creates a base-pay program that reinforces the company's new broader jobs, skills training, and performance feedback for teams and individuals. The Strategy-based Pay® process entails the following action steps:

- Review business objectives, team and individual performance objectives
- Review current compensation strategy and total compensation package
- Determine the company's ability to pay
- Review internal and external equity positions
- Establish a new job grade structure for the new broad jobs
- Design pay distribution and guidelines
- Model career progression in the new structure

Strategy-based Pay® is designed to produce a base-pay program tailored to the inputs from process steps 1 through 6. The resulting pay supports the company's strategic success factors, operational business objectives, and initiatives as reflected in weighted team and individual performance factors.

The actual pay structure might take any one of a number of forms (e.g., broad banding). The actual form selected would control an individual's progression to meet the company's business objectives.

2. Performance-based rewards can reinforce and encourage performance improvement from large groups or facilities by sharing the benefits of improved performance. This rewards system—typically labeled as gain sharing—is not usually implemented until after a new strategy-based pay system is in effect, and until the tools, training, and initiatives are in place to produce improvement. Until these elements are in place, there will be no "gain" for the company to "share." And in the absence of gain, employee expectations are dashed and the system de-motivates, rather than encourages, improvement.

Traditional performance-based gain-sharing plans, such as Scanlon, Rucker, or *Improshare®*, are giving way slowly to contemporary systems that stress breakthrough performance. These more future-looking plans are referred to as "goal sharing" or results-sharing programs—they focus on a mix of operational and financial performance indicators.

As with Strategy-based Pay®, the design of performance-based rewards flows from the results of the first six process steps of the ten-step People Systems Process. Creating successful performance-based rewards requires that the company take an iterative approach at answering the following nine questions:

1. What improvements are desired? Based on the company's strategic direction, where is significant improvement required?
2. What planned initiatives will achieve the improved performance? How will the initiatives improve performance?
3. How will the improved performance be measured for each factor? When? By whom? And under what conditions?
4. What individual behaviors contribute to improved performance for each identified factor?
5. On which factors will the improvement and reward strategy focus?
6. What is the process for tracking each measure? How will it be tracked? By whom? At what time intervals? Will employees be involved in the tracking?
7. What does performance improvement have to look like to generate a payout? What are the funding formulas?
8. How will pay be distributed? Who participates? How often?
9. What special considerations must be made for possible contingencies?

## *Successful Implementation*

Recent compensation studies reveal a list of design elements that enhance the success of alternative new compensation systems like *NewComp®*:

- A clear vision of the organization's strategy and culture
- Reward linked to long-term strategic objectives, rather than solely to current business conditions
- Designs clearly tied to business priorities
- A high degree of involvement from all levels of management
- A defined notion of intended results of the programs
- Involving employees in the design and implementation
- On-going evaluation and monitoring against intended results
- Flexibility that allows for Continuous Improvement

The *NewComp®* process employs these design characteristics. Applied to a variety of organizational situations, it produces customized pay and rewards systems that ensure a return on the company's human assets.

## KEY CONCEPTS

**Broad banding**: A base-pay structure often incorporated into strategy-based pay. It moves pay progression laterally through a broad pay range based on established criteria such as performance, skill acquisition, competencies, etc.

**Drivers of change**: Compelling reasons for companies to change from their traditional operating environments. These generally consist of an impending threat to survival or to continued growth and prosperity.

**Empowerment**: That state in which the company's people have been enabled and permitted to share in the control and responsibility for the "performances" that make up the *performance* of the company.

**Entitlement mind-set**: When employees believe that they do not have to earn their pay but rather are owed it because they put in time at work. This leads to an environment in which there is little relationship between performance and pay.

**Expectation mind-set**: The state in which a company and its employees expect that performance counts—that pay and rewards are linked directly to individual and team performance. It produces an environment in which there is a direct relationship between performance and pay.

**High performance operating environment**: An environment built on an expectation mind set. This operating environment is characterized by the fact that performance counts and that the context for performance is empowerment.

**High Performance People Systems**: "Reinvented" people systems that acknowledge, enable, and support the business objectives of the company. They provide the focus, alignment, integration, and system of a hard, but open, process for Continuous Improvement and renewal.

**Operational business objectives**: Measurable, operational business goals that underlie the company's strategy for meeting its long-term goals.

**Pay**: Base pay, the fixed pay rate that a person makes per hour, week, biweekly, semimonthly, or monthly. It is the rate used as the basis to calculate pay premiums such as overtime and shift differentials.

**Pay-for-skills or skill-based pay**: A base-pay system in which pay progression is directly tied to skill acquisition.

**Performance-based rewards**: A form of variable compensation that focuses on reinforcing improvement of shared and common goals among members of an organizational unit. It is often referred to as gain sharing, goal sharing, results sharing, etc.

**Skills**:
 **Core skills**: A group of skills that constitute minimum knowledge or expertise required to perform work in all jobs. Core skills are represented by skills such as reading, basic math, an understanding of the company's initiatives, safety, and housekeeping.

 **Support skills**: Skills particular to the new broader job but not directly related to work performed in the process or on the product These are generally skills that do not add value, and may include material handling, inspection, expediting, etc.

**Operational skills**: Skills that represent the meat of the job—the primary skills that generally add value. In the new broader job, an operational skill may represent what used to be an entire discrete narrow job.

**Technical skills**: Skills that represent an advanced level of basic operational skills or an incremental level of expertise (e.g., not only operating and setting up the machine but also repairing the machine).

**Strategic success factors**: Major themes or areas of change and improvement. Also, broad, general goals identifying the major achievements that over time will enable the company to complete its mission and fulfill its vision.

**Strategy-based Pay®**: A compensation method that aligns and integrates the company's pay systems with its business objectives and a high performance operating environment.

**Traditional compensation**: The pay and rewards systems of the traditional operating environment, which focus on control and consistency and are not linked to the business objectives of the company.

## ACTION STEPS

- Assess the company's readiness to take on the design, development, implementation, and Continuous Improvement of its people systems, including compensation.
- Select a managed project approach to creating world class people systems, including a compensation system appropriate to the company's strategic direction and business objectives.
- Educate management on the process for creating the High Performance Enterprise.
- Using the results of the company assessment as a foundation, complete deficient elements of the strategic process. The output of

this part of the process will become critical input for the People Systems Process. It will also determine the exact charter for the design team.

- Complete all ten steps of the People Systems Process to ensure the creation of a high performance operating environment and the compensation system to enable and sustain it.

## PROBLEM-SOLVING

*"We're doing lean manufacturing and teams, and we're having a problem with compensation. We need a new compensation program for our teams."*

Don't begin with compensation—begin at the beginning! Compensation is only one step in a multistep process . . . and it's way down in the process. Begin with the strategic process, and then proceed step-by-step through the ten-step People Systems Process until a solid foundation is built. The company can apply the *New-Comp®* process to that foundation.

*"Why can't we just do the compensation part of the process? The full process looks as though it takes too much work."*

Compensation is reinforcement. What it reinforces is determined either by design or default. If it doesn't matter to your company what is reinforced, then by default, any compensation approach will do. If the company is implementing initiatives such as teams, lean manufacturing, or TQM—in other words, if the company is redesigning the way it does business—then it must redesign the people side of the business, as well. The ten steps of the High Performance People Systems Process do just that.

## SUMMARY

- Traditional compensation systems are seldom linked to the business objectives and strategies of the company and, as a result, do little to improve company performance.

- *NewComp®*, as part of the ten-step People Systems Process, seeks a greater return on human assets by focusing on compensation as a tool for reinforcing the business objectives of the company.
- The High Performance Enterprise is the product of a Strategic Progress and of a People Systems Process. Compensation design is just one of the steps in the People System Process.
- *NewComp®* combines Strategy-based Pay® and performance-based rewards systems. Together, they support the higher performing working environments that world class companies are moving toward.

## INFORMATION RESOURCES

*The High Performance Enterprise: Reinventing the People Side of Your Business,* Donna R. Neusch and Alan F. Siebenaler, Oliver Wight Publications, 1993.

*Rewards and Renewal: America's Search for Competitive Advantage Through Alternative Pay Strategies,* Marc J. Wallace, American Compensation Association, 1990.

*Strategic Pay,* Edward Lawler, Jossey-Bass Inc., 1990.

*Capitalizing on Human Assets,* Jerry L. McAdams and Elizabeth J. Hawk, American Compensation Association, 1992.

## INTERNAL CROSS-REFERENCE

Your understanding of this topic may be enhanced by the following chapters:

III–1. Building a Learning Organization

III–2. Making Employee Empowerment Work

VII–1. Measuring Customer Satisfaction

VII–2. Performance Measurements That Support World Class Manufacturing

## About the Authors

Donna R. Neusch and Alan F. Siebenaler are partners in Millennium Management Tools, Inc., a management consulting and education firm located in Evergreen, Colorado. Donna holds a Ph.D. in educational psychology and is a certified compensation professional. She has held senior management positions with Motorola and Tellabs. Alan Siebenaler worked at GTE and Tellabs, where he held senior positions in operations, manufacturing, product development, and quality and design technologies. His hands-on experience spans initiatives such as strategic quality management, demand flow manufacturing, MRP II, focused factories, self-directed work teams, process perfection teams, and pay-for-skills compensation plans.

# PART IV
# CONTINUOUS IMPROVEMENT

**1. Total Quality Management (TQM)**
*Joseph Colletti*

**2. Tools for Total Quality Management (TQM)**
*Bill Montgomery*

**3. Benchmarking the Best-in-Class**
*Pete Landry*

**4. Just-in-Time: Driver for Continuous Improvement**
*William M. Boyst, Jr. (III)*

**5. The Malcolm Baldrige National Quality Award Program**
*Stephen George*

**6. ISO 9000: The International Quality Standard**
*Robert L. Jones and Joseph R. Tunner*

**7. Discovering Improvement Opportunities Through Quality Auditing**
*Greg Hutchins*

IF PEOPLE ARE the heart of the enterprise, then Continuous Improvement is its conscience. A mind set of Continuous Improvement (called "Kaizen" in Japan) fosters a creative discontent with the status quo, If we're still doing it the same way as we were six months ago, we're probably not doing it as well as we could. How can we do it better?

The two opening chapters in Part IV go hand in hand. First, Joe Colletti of Goal/QPC, writing on **Total Quality Management (TQM)**, describes how this superb approach enables companies to continuously improve and respond effectively to change. Next Bill Montgomery, also from Goal/QPC, shows us how the specific **Tools for Total Quality Management** are used in a world class environment. Pete Landry lived and breathed benchmarking during his years at Xerox, and he shares his knowledge with us in **Benchmarking the Best-in-Class.** In the next chapter, Bill Boyst focuses on **Just-in-Time: Driver for Continuous Improvement.**

No discussion of Total Quality would be complete without a discussion of the Baldrige Award and also ISO 9000. This is accomplished in Stephen George's chapter on **The Malcolm Baldrige National Quality Award Program** and **ISO 9000: The International Quality Standard** by Bob Jones and Joe Tunner. Part IV concludes with Greg Hutchins's chapter on **Discovering Improvement Opportunities Through Quality Auditing.**

# IV-1

# Total Quality Management (TQM)
## *Joseph Colletti*

### IN A NUTSHELL

Total Quality Management (TQM) in a manufacturing environment is sometimes difficult to differentiate from traditional quality practices. Charts and graphs have been used in manufacturing for years. People focus on processes and control systems. There are audits and review teams. People worry about scrap, waste, and rework. Discussions often center on output, efficiency, and productivity.

So what's different about TQM? The best answer may be found in this short definition: Total Quality Management is a *new way of working together*.

TQM is based on a process approach to everything in the organization. It is new in that its focus is not limited to problem-solving, but extends to making the best better. In TQM, everyone works both to fix problems and to amplify the excellent things already being done. Its focus is on how to make systems and processes dynamic, not static. This is quite different from the traditional view of organizations as machines.

TQM is a new way in that significant attention is paid to process visibility and process flow. Likewise, there is a focus on the voice of the customer and how it is integrated through design and development into the manufacturing and delivery systems. Heavy emphasis is placed on process visibility created through the use of management tools that make data, information, and concepts visible.

Working means approaching our jobs smarter and harder. We work smarter because TQM provides excellent tools for assessment, analysis and planning. People work harder because they have ownership of the processes in which they participate.

Finally, TQM means working *together*. This is not *empowerment* as commonly understood. Rather it is a *collaboration of efforts* within the strategic goals of the organization. Blind empowerment leads to destructive optimization of individual processes at the expense of the whole organization. Activities that are collaboratively performed lead to successful results.

To repeat: Total Quality Management is a *new way of working together*.

## *Quality in Manufacturing: A Dynamic Model*

A model is helpful in understanding the TQM philosophy and its use in managing a manufacturing organization. Figure 1 captures most dimensions of this model.

To fully understand the message conveyed in Figure 1, we need to examine each section of the figure individually, by the three distinct yet interrelated dimensions to quality:

- The customer dimension, the focus of the organization's efforts
- The operational dimension, which captures the organization's quality strategy in responding to customer requirements
- The organizational dimension, which combines the human and technical components that make the successful achievement of quality efforts possible

These three dimensions do not exist in a vacuum, but within the context of an annual operational plan that is, in turn, part of a long-

**FIGURE 1. TQM: THE ORGANIZATIONAL CHANGE GENERATOR**

©The Woodledge Group. Reproduced with permission.

term strategic plan. Understanding how these dimensions interrelate is critical to the successful implementation of TQM.

*The Customer Dimension* With respect to quality, there are three types of customer demands: Delighting, Requested, and Assumed (see Figure 2). The most obvious is Requested because these are the

**FIGURE 2. THE CUSTOMER DIMENSION**

demands that customers specifically ask for. When a manufacturer delivers a product or service that goes beyond the Requested level of quality, it provides Delighting quality. Finally there is an entire level of quality that is not requested because it is Assumed by the customer. A car buyer *assumes* that the car body will not rust during the first few years of ownership. This same car buyer *requests* the color of choice and is *delighted* when the car responds assertively to the accelerator as it merges onto the expressway.

The key to understanding these variables is to recognize two significant points:

1. This a dynamic model. What is Delighting quality today becomes Requested tomorrow, and Assumed quality before long. Therefore any commitment to quality must be a commitment to continuous and ongoing change. Unless processes and systems have a generative capability, they become obsolete.

2. These dimensions exist in an ordered hierarchy. An organization must meet Assumed quality requirements *before* Requested quality can be addressed. Likewise, the Requested level of quality must be satisfied before there can be Delighting quality. Failure to deliver on Assumed quality will devastate the quality efforts of any manufacturing or service organization.

*The Operational Dimension* The operation dimension of TQM exists to satisfy the customer dimension. In the TQM model, these take the form of Regulated quality, Defect-Free Performance quality, and Feature/Characteristic quality (see Figure 3).

**FIGURE 3. THE OPERATIONAL DIMENSION**

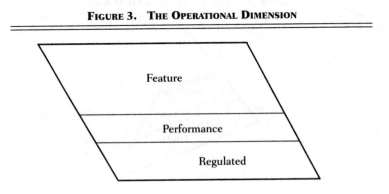

To ensure that there are no breaches in Assumed quality, a TQM organization engages in Regulated quality—typically through a program of quality control and quality assurance. These activities do not add value directly to the product or service, but they minimize the possibility of failures in Assumed quality that would negatively impact the organization's market performance. Without Regulated quality, an organization can't even get into the game and compete. Recent emphasis on ISO 9000 is a good example of Regulated quality.

Defect-Free Performance reflects the manufacturing organization's efforts to create a product that meets all Requested requirements. At the same time it means that the internal processes and systems of the manufacturing operation function without waste or rework.

Finally, there is Feature/Characteristic quality, in which a particular feature of the product itself (e.g., fifty miles per gallon fuel consumption for an automobile) or the processes that produce the product (delivery in ten minutes or less) exceeds customer expectations. These are the characteristics that truly surprise and Delight the customer.

*The Organizational Dimension* The Customer and Operational dimensions of TQM are the most visible aspects of a TQM program. Less visible, but as important, is the Organizational dimension, which acts as their foundation. It is through organizations, after all, that important tasks are undertaken and mastered.

To meet or exceed customer requirements and to manage its operations, the organization must mobilize all of its Human Resources and Technological Capabilities. (See Figure 4.)

Technological capabilities must be at a level that can support the organization's objectives, and they must be enhanced on a continuous basis to support product development and manufacturing process improvements. From a human resource perspective, the organization uses both individual and team efforts to move forward. Team efforts may take a variety of forms: self-directed teams, quality circles, cross-functional teams, and so forth. Teams combine the

## FIGURE 4. THE ORGANIZATIONAL DIMENSION

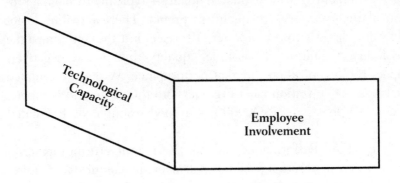

talents, abilities, and resources of individuals and use them in achieving particular objectives. Using teams, an organization can link the entire process chain together—from suppliers, through manufacturing, to the customer.

*Strategic Linkages* What has been described so far of the model represents a change generator. But this change must be guided in a direction determined by an annual plan within a strategic plan. (See Figure 5.) The strategic plan is a multiyear set of objectives that define the breakthroughs, incremental improvements, standardizations, and process terminations required to ensure the success of the organization over the long term. These objectives are, in turn, cap-

## FIGURE 5. STRATEGIC LINKAGES

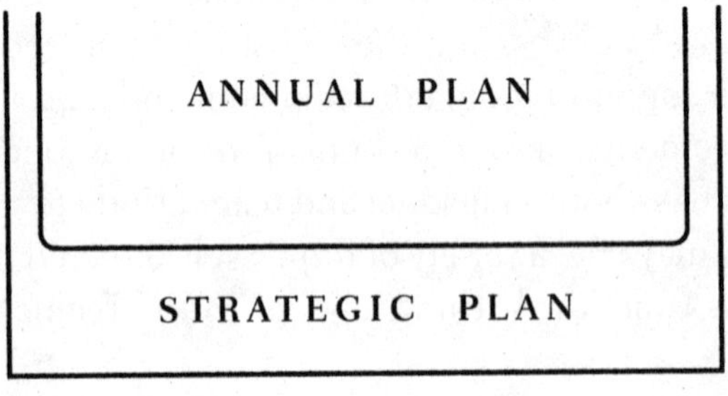

ANNUAL PLAN

STRATEGIC PLAN

tured in the organization's annual operational plan—the template within which the improvement efforts of the organization are focused.

*Partnerships* TQM is based on a process and system perspective. It should be no surprise, then, that no TQM organization stands separate from its suppliers and customers. All are bound together. The quality of raw materials and the information provided by a supplier, for example, have a direct impact on the quality of the user's product or service. No matter where or at what level one looks at an organization's systems, the view always includes the linking of suppliers and customers. This applies to internal as well as external suppliers and customers.

## *The Tools of Total Quality Management*

Since Total Quality Management focuses on data and visibility, it is not surprising that it has tools that capture both data and information in a form that can be analyzed and manipulated. There are the traditional quality-control tools: flowcharts, Pareto charts, data-collection sheets, trend/run charts, control charts, and fishbone charts. These tools are used extensively in problem-solving and process control. And there are new tools, such as the affinity chart, relationship diagram, radar chart, matrix, sequence chart, and contingency tree. These are tools designed to make information available in forms that can be sorted, classified, analyzed, and sequenced by the user. (Please see chapter IV–2 for more information on quality tools.)

## *Implementation*

Successful implementation of TQM in a manufacturing enterprise is contingent upon several prerequisites:

- *A perceived, urgent need for change in the operations of the organization.* Since TQM requires a major management shift, most leadership groups are apprehensive about making the changes needed to create and maintain a TQM environment. The more successful an organization has been in the past, the greater is the reluctance to change behaviors. That reluctance should not be allowed, however, to obscure management's perception that things must change if the company is to survive and prosper.

- *An understanding that TQM is a journey, not a destination.* American organizations often look for short-term fixes and quick solutions. TQM is neither. TQM is a dynamic process that requires constancy and consistency in application, often for years.
- *A willingness to redistribute power and authority.* With its emphasis on customers, collaboration, and the use of teams, TQM alters the distribution of power and authority in most organizations. Autocratic organizations have great difficulty in implementing TQM because decision making is driven down to the lowest appropriate levels in the business.

## *Benefits*

- *Internal processes and systems become generative.* Using the Plan-Do-Check-Act Cycle (described in the Key Concepts section) as a process template, an organization can make adjustments in its processes to adapt to the ever-changing environment. This means that an organization can be flexible in the face of both expected and unexpected change.
- *TQM leads to competitive advantage.* Using TQM, an organization can reduce cycle time, scrap, and rework, improve productivity, and increase customer satisfaction. These elements combine to make the organization a strong competitor.
- *TQM fosters total employee involvement.* The TQM focus on process improvement, customer-supplier partnerships and cross-functional communication encourages personnel at all levels to make daily improvements to the quality of its work. Having more direct control over one's work leads to a greater assumption of responsibility for process outcomes. TQM also capitalizes on the collective genius of teams in solving the problems facing the organization.

## KEY CONCEPTS

**Customer focus**: The voice of the customer is integrated into each process and system in the organization. Meeting and exceeding customer demands are the ultimate objective. For any process there are downstream customers and ultimate customers. Downstream customers are other processes that utilize the output of a specific process. These customers are all those processes between the specific process and the ultimate customer.

**Plan-Do-Check-Act (PDCA) Cycle**: In a changing environment, every process must be able to regenerate itself if it hopes to survive for the long term. The PDCA Cycle ensures this capability. Each process has a "Plan" step that creates the strategy by which the process is organized and performed. The "Do" step transforms inputs into outputs. The "Check" step analyzes the results and the effectiveness of the process itself. Finally, the "Act" step either upgrades the process or standardizes it so that it can be consistently performed at the highest level of effectiveness.

**Process Control/Management**: TQM centers on the premise that all organizational activities are processes—i.e., sequences of activities, or steps, that transform inputs of raw material or data to outputs. Further, no process step stands alone; its interaction is what produces the output. Because interactions take place between a process and its environment, there is variability in the output of processes. Therefore, the control and management of organizational processes are critical to the success of the business.

**Reliance on facts**: TQM is focused on what can be demonstrated through evidence. It is a fact-based management approach. Data and information visibility is critical. Gut feel and experience have to be translated into usable information. Assumptions are continually challenged.

## ACTION STEPS

There is no perfect way to implement Total Quality Management in a manufacturing enterprise. Experience has shown that each organization develops its own implementation based on what is useful and effective. Top-down implementation historically is faster and more efficient; here, the commitment and support of senior management are critical. Figure 6 represents a top-down approach to TQM implementation:

*Step 1. Leadership Commitment* This critical step is the basis for all that follows. It consists primarily of the senior management's initial education on TQM. This may involve visits to locations currently using TQM, reading about TQM, and discussion of TQM's applicability for the organization. After this review the senior leadership group makes a formal commitment to implementing TQM in the organization.

*Step 2. Leadership Practice* The leadership team reviews the processes and systems it currently manages. Processes are made visible in macro flowcharts and the vital signs (measurements) of those processes are identified, charted, and monitored. The extent to which the PDCA Cycle is used in various processes is determined. Customers and their demands on the processes are also identified, and the performance against those demands is assessed.

This accomplished, the leadership team reviews the strategic plan of the organization and identifies its major objectives. It then selects several improvement topics and assigns them to teams. The team process is initiated and the leadership group learns about the dynamics of managing teams in a TQM setting.

The leadership team also evaluates its own management and decision-making activities with respect to TQM principles. Emphasis is on "walking the talk." This evaluation becomes an on-going critique.

Finally, the leadership team develops an implementation plan for cascading and integrating TQM into the organization. It sets up and

**FIGURE 6. TQM IMPLEMENTATION FLOWCHART**

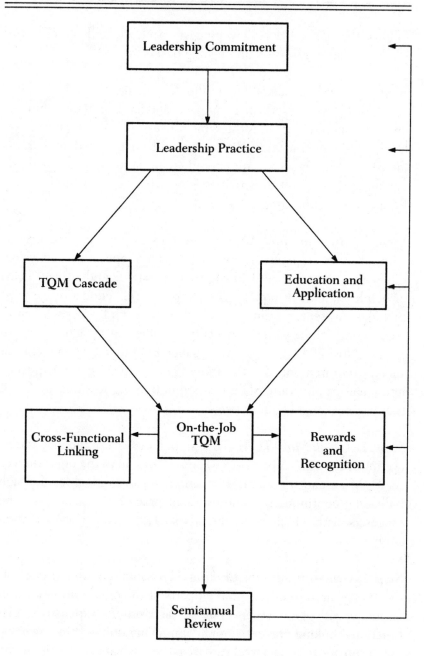

follows through on a review process to check and upgrade this implementation effort on an ongoing basis.

***Step 3. TQM Cascade*** Once the leadership team has cycled through at least one set of team projects and has begun to monitor its own vital signs, it cascades the same process down to the next lower level in the organization. Processes and customer demands are identified. Vital signs are monitored. Team activity is assigned and encouraged. This set of activities is progressively repeated at each level of the organization

***Step 4. Education and Application*** This step is run concurrently with all other steps of the process. It is a supportive activity that raises the ability of individuals to understand and utilize TQM principles and techniques. The scope of the education process includes awareness training, tool utilization, and process analysis techniques. There is also specialty training, on design of experiments, Hoshin Planning, and Quality Function Deployment for specific requirements. For this training to be effective, there must be immediate application. Skills learned in training sessions are lost if they are not quickly put to use.

***Step 5. On-the-Job TQM*** This step focuses on the day-to-day cycling of the PDCA process by each individual in the organization. As TQM cascades down to the various organizational levels, each individual continues the improvement process to ensure that the processes with which he or she is associated are performed effectively.

***Step 6. Cross-Functional Linking*** Horizontal coordination of efforts is required to ensure that all parts of the organization grow in harmony with each other—not at each other's expense. Cross-functional linking prevents rapidly improving units of the organization from moving so far ahead that their advances result in the suboptimization in other units. Management plays a key role in this linking step. Once these internal linkages are strong and well defined, external suppliers and customers can be brought into closer partnership with the organization.

*Step 7. Rewards and Recognition* Culture change will occur only if it is reinforced through rewards and recognition. Rewards and recognition systems are established to support both team and individual improvement efforts. Internal cooperation is as deserving of reward in these systems as internal competition.

*Step 8. Semiannual Review and Upgrade* This implementation process is not exempt from the PDCA Cycle. Accordingly, the leadership team assesses the organizational process versus its plan at least twice a year. Both implementation results and the implementation process itself are analyzed. Problem-solving is conducted on issues and process breakdowns. Lessons learned are identified, evaluated, and, if appropriate, incorporated into the process itself. In this way the TQM process gets better and better over time.

## PROBLEM-SOLVING

*"What happens when we don't get the support of senior management—when they don't 'walk the talk'?"*

This is one of the most common problems faced by those trying to implement TQM. There may be a variety of causes of senior management inconsistency: a misunderstanding of the nature of TQM, resistance to loss of power, a lack of understanding of internal processes and systems, or a misuse of the TQM tools. The best solution is to determine the causes of this problem in your particular situation. An aggressive education program for managers is obviously a must. Follow-up and ongoing audit/review of management practice can also be helpful. In most cases, demonstration of TQM effectiveness at lower levels is the best catalyst for management commitment.

*"Our senior management said TQM is important and gave middle managers an overview. It then got all the employees involved. There are many random ideas being generated and employee expectations of operational change are now escalating. This is turning into chaos. The middle managers have been kept out of the loop and, frankly, we don't know what to do."*

This situation arises when company leaders have not taken the time to figure out how the TQM effort will be managed. The chaos you describe can be the result. The key is for managers to decide how change will be managed. This will have a direct impact on who gets assigned to teams and how recommendations get implemented.

*"We've been doing TQM for several years. At first there were a lot of successes, but now things are more complex and take more time. What are we doing wrong?"*

There is nothing *wrong*. This is the normal path of TQM development in an organization. First the organization "grabs the low hanging fruit." After these easy victories have been won, the organization moves on to more complex analysis and problem-solving. The gains achieved here are more complex, but they are more far reaching in terms of time and money.

### SUMMARY

Implementing TQM in a manufacturing environment is, in essence, the application of sound manufacturing techniques. The statistical process-control tools are the same, there is an emphasis on processes and flows, and teams are often used to ensure cross-functional compatibility of new system ideas and procedures. The major distinction is that the guiding management philosophy aims to "make our best better." Quality becomes part and parcel of the way the organization is run. There is no distinction between quality and the work that one does. The benefits are:

- An aligned workforce
- Continuously improving processes and systems

- Linkages to the voice of the customer
- Visibility and control of processes and systems that enhance the organization's ability to respond to the chaos of ongoing change
- Competitive advantage

## INFORMATION RESOURCES

"Attractive Quality and Must-Be Quality," *Noriaki Kano, Translations Book* 3. GOAL/QPC, 1988. [Refer to this work for the three types of customer demand.]
*A TQM Approach to Achieving Manufacturing Excellence*, Richard Shores, Quality Press, 1990.
*A Quality Technology Primer for Managers*, Joseph R. Tunner, Quality Press, 1990.
*Achieving Total Quality Management*, Michel Perigord, Productivity Press, 1990.
*Attaining Manufacturing Excellence*, Robert Hall, Business One Irwin, 1987.
*Company-wide Total Quality Control*, Shigeru Mizuno, Asian Productivity Organization, 1989.
*Japanese Manufacturing Techniques: Nine Hidden Lessons in Simplicity*, Richard J. Schonberger, The Free Press, 1982.
*Quality Planning and Analysis*, Joseph Juran, McGraw-Hill, 1980.
*Reinventing the Factory: Productivity Breakthroughs in Manufacturing Today*, Roy Harmon and Leroy Peterson, The Free Press, 1990.

## INTERNAL CROSS-REFERENCE

Your understanding of this topic may be enhanced by the following chapters:

I–1. Hallmarks of Excellence

I–4. Hoshin Planning: Breakthrough Tool for Strategy Deployment

II–6. Quality Function Deployment: Breakthrough Tool for Product Development

IV–2. Tools for Total Quality Management (TQM)

IV–4. Just-in-Time: Driver for Continuous Improvement

VI–2. Supplier Quality Management (SQM)

## *About the Author*

Joseph Colletti is a consultant, educator, and author specializing in the areas of TQM implementation, strategic planning, and team facilitation. He has consulted extensively with a variety of major U.S. corporations and has been internationally recognized for his expertise in TQM. His work experience ranges from shop-floor machinist to executive staff member of a Fortune 500 company. Mr. Colletti is a co-author of *Making Daily Management Work* and author of *Focused Planning: Hoshin Kanri American Style.*

# IV-2

# Tools for Total Quality Management (TQM)
## Bill Montgomery

*Editor's note: You'll find the format of this chapter to be substantially different from others in this Guide. The nature of the material—covering a wide range of tools used in Total Quality Management (TQM)—requires that it be presented in an alternative format for maximum clarity and ease of understanding.*

## IN A NUTSHELL

Becoming a world class manufacturer involves improving work flows in the company. It requires a focus on the customer, on employee involvement, on lower cost, and on less waste. These work flows may be found on the manufacturing line or in administration, sales, product development, testing, shipping, or any area of the company.

The common ground of every job is this: A job is a process. The work we do is one, or several, or even many processes. We define process as *a set of interconnected steps with an input and an output*. A process converts that input into a finished product or service for the customer.

The TQM tools described here help people find and correct problems or inefficiencies in processes. These tools are practical and effective, and they're easy to understand and use. Further, they make data and ideas visible for everyone to see and understand. The reason these tools are so effective in process improvement is that they help people both to communicate and to make sound, fact-based decisions.

Each tool, beginning with brainstorming, will be presented using the following sequence:

- What is it?
- Why use it?
- Discussion
- Construction

## *Brainstorming*

*What is it?*
A way to generate ideas, build on each other's ideas, and arrive at a new set of possibilities.

*Why use it?*
- To identify new possibilities
- To develop new strategies
- To involve others in the creation of new approaches

DISCUSSION

Most people have been involved in brainstorming and think that they understand it. As a tool, brainstorming is both valuable and easy to use, but it is also easy to misuse. To be as effective as possible with brainstorming, it is important to pay attention to the guidelines given in the construction section below. Perhaps the most important point is to be clear about the objectives of brainstorming, which should be clear to everyone on the team.

One common objective of brainstorming is to create a long list of ideas (30 to 40) from which 4 or 5 can be explored in depth.

Unfortunately, this leaves 25 or 35 ideas unaddressed, with the result that certain members—backers of those ideas—may feel left out of the brainstorming process. They see their ideas, in effect, consigned to the recycling bin. These situations can generally be avoided. First, if the objective is to address all of the activities needed to achieve a project, use an Affinity Diagram, which is discussed next. No ideas are lost with an Affinity Diagram.

Second, if the objective is to achieve breakthrough thinking, or "out of the box" thinking, then brainstorming is the tool to use. Here, each idea is used as a building block to help generate that one idea that is unusual, different, and, perhaps, even exciting.

## Construction

Begin by being clear about the issue to brainstorm. The issue may be: How can we reduce the cost of shipping this product? Then be clear about why you are brainstorming, as discussed above. Is it to achieve a breakthrough, or simply to make a list of all the possibilities from which a few items will be selected?

Agree to the objective as a team before beginning. Then be certain that each person understands the *rules* of brainstorming, which are:

- No criticism of ideas. All ideas are good ones.
- Limited clarification is allowed. Clarification is permitted because others must understand an idea if they are going to build on it. But long discussions can disrupt the flow of ideas.
- Listen to each other. Really listen.
- Everyone is invited to share his or her ideas. Whether you go around the circle to gather ideas, or allow people to speak up spontaneously, all ideas must be welcomed.

With these rules in mind, each person silently makes his or her own list of ideas. Allow about one minute for this. Most brainstorming teams do not do this, but we have found it extremely effective. Once each person has a list, each can concentrate on what others are saying in the brainstorming session that follows. They will not be concerned about not having an idea when their turn to offer an idea comes around!

The next step is to gather ideas from everyone. A "scribe" records all ideas or comments on a flip chart exactly as they are presented. Where possible, combine similar items, but only if the contributors agree.

When everyone has participated and all ideas are on the flip chart, discuss each idea. Be certain they are fully understood by all participants.

The list is now complete. Your team has generated and finalized a list of brainstormed items and ideas about the issues at hand.

## *Affinity Diagram*

*What is it?*
An Affinity Diagram is a collection of ideas organized into vertical columns. Each column has a "header card" placed at the top that captures the theme of the column of ideas.

*Why use it?*
- To identify the elements for success of a project
- These elements are described by the header cards
- To involve all team members in the process of describing actions to be taken
- To create expansive thinking on an issue
- To create order out of chaos
- To begin a proactive planning effort

DISCUSSION

An Affinity Diagram is a relatively new tool that few people have yet tried. Those who have used it have found it to be a valuable tool for identifying and documenting the actions and items that need to be considered in addressing any issue. Some may think of the Affinity Diagram as merely a mechanical set of steps. It can, however, provide a dynamic experience for teams.

## Construction

Be clear about the issue to be addressed. Write the issue on a flip chart and discuss it to be certain that all team members understand it and agree with the wording. The issue can be anything: What must we do to correct this problem? Or, in the sample Affinity Diagram in Figure 1, What are all the activities needed to achieve our customer-service goal?

Once the issue is understood and clearly articulated, the members start with a dozen or so Post-It™ notes (or other self-sticking note card) upon which they write their ideas in response to the stated issue. Use only a few words on each note card, and begin each with a verb, such as "increase," "gather," "survey," or other action words.

Ideas should be generated through interaction. Thus, talking and sharing are useful during this phase. Do not be concerned about duplications because two note cards that read the same often have slightly different meanings.

Once the cards have been generated, place them randomly on a large flat surface—a wall being a good choice. Then spend a few minutes discussing them and looking for missing action items and ideas. At this point, you can begin organizing the cards into columns as shown in Figure 1. Everyone should silently participate in placing the cards. If two people want one card in two different columns, simply duplicate that card. It can be in both columns.

Once the columns have been formed, create and place header cards at the top of each. The team should talk as they create these headers. Again, use a verb in each header card. The Affinity Diagram is now complete. The header cards represent the key elements that underlie the issue statement.

I have found the Affinity Diagram to be about 80 percent complete the first time it is created. Over time, as the team works on the project, the Affinity Diagram may grow as more items and ideas are added to it, but the first creation of it is nearly complete.

#### FIGURE 1. AFFINITY DIAGRAM

What are all the activities needed to achieve our customer-service goal?

| Develop Employees | Allocate Equipment | Allocate Time | Construct Space | Develop Feedback Approaches |
|---|---|---|---|---|
| Train employees in new methods | Purchase new technology | Make time for planning sessions | Contact contractors | Monitor performance |
| Hire sufficient staff | Buy work station equipment | Prioritize efforts | Determine work areas needed | Develop suggestion system |
| Evaluate skills | Locate unused components | Schedule meetings | Establish budget for new work areas | Compare performance to customer requirements |
| Develop performance evaluation | | Decide key events | | |
| Develop career paths | | | | |

## *Column Flow Chart*<sup>SM</sup>

*What is it?*
A drawing that shows the steps of a process from a high level overview—that is, without details. These steps are placed in columns corresponding to the departments, work groups, or functional areas that do them.

*Why use it?*

- To see all the work groups involved in the process, or to see the functional areas if only one work group is involved
- To describe the process at high level before filling in the details in a Basic Flow Chart
- To uncover bottlenecks
- To identify points within the flow for collection of specific data on the number of errors, time intervals, and similar performance measures
- To begin streamlining the process

DISCUSSION

A Column Flow Chart may be new to you. It is not commonly known, yet it has proven to be valuable for documenting, studying, and improving work flows and manufacturing flows.

The Column Flow Chart is a high-level view that is useful to have before constructing the more detailed flow chart. By constructing the Column Flow Chart you will better understand where a process—or work flow—begins and ends, the work groups or the people involved, and the degree of complexity. Bottlenecks, loops, and dead-ends will be visible.

Very often the team will say "Sure we know the XYZ process, we work in it every day!" But as they begin to discuss it, they may find that the boundaries are unclear. Where does the process start and end? The Column Flow Chart adds clarity. It allows team members and others to see the beginning and ending points of a job or work flow. It shows the overall picture and provides a base from which to begin detailed study and improvement.

CONSTRUCTION

Begin by deciding on a name for the work flow or process under study, such as "the billing process" or "the process for handling customer complaints." In Figure 2, the process is chair manufacturing.

Then identify the output of the process. What does it produce? Who is the customer for that output? There may be multiple cus-

**FIGURE 2. COLUMN FLOW CHART
PROCESS CHAIR MANUFACTURING**

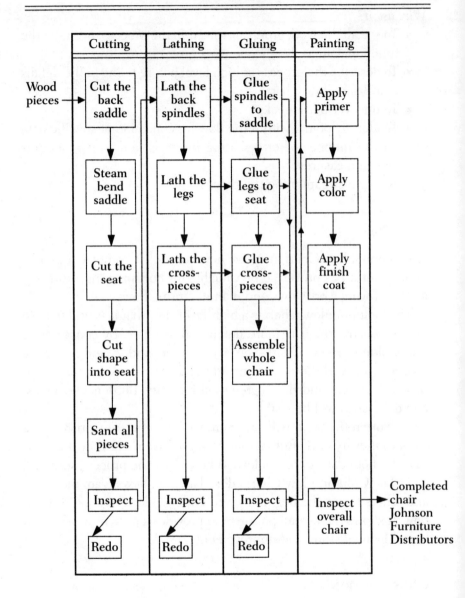

tomers for the product or service generated by the process. In Figure 2, the output is "Completed chair," and the customer is a furniture distributor. Next, identify both the inputs needed to generate that output and the suppliers of those inputs. Inputs are usually raw materials or information. Now, draw a large box and show the output coming from the lower right-hand corner. The inputs come in at the upper left-hand corner.

The next step is to identify the departments, work groups, or the individuals involved in creating that output. Identify all of them. Alternatively you may identify the functions performed. For example, if the entire ordering process is being drawn, departments—such as marketing, sales, customer service, warehouse, shipping, and billing—might be shown at the top. If, on the other hand, the process you are drawing is for the manufacturing of a chair, and if the entire process takes place on the assembly line, you probably want to show the functions at the top of the Column Flow Chart. These functions might be cutting, lathing, gluing, and painting, as shown in Figure 2.

Separate each department or functional area with vertical lines. By doing this you create the columns for which this tool is named. Now each column shows the people or functions involved.

The next step is to specify the activities that take place in each column. These are the activities that convert the input to the desired output. In Figure 2, wood will be converted into a chair. Details are not needed, just general statements about the activities that take place. Use self-sticking notes to show the activities; these make changes easy. Connect the activities with lines and arrows. Draw the flow as it occurs, going from one activity to another. One activity may have multiple outputs or even multiple inputs. The last line out of the last activity box represents the output that the process generates for the customer.

## Basic Flow Chart

*What is it?*
A pictorial description—a drawing of rectangles and diamond shapes—that shows the flow of a process.

*Why use it?*
- To make the process flow visible and understandable to everyone
- To locate potential bottlenecks, activities that could lead to delays, and areas where mistakes are likely
- To facilitate streamlining and cost reduction of the process

DISCUSSION

A process is a set of interconnected steps with an input and an output. A flow chart is a tool for showing those steps. Teams working to streamline a process they all know and work with on a daily basis are often surprised by how difficult it is to flow chart this process. They may find themselves in disagreement as to the order of the steps; in some cases they cannot even agree on the process starting point. These disagreements can be frustrating, leading team members to feel that the flow charting tool is simply not working because people see their job differently, or that the "flow chart does not apply." These differences as to how work is carried out may, in fact, represent the cause of difficulties for customers, higher costs, and even delays. True, there are situations where A can be done before B and it does not matter. In these cases, simply pick one sequence to represent on the flow chart and move on. In cases when it does matter whether A precedes B, and both ways are practiced, make a note of it. If a resolution cannot be made fairly quickly, show both ways on the flow chart or make two different flow charts. Make a note of why they happen and the difficulties that can result, and move on.

Remember, the purpose of a flow chart is to better understand the flow of a process, including differences and difficulties. Find those differences and difficulties, and represent them in the chart. Later, when the team is ready to explore changes and improvements, the flow chart will be there to facilitate the discussion and any data collection planning. The flow chart is an essential tool in studying any job or process we undertake.

CONSTRUCTION

Only two symbols are needed to construct any basic flow chart—a rectangle and a diamond. Rectangles describe activities, with one activity per rectangle. Diamonds indicate where decisions are made within the process. Two lines emanate from a decision diamond, most often one line is for "yes" and the other for "no." For example, for a diamond containing the words "Is the work order complete?" one path is for "yes", and a different path for "no."

To construct a flow chart, first agree on the end point, which you may have documented with the Column Flow Chart described earlier. Before we can determine what needs to come into a process, we need to determine what we are trying to produce. Then agree on the starting point and what comes into the process? What are the inputs needed to generate that output?

Now you are ready to draw rectangles and diamonds. Figure 3 is a Basic Flow Chart for the chair "painting" activities first described in the Column Flow Chart discussed earlier. This figure expands the painting function into greater detail.

Decide what occurs first in the process. What is the first thing that happens? It may be a decision, or it may be an activity. Draw the box or the diamond, write the activity or the decision question inside, draw lines coming out, and move to the next activity or decision. Keep going until the desired output is generated.

Loops are sometimes formed in the flow chart; that is, the output of a rectangle or a diamond may circle back to a previous rectangle. This circling back occurs when something is not complete and an activity must be repeated. In Figure 3, these looping back steps occur at the decision diamonds that ask if the paint is dry. In each case, if the answer is "no," the flow returns to the air blower activity.

After completing the flow chart, show it to others who work in the process but are not on your team. Ask for their views as to its

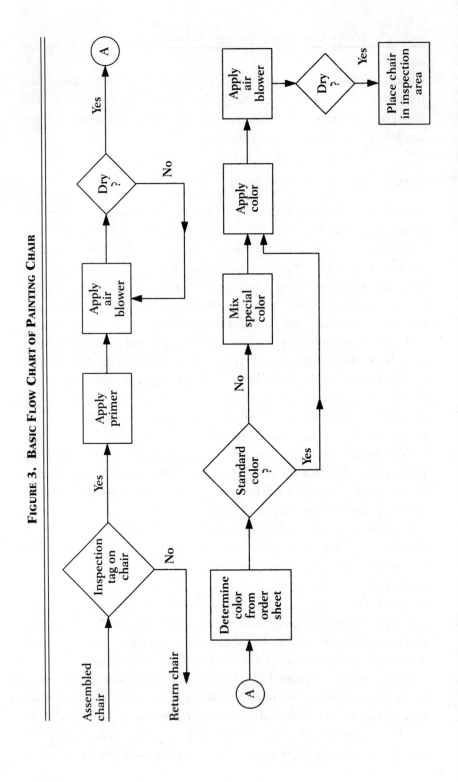

FIGURE 3. BASIC FLOW CHART OF PAINTING CHAIR

accuracy. Solicit their ideas for improving the flow chart. Remember that the chart will be a living document representing an existing process, and that it will change as you improve the process.

## *Pie Chart*

*What is it?*
A circle divided into parts that show the relative proportion of items or events.

*Why use it?*
- Reduces quantitative information into an easy-to-interpret visual
- Shows the relative proportion of events, allowing easy comparison
- Assists in determining what to address first
- Provides a base of current performance, such as percentage of certain types of errors
- Relatively easy to construct, either manually or with a software program

DISCUSSION

Pie charts have a perfectly descriptive name. We all remember cutting pies as kids and looking carefully at the size of each before handing them out. The size of a slice has real meaning.

Size notwithstanding, every pie slice is a fractional portion of the very same thing. That "thing" may be blueberry, or apple, or peach, or even mixed fruit pie, but it is one type of pie.

When used in process improvement work, a pie chart gives a clear visual picture of the magnitude of one or several factors relative to the whole. So, if we are concerned with the causes of customer complaints, as in Figure 4, the relative proportion of each category of complaint (poor finish, loose piece, etc.) can be easily seen.

Examples of conditions or events that are typically displayed on pie charts are: types of errors in assembling a product; types of billing mistakes; types of products sold; and different sources of revenues.

**FIGURE 4. PIE CHART
CUSTOMER COMPLAINTS**

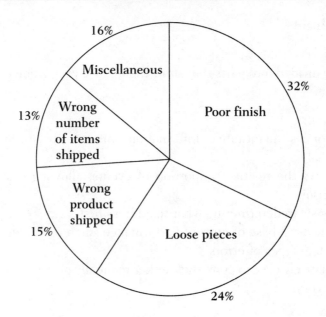

CONSTRUCTION

Collect data on each item to be represented in the pie chart. The data will actually be a kind of frequency for each item, such as dollars of sales for product A, or number of errors of Type X. Place the item with the highest data value or frequency first, the next highest frequency second, and so forth until all are listed. Then calculate the percentage each item is of the whole.

Finally, represent those percentages on the pie chart by simply remembering that 25 percent, for example, is one-fourth of the pie, or 90 degrees of the 360 degrees that constitute the entire pie. Use shading or color to separate the different categories and to help enhance the visual picture created by the data.

## Bar Chart

*What is it?*
Vertical or horizontal bars showing the magnitude of the data for each item, much like a thermometer.

*Why use it?*
- Bars are natural ways to display individual data items
- Trends or changes in trends in the data can often be seen
- Bar charts facilitate a visual comparison of mandated versus actual performance levels
- Two or three different sets of data can usually be displayed clearly on one chart

DISCUSSION

The meaning of bar charts, like that of pie charts, is very easy to determine. No one needs training to understand them. The common fever thermometer is a simple bar chart, and any person of average intelligence can understand that the red bar rises with rising temperatures.

Bar charts have several advantages over pie charts:

- They allow us to see small differences in the data because the bars are adjacent. By comparison, small differences in individual segments of pie charts are difficult to perceive when the segments are nonadjacent.
- When bars are arranged by consecutive time periods—weeks, months, or years—trends can be observed.

Figure 5 is a bar chart containing multiple sets of data displayed over time: cost of manufacturing, segmented by labor and material components; and cost of manufacture on a time-sequenced basis—from 1989 through 1997. The reader can easily obtain and interpret the rich trove of data about manufacturing costs contained in this single chart. Figure 6 is also a bar chart disclosing weekly sales volume by number of units. The indication of a new product intro-

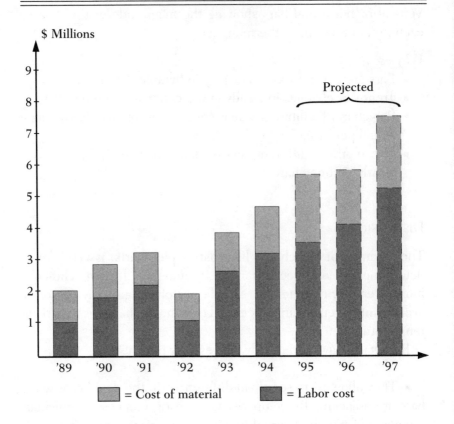

**FIGURE 5. BAR CHART
COST OF MANUFACTURING PRODUCT A EACH YEAR**

duction in week 9 helps the reader to draw inferences as to a subsequent trend of increasing sales.

Bar charts are not nearly as effective as pie charts, however, when it comes to showing the relative proportions of different items. Also, while bar charts are able to handle many different sets of data at one time, clarity can be a problem. We do not recommend that more than two or three data sets be shown on a single chart because it can be confusing and difficult to interpret. Line charts, as we will see shortly, are able to handle multiple data sets while preserving clarity.

## Tools for Total Quality Management (TQM)

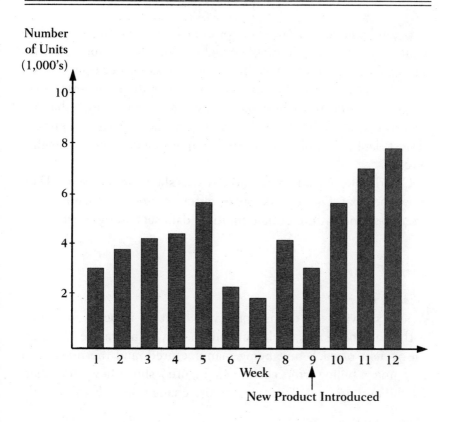

**FIGURE 6. BAR CHART
VOLUME OF SALES EACH WEEK**

## CONSTRUCTION

The construction being described here is for a vertical bar chart. These charts are generally drawn in two dimensions, along x and y axes. In Figure 5, for example, the x axis contains the years 1989 through 1997; the y axis indicates dollars in millions.

Horizontal bar charts simply have the x axis and y axis switched in order to create a different visual image of the data. While vertical bar charts are most often the choice, you can construct a horizontal chart from the description below by simply exchanging the instructions for the x axis and the y axis.

The vertical, or y, axis of a bar chart always shows the value of the data for the item that was measured. The horizontal, or x, axis, always shows the items themselves. These may be years, products, types of errors, types of materials, types of jobs completed, and the like.

Begin by collecting the data for each item. Then determine the scale on the y axis by finding the highest data item. Experience has shown that multiplying that highest value by 1.25 or even 1.5 is a useful way to arrive at the top scale for the bar chart. The extra 25 to 50 percent over the highest value provides an extra margin that has proven useful when future data points are larger than the current largest data point, or when customer requirements are at a higher level.

Clearly label each item on the x axis, as shown in the figure. Then draw each bar. Different colors or different cross-hatched patterns are important to differentiate multiple data sets on the x axis.

## *Line Chart*

*What is it?*
A line showing the change of a variable that is being measured within a process. Examples include hourly temperature readings, the weight of each unit being manufactured, and the number of shipping or billing errors each week. Figure 7 shows how a line chart can be used to track daily temperature changes in a chemical bath.

*Why use it?*
- Provides a visual display of the change of a variable over time
- Shows upward or downward trends
- Shows patterns, such as higher readings on Mondays
- To compare patterns of one data set with another
- To compare actual performance with customer requirements

DISCUSSION

All processes have variation. Any work we do will vary somewhat from hour to hour or day to day. Likewise, any product or unit that we manufacture will have some variation when compared to another

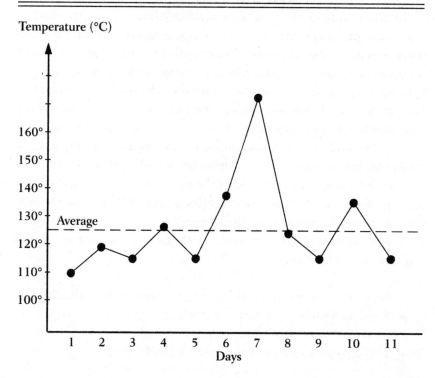

**FIGURE 7. LINE CHART
DAILY TEMPERATURE OF CHEMICAL BATH**

unit. The variation may be small, perhaps too small to easily measure, but it is there. We must, therefore, expect variation in processes and in products and services, but we want to contain that variation within an acceptable range. For example, if a steel cylinder is designed to a 4mm diameter specification, the acceptable range may be 3.95mm and 4.05mm. Variation outside that range may fail to meet customer expectations, or the cylinder may not fit into a larger assembly later in the manufacturing process.

We can accept, for example, air pressure in our car tires of between about 25 and 32 pounds. More or less than that and we have a poor ride and fast-wearing tires. Yet the tire pressure varies not only among the four tires, but one tire will show a different pressure each time it is measured just because some days are hotter than other days.

If variation is normal and acceptable within limits, a line chart is a perfect tool for showing us the degree of variation, and for comparing that variation to acceptable limits.

In addition to comparing the variations shown on a line chart to the customer requirements, we can also apply three "run tests," as they are called. The idea here is that while processes vary, we expect them to vary randomly, which simply means that we cannot predict what the next value will be. Random events happen in a completely unordered way. Likewise, random measurements or data points are unordered and unpredictable. That is what we expect of our processes. We know that a temperature will be around 100 degrees, for example, but we cannot predict whether it will be 100.1 or 100.9. If, on the other hand, we can predict the measurement because of past history, then we say that "special effects," as W. Edwards Deming called them, are influencing the process.

The three run tests that suggest that the process has special effects, are as follows:

- Nine data points in a row are on the same side of the average
- Six data points in a row have a continuous rising or falling pattern
- The data exhibits a wave or saw-toothed pattern

Examples of these patterns are shown in Figure 8, a line chart that shows annual sales revenues for three different products. If the data satisfies any one of the above three tests, then the process is said to be *nonrandom*, or under the influence of special effects. This may not be a bad or undesirable circumstance.

Sometimes we want our processes to show a pattern that is up on Monday and down on Tuesday, for example. We may actually design it that way. On the other hand, if the length of bars coming off a lathe is 1 millimeter too long nine or more times in a row, then something has probably changed in the milling process and it is time to investigate the cause and correct it. Perhaps the cutting tool was changed; perhaps the lathe operator does not understand the specifications. The probability of the data's satisfying any one of the above tests by chance, or accidentally, is only one out of 750; so if a test is

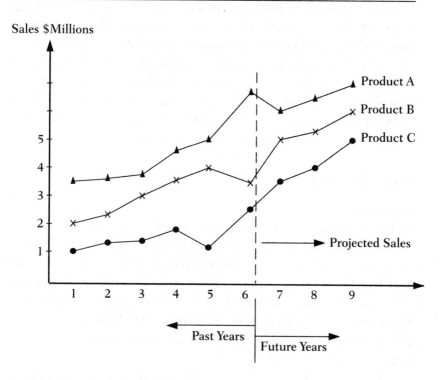

**FIGURE 8. LINE CHART**
**SALES OF PRODUCTS EACH YEAR**

satisfied, it is likely that something has happened to change the performance of the process. Some special effect is at work.

CONSTRUCTION

The horizontal, or x, axis of the line chart shows time or sequence number. The time may be, for example, in minutes, hours, days, etc. A measurement taken the first hour, for example, will simply be plotted above the first hour mark on the x axis. The measurement for the second hour will be plotted above the second hour mark. If the data points are plotted by sequence, that simply means that the first data point is plotted, then the second, etc. The label on the x axis in this case simply displays the sequence numbers 1,2,3,4,5. . . .

First draw the x and y lines, then label each. If time is the variable on the x axis, the label will say the units of time, such as hours, or may even show clock time, such as 9 A.M., and 10 A.M. If sequence is being used, then the x axis label says "measurement number", for example. Then place the label on the y axis that reflects the measurement being taken, such as "temperature in degrees," or "air pressure," or "number of billing errors." Then place a scale on the y axis. We suggest that you use 1.5 times the highest data point because that provides room above the highest data point in case future points are higher, just as with a bar chart. Finally, different colors or different line patterns like dots or dashes are useful to show the lines for different sets of data on a single x-y chart.

## *Pareto Chart*

*What is it?*
A chart with vertical bars, the height of each bar representing the frequency of a particular error or event. The highest bar is placed first on the chart, then the next highest, and so on. Figure 9 is a Pareto Chart based on data from the author's work group, indicating, in descending order, the most frequent reasons given for being late to work during a specified period (January through March 1994). Here, car trouble is the leading cause, followed by "alarm not set," and so on.

*Why use it?*
- To identify those few errors or events that create most of the difficulty
- To focus attention on those few items that, if corrected, can improve the quality of the product or service provided to customers
- To create a visual display of data error rates
- To compare process error rate performance to specifications of the company or of the customer

DISCUSSION
Vilfredo Pareto was an Italian philosopher who discovered that 80 percent of the land in Italy at that time (around 1880–1900) was owned by 20 percent of the people. This discovery led to the *80/20*

### TOOLS FOR TOTAL QUALITY MANAGEMENT (TQM)     247

**FIGURE 9. PARETO CHART**
**REASONS FOR BEING LATE FOR WORK**

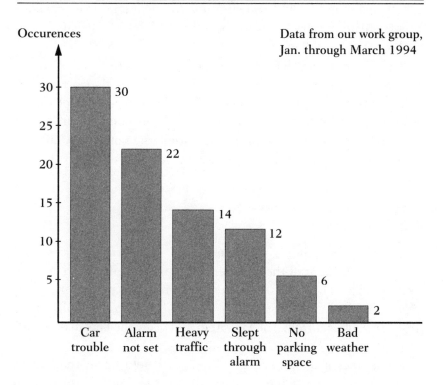

*rule.* Dr. Joseph Juran and other early students of quality in manufacturing realized that Pareto's 80/20 rule could apply to finding and correcting problems. In fact, it has broad application in business management. For example, we often find that 80 percent of sales are to 20 percent of our clients. Also, 80 percent of inventory costs are often associated with just 20 percent of the items. Likewise, in working to improve our processes, we find that 80 percent of the money we spend fixing mistakes or redoing work is caused by about 20 percent of all the errors. Most of the errors do not happen often or are not serious when they do occur. A relatively few number of errors are serious and expensive.

While the Pareto Chart is a useful tool, caution must be exercised in its use. In particular, the item or error with the highest bar is the one that happens most often, and is usually the one that logic compells us to address first. However, another less frequent error may in actuality be the one to address first simply because it can be fixed quickly and easily. Fixing this less frequent error may provide a much greater payback, given the time and costs associated with making the correction.

The Pareto Chart, like all team tools, is a guide, a way of seeing the data. It does not automatically tell us what to address first. You must consider the time and cost of fixing that type of error that is occurring most often, the value to the customer, and the impact on the rest of the process. These considerations are not usually difficult to address and they help assure a wise decision that is customer-focused.

## Construction

A Pareto Chart always has "words" on the horizontal axis, and frequency (a count of the number of times an event occurs) on the vertical axis. The words are events, items, or types of errors, as shown in Figure 9. Construct the vertical bars corresponding to the frequency of occurrence of each item and place the bars in descending order.

Sometimes it makes sense to create a Pareto Chart that shows each type of error as a percentage of the total number of errors. To do this, simply convert each error count into a percentage by dividing by the total number of errors. For example, the counts for error types W, X, Y, and Z might be 50, 40, 25, and 10. The percentages would be calculated by dividing each frequency by the total, which is 125. The resultant percentages are 40, 32, 20, and 8. The advantage of showing percentages on the chart is that the relative proportion of each error is made clearer. We can say there are 50 errors of type W, but there can be more information when we say that 40 percent of all errors are of type W. In addition, we can see the relative magnitude of each on the Pareto Chart.

## Histogram

*What is it?*
A set of vertical bars, one bar for each of several measurement intervals, that show the frequency of occurrence of data points falling into each interval.

*Why use it?*
- To see the shape or distribution of the data from a process
- To see the average value of the data and how much the process varies on either side of that average
- To compare process performance to customer requirements
- To form a baseline visual display that will change and improve as the process is improved

DISCUSSION

Process measurements are the key to understanding and tracking performance. A histogram is an excellent way to display that performance data. Suppose, for example, that you have collected dozens of data points, each one representing how long it took to fill an order. Each order was tracked and the time to fill it was recorded. How can you display that data to see the spread of the time intervals, along with the average, the frequency of each time interval, and a comparison with customer requirements? A histogram does all of these.

The most common shape that occurs in a histogram is a *bell* shape, as shown in Figure 10. Bell-shaped distributions occur frequently in manufacturing. For example, if you weighed 100 or so units coming off the assembly line and plotted those 100 data points on a histogram, you could expect a bell-shaped curve to result.

If some other shape occurs, it may be because something abnormal is happening in the process. A bimodal distribution, shown here as Figure 11, suggests that two populations exist within one set of data. In other words, the lower data points may result from one assembly line, and the higher data points from another. That may be a clue that the processes differ when they should not.

**FIGURE 10. BELL-SHAPED HISTOGRAM**

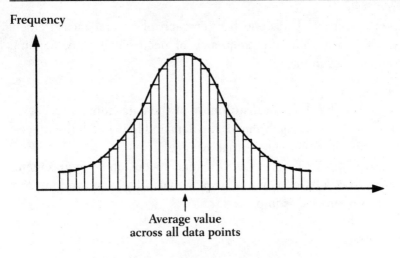

Average value
across all data points

**FIGURE 11. BIMODAL DISTRIBUTION**

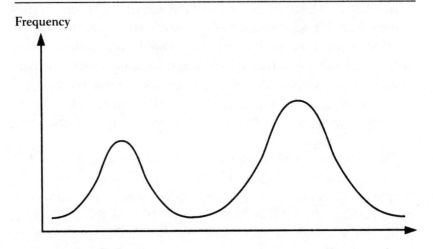

CONSTRUCTION

A histogram is not difficult to construct. Several software packages, including popular spreadsheets like Lotus 123 and Excel, facilitate histogram generation. Manual construction is also easy and often provides better insight than computer generation because it requires working closely with the data.

Thirty or more data points are needed to generate a reliable histogram. More the better, but once you have around 200 data points there is little advantage to collecting more. Begin by ordering the data from low to high frequency. Count the number of data points and call that N. All we need to do now is select the number and size of the measurement intervals that we will have on the horizontal axis of the histogram. Select the number of intervals for the horizontal axis by taking the square root of N. If N is 36, the number of intervals is 6. If N is 100, the number of intervals to use is 10. If N is not exactly a squared number, like 52, use the closest square root, such as 7. Taking the square root is only a guide.

Call the number of intervals that you select K. The numerical width of each interval will be R/K (R divided by K) where R is the range of the data, the difference between the highest and the lowest data points. Simply place the intervals on the horizontal axis starting at the lowest data point and you are ready to construct the vertical bars.

For each interval count the number of data points that fall into it, and that will be the height of the bar for that interval. If a data point falls right on the line that separates intervals, simply decide whether to count that point as falling to the left or the right, and do that consistently for all other data points that fall on the line.

Here is an example: Data on the weight of units coming off the assembly lines. Weight is shown in pounds.

| 1.2 | 1.2 | 1.3 | 1.5 | 1.5 | 1.6 | 1.6 | 1.7 | 1.8 | 1.9 |
| 1.9 | 2.0 | 2.0 | 2.1 | 2.1 | 2.1 | 2.1 | 2.2 | 2.2 | 2.2 |
| 2.2 | 2.3 | 2.3 | 2.3 | 2.4 | 2.4 | 2.4 | 2.5 | 2.5 | 2.5 |

Thirty data points have been collected and the data has been placed in ascending order. With N = 30, we can chose 5 or 6 intervals (the square root of 30 is between 5 and 6). We will chose 5, so that K = 5. The range of the data is the difference between the highest and lowest data points. Thus, R = 2.5 minus 1.2, or R = 1.3. The width of each interval will be 1.3/5, which we will round-off to 0.3. This all means that we will have 5 intervals, each being 0.3 unit in length and starting at 1.2 on the x axis. Figure 12 is a histogram based on the data just given, with 5 intervals of 1.3 pounds each.

Now we simply count the number of data points in the first

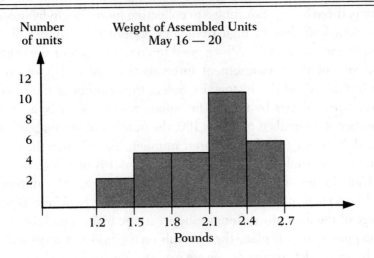

**FIGURE 12. HISTOGRAM**

interval. Counting data points as falling to the right, we find three data points in the first interval. The following table shows the count for each interval:

| | |
|---|---|
| 1.2 - 1.5 | 3 units |
| 1.5 - 1.8 | 5 units |
| 1.8 - 2.1 | 5 units |
| 2.1 - 2.4 | 11 units |
| 2.4 - 2.7 | 6 units |

Thus, the bars of the histogram will be the heights shown above: 3, 5, 5, 11, and 6.

The histogram is now complete, but it is useful to also show the specifications for the measurement. Specifications for the weight of the assembled units, for example, may be 1.5 to 2.4 pounds—these are the upper and lower limits within which weight variations are tolerated—in which case the process has generated 3 units that are too light and 6 that are too heavy. To meet the specifications, this process will require some improvement. The Cause-and-Effect Diagram discussed next is a useful tool for uncovering the causes of such problems.

## Cause-and-Effect Diagram

*What is it?*
A diagram that captures possible causes of a problem and shows the interrelationship of those possible causes. The diagram resembles the skeleton of a fish and is often called a "fishbone diagram."

*Why use it?*
- To identify likely root, or primary, causes of a problem
- To display weaknesses and opportunities for improvement in a process
- To explore new possibilities and capabilities

### DISCUSSION

The Cause-and-Effect (C/E) Diagram is very popular in industry. It provides an excellent means for people to investigate possible causes of a problem, and to conduct that investigation in a way that goes to deeper and deeper levels in uncovering the primary cause. The primary or root cause means the underlying cause of a problem. For example, a headache can be caused by many things, such as, allergies, stress, eye strain, certain foods, lack of food, noise, lack of sleep, and so forth. Before a physician can recommend a solution the cause must be determined. The above list, however, is insufficient in that root causes are not shown. Allergies, for example, are of many different types and causes. The root cause here may be an allergy to ragweed, in which case the solution is to avoid it. If, on the other hand the allergy is to dog hair, the solution is to avoid dogs that shed and not to worry about ragweed. We need as much as possible to understand the root cause of our headache, including any headache that is in our manufacturing process. The C/E Diagram helps us locate the root cause.

### CONSTRUCTION

Begin by being clear about the problem. Write the problem for all to see and to discuss the wording. This is important because everyone on the team needs to address the same issue and with the same intention.

Next place that problem statement (or a short form of it) in the box on the right-hand side of the C/E Diagram. In Figure 13, the problem statement is "Car Trouble Going to Work;" this picks up on our earlier discussion of the Pareto Chart. Draw the horizontal line and the angled lines that spring off of that horizontal line. Now place the names of various categories on these angled lines. You may have categories from a Pareto diagram, or your team may know the categories from some previous work that was done in studying the process. If no categories are obvious to use, the generic ones that Isakawa, the inventor of this tool, recommends are: materials, methods, people, and machines, as shown in Figure 13. These work well in virtually all cases.

Next, all of the team members should participate in generating ideas on the likely causes of the problem. Stay within one category, such as machines, and ask "What are the possible causes of this problem at the head of the C/E Diagram that have to do with machinery?" State the possible causes in a negative way, such as "overheats" or "flat tire." Identify truly possible causes, feasible causes, and causes that have been known to be the case. Then, for each of these major possibilities, ask why it occurs and write the reason on a line that connects to the major possibility. Then ask why that second-level item occurs, and so on until there is an answer. Isakawa said to "ask why five times," meaning that we need to keep asking *why* until we get to an automatic stopping point. Remember that we are seeking the root cause. You will find that after asking why two or three times, you will usually reach an automatic end beyond which there is no further reason.

After completing the diagram, the result will look similar to the one in the figure. The next activity is to circle two or three causes on the diagram that the team believes are root or primary causes of the problem. Then arrange to collect data to verify that these are root causes, or to find which occurs more often and is therefore the root cause of significance.

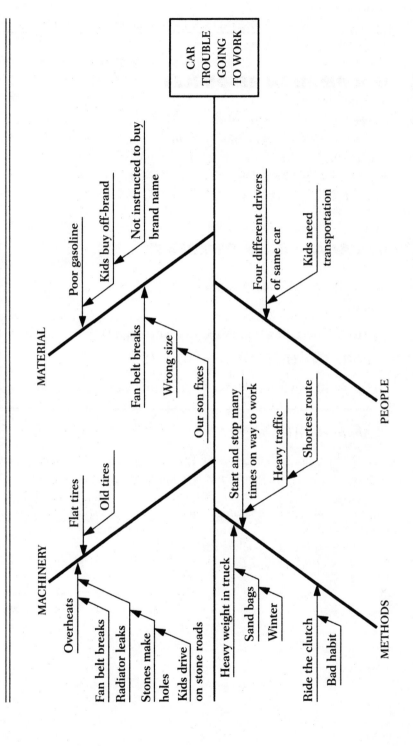

FIGURE 13. CAUSE AND EFFECT DIAGRAM

## INFORMATION RESOURCES

*Power-Up TQM: Learn New Approaches to Team Effectiveness by Unlocking the Power in TQM Tools and Techniques*, Bill Montgomery, The Montgomery Group, 1994.

*The Memory Jogger: A Pocket Guide of Tools for Continuous Improvement*, Michael Brassard, Goal/QPC, 1988

## INTERNAL CROSS-REFERENCE

Your understanding of this topic may be enhanced by the following chapters:

III–3. Energizing Your Workforce with High Performance Teams

IV–1. Total Quality Management (TQM)

IV–4. Just-in-Time: Driver for Continuous Improvement

---

### About the Author

Bill Montgomery is founder of The Montgomery Group, headquartered in Pittstown, New Jersey. He has worked with a wide range of manufacturing and service companies, specializing in process improvement, effective strategic planning, various aspects of management skills training, facilitator training, and team leader training. Dr. Montgomery's new book is *Power-Up TQM: Learn New Approaches to Team Effectiveness by Unlocking the Power in TQM Tools and Techniques*.

# IV-3

# Benchmarking the Best-in-Class
## Pete Landry

**IN A NUTSHELL**

Most manufacturing executives understand the importance of Continuous Improvement. Many, however, struggle with *what* should be improved, *how* it should be improved, and *how much* improvement is required to establish market leadership. More often than not, improvement is driven from a historical perspective or gut feel that fails to match the reality of the competitive environment. As a driver to Continuous Improvement, benchmarking provides answers to the what, how, and how much of Continuous Improvement.

Benchmarking is the process of measuring products, services, and practices against those of leading companies. The benchmarking firm looks outward, measuring its performance and practices against those of best-in-class companies; through analysis of these measures, it makes changes designed to bring its own operations to a level that will match or surpass best-in-class performance.

Benchmarking is also a tool used to identify, establish, and achieve standards of excellence based on the realities of the marketplace.

## *Origins*

North American quality programs of the 1970s and early 1980s provide a good example of the dangers associated with being internally focused and approaching performance improvements from a historical perspective. Plans for improving Acceptable Quality Levels (AQL) by 5 to 10 percent per year were commonplace during those years. Quality performance in the 96 to 98 percent range was considered excellent, and a 99 percent level was viewed as an unreasonable expectation. Meanwhile, Japanese competitors were measuring quality performance in terms of a few hundred parts per million (PPM). (Note: As a point of reference, 99 percent is equivalent to 10,000 defects per million.)

From a historical perspective, 10 percent year over year improvements appeared reasonable. But from a competitive standpoint, North American companies were far behind the Japanese and losing ground. Misplaced expectations about productivity, product costs, product reliability, customer service, and other vital measures contributed to significant loss of market share in many industries. Fortunately, a few enlightened companies recognized that the traditional, evolutionary approach to change would not yield the dramatic improvements required to regain competitive standing in the global marketplace. An externally focused approach, one based on best practices—regardless of industry—would be required. Xerox and Motorola were two U.S. companies that pioneered this external approach. Both recognized the potential of benchmarking as a driver of Continuous Improvement and responded to the competitive challenge from abroad with the result that both firms regained market share from Japanese rivals.

Benchmarking was instrumental in providing the much-needed wake-up call to Xerox in the early 1980s and led to its tossing out many traditional practices for managing its business. Benchmarking pointed the way to quantum improvements in product quality, reliability, cost, time-to-market, and total customer satisfaction. The changes were so positive that Xerox applied for and won the Malcolm Baldrige National Quality Award in 1989. Today, benchmarking is fully integrated into the Xerox management process.

For companies seeking the Malcolm Baldrige Award, the application guidelines specify benchmarking as a mandatory management process. A recent survey indicated that approximately 40 percent of the Fortune 500 companies are using the benchmarking process to drive improvements in customer satisfaction.

## The Benchmarking Process

The benchmarking process has four phases: Planning and Data Gathering, Analysis, Integration, and Action.

*1. Planning and Data Gathering Phase* Unfortunately, the planning part of this phase is often neglected. The urge to make a few telephone calls to line up a site visit with a world class company (Malcolm Baldrige Award winners are popular sites) must be held in check until a comprehensive benchmarking plan has been formulated. Poorly planned benchmarking visits result in wasted time for the visiting and host company alike. If the planning phase is properly conducted, the company may even choose an information-gathering technique other than a site visit (mail or telephone survey, library search, etc.). Careful planning will also help pinpoint the most compatible benchmarking partner.

The key questions that should be addressed during the planning phase include:

- What will be benchmarked? A review of corporate, business and functional priorities and critical success factors provides a good start to answering this question. Often, a specific problem area—such as slow order fulfillment—will dictate the focus of the benchmarking effort.
- Who should be benchmarked? Without losing sight of your competitors, remember that, for specific functions, your competitors' performance may not be best-in-class or worthy of emulation. More often than not the company with be best performance on a

function will be found outside your industry. In what has become the classic benchmarking case, Xerox found L.L.Bean, a mail-order clothing and outdoor gear distributor, to be best-in-class in the area of warehousing and distribution. As a benchmarking partner, L.L.Bean showed a Xerox benchmarking team the processes and practices that made its warehousing and distribution so effective. This study led to the discovery of a number of concepts and practices that Xerox could adopt, resulting in significant improvements in its own warehousing and distribution functions.

- How will the data be gathered? There is no cookbook approach to gathering benchmarking data; imagination and creativity are called for. A library search can provide information on world class performance; you'll find it documented in books, trade periodicals, and journals. Professional networks and trade associations are also excellent sources of data on specific functions or processes. More specific data can be gathered through telephone and mail surveys. Detailed data gathering on processes, practices, and methods, however, often require direct contact with the benchmark partner.

*2. Analysis Phase* The objective of this phase is to understand the data acquired from the benchmarking study and to make comparisons against your own performance. A poor understanding of your own practices and methods is a common problem in this phase. One remedy is to flowchart your operational process. Both quantitative and qualitative data needs to be fully analyzed before you can formulate a valid comparison and take action. Quantitative analysis indicates the size of the opportunity. Qualitative analysis reveals the operational opportunity. Key questions to be answered during this phase are: Is the performance of the benchmarked company better than yours? How much better? What can you learn from the benchmark company? How can you apply what you have learned?

*3. Integration Phase* Once you have hard data and fully understand the specific operational areas requiring improvements, you are ready to set objectives for meeting and surpassing benchmark performance. The first step is for management to accept the results of the benchmarking analysis and make a commitment to developing action plans. Management will often question the result, especially if it points to a significant performance gap. Functional managers may become defensive if the benchmarking analysis reflects badly on their performance. For that reason, functional managers must be involved early in the planning phases of the study and be allowed to participate in the discovery and learning aspects of the benchmarking process. Analysis must also be well documented and conclusive.

**4. *Action Phase*** Here specific and measurable goals are made part of your operating and long-range plans. Performance measurements must be established and used to track progress. This phase must also provide for periodic updating of benchmarks. The standards for operating and performance in best-in-class companies, by definition, improve continuously. If you intend to match or exceed the standards of these companies, then you cannot aim for where they *were* at the time of your benchmark study, but where you anticipate their improvements will take them. Analyzing products of a best-in-class companies through reverse engineering, for example, tells you what those companies did *in the past* with respect to product design, materials, and technology; the products in their new product pipeline may be much different and much improved. Anticipating their rate of improvement—"shooting ahead of the duck"—is critical if you are to keep pace with, or stay ahead of, best-in-class companies.

## *Implementation*

To make the most of a benchmarking study, always observe the following:

- Any benchmarking initiative should start with education. Consultants who have had hands-on benchmarking experience can be especially helpful in providing education as well as guidance on the actual benchmarking study.
- Benchmarking studies are most effective when performed by the managers who have a stake in the results—namely, those responsible for the function being studied in another company and

those who have the authority to make changes in operational processes.

- Benchmarking is a continuous process. It should be integrated into the formal operating and strategic planning processes.

## KEY CONCEPTS

**Benchmarking**: The process of measuring products, services, and practices against those of leading companies. It focuses on best practices and methods of world class leaders, regardless of industry.

**Benchmarking partner**: A best-in-class organization or company willing to participate in a benchmarking study and prepared to share information as to practices, methods, processes, and performance measurements.

**Competitive analysis**: Focuses on competitive strategies and tactics, the source of information being limited to competitors and industry analysis. Benchmarking starts where competitive analysis leaves off.

**Recalibration of benchmark**: Periodic recalibration of a benchmark is required to validate our assumptions on the rate of improvement, recognize any new best-in-class competitors, and to ensure that our performance measures are still appropriate in view of changing industry dynamics.

**Reverse engineering**: Focuses on the comparison of product characteristics and functionality of competitor products.

**Search for best-in-class**: The process of identifying potential benchmarking partners. Sources of information include library search (books, periodicals, journals), professional networks and trade associations, annual reports, consultants, customers, suppliers, etc.

## ACTION STEPS

Each of the following steps must be carried out by Top Management in implementing benchmarking:

- Learn the mechanism of benchmarking, what it is, and how it can become a "driver" to Continuous Improvement.
- Create an environment in which the status quo is unacceptable and the standards of performance are best-in-class.
- Provide for the education of all functional managers in the techniques of benchmarking.
- Establish benchmarking teams and initialize pilots in each major functional areas. Establish checkpoint reviews to ensure adherence to the process.
- Establish an internal network of benchmarkers to promote, facilitate, and improve the benchmarking process.
- Integrate benchmarking into the formal operating and strategic planning processes of the company.

## PROBLEM-SOLVING

*"Recognizing that we must continually improve if we are to remain competitive, how do we establish goals that are both realistic and capable of keeping us in the competitive arena?"*

Benchmarking stimulates an external focus on being competitive and provides creditable data for establishing aggressive yet attainable goals—aggressive in that we are measuring ourselves against best-in-class and attainable in that someone is actually performing at those levels.

*"Our managers doubt that the goals are either realistic or attainable."*

Benchmarking is a learning experience and a discovery process. The real benefit is uncovering the practices and methods supporting the good performance metrics. Discovering the how to will often result in breakthroughs, process improvements in your own operations.

*"How do we know that we are measuring the right things?"*

Without benchmarking, the focus of your measurement system often centers on the things you do very well (pet projects, route of least resistance, etc.). Benchmarking helps you to understand your strengths and weaknesses. Benchmarking analysis identifies the real problems that require resolution and the appropriate measurements.

## SUMMARY

- Benchmarking is a continuous process of measuring your product, services, and practices against those of your toughest competitors or other leading companies.
- Benchmarking is a tool for identifying, establishing, and achieving standards of excellence, based on the realities of the marketplace.
- Benchmarking is both a learning experience and a discovery process.
- Benchmarking has four phases: Planning and Data Gathering, Analysis, Integration, and Action.
- To be effective, benchmarking should be integrated in the operating and strategic planning processes.

## INFORMATION RESOURCES

*Benchmarking: The Search for the Industry's Best Practices That Lead to Superior Performance*, Robert C. Camp, ASQC Quality Press and UNIPUB/Quality Resources, 1989.

*Benchmarking: A Competitive Strategy for the 1990s*, Pete Landry, APICS, 35th International Conference Proceedings, October 1992.

"Benchmarking: A Self-Improvement Strategy," Lawrence S. Pryor, *The Journal of Business Strategy*, November–December 1989.

"The Benchmarking Bandwagon," *Quality Progress*, January 1991.

*Strategic Benchmarking*, Gregory H. Watson, John Wiley & Sons, Inc., 1993.

## INTERNAL CROSS-REFERENCE

Your understanding of this topic may be enhanced by the following chapters:

I–1. Hallmarks of Excellence

II–1. Being a World Class Customer

III–1. Building a Learning Organization

IV–5. The Malcolm Baldrige National Quality Award Program

---

### About the Author

Pete Landry is a management consultant, a principal of the Oliver Wight Companies, and a former executive of the Xerox Corporation. During his twenty years at Xerox, he held various staff and line positions, including materials manager for a major manufacturing division and manager, supplier development, with responsibility for developing and implementing strategies to improve supplier performance. Mr. Landry participated in the development and use of the Xerox benchmarking process.

# Just-in-Time: Driver for Continuous Improvement
## *William M. Boyst, Jr. (III)*

## IN A NUTSHELL

Just-in-Time (JIT) is an approach to manufacturing based on two concepts: 1) the planned elimination of all waste, and 2) Continuous Improvement in productivity. Just-in-Time encompasses all manufacturing activities required to produce a final product and aims to:

- Have only the required inventory on hand when needed
- Improve quality to zero defects
- Reduce lead times by reducing setup times, queue lengths, and lot sizes
- Incrementally revise operations
- Accomplish all of the above at minimum cost

### *Waste Elimination*

JIT continuously seeks to eliminate waste—waste being defined as any activity that does not add value to the product for the customer.

Waste must be eliminated not only because it adds cost without value, but because it constrains our ability to respond to change. The following activities are traditionally considered to be essential in running a business, yet not one adds value to the product for the customer:

| | |
|---|---|
| Purchase orders | Acknowledgments |
| Work orders | Inspecting |
| Expediting | Scrap/rework |
| Receiving reports | Sorting |
| Returns to suppliers | Storing |
| Moving materials | Invoices |
| Material requisitions | Counting |

JIT asks the question: How can we eliminate the need for these nonvalue-adding activities? Let's consider how one of these—work orders—can be eliminated.

Work orders are the basis for an informational-based material control system. They represent lots of paperwork, lots of transactions, and lots of people to keep track of both. Work orders can be replaced by *kanbans*. Kanbans are a simple, efficient, and highly visible way to authorize the production and movement of materials.

*Product-dependent kanbans* These are the technique of choice for high-volume/low-mix environments. Product-dependent kanbans provide a visible signal of what to do and when to do it. When a kanban becomes empty, you simply replace what was there with another just like it. For example, the kanban for a drill press work station might be a bin in which items are placed after the work is done. Once the next work station empties this bin, the drill press operator knows to drill more pieces and refill the bin. No paperwork is generated, checked, or stored. (See Figure 1.)

*Product-independent kanbans* These are the technique of choice for low-volume/high-mix environments. Product-independent kanbans provide a visible signal of when it is time to do something but not what to do. The what to do must be communicated independently of the kanban signal by an external method. For example, the

**FIGURE 1. PRODUCT-DEPENDENT KANBANS (1 PRODUCT)**

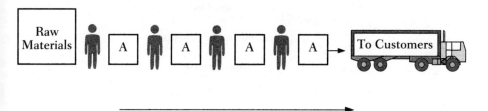

Work Flow

MRP dispatch list, a final assembly schedule, or a customer order. The process works like this: Whenever a customer pulls material from your kanban, you in turn pull material into your work station. The process continues (each customer pulling from his supplier) until the kanban at the starting work station is pulled. The empty kanban at the starting work station will be the signal to begin production of the next item on the schedule. (See Figure 2.)

The schedule tells the people what to make; product-independent kanbans tell them when to make it. In his book *Just-in-Time: Making It Happen*, Bill Sandras refers to these as "generic kanbans" and to the product-dependent variety as "brand-name kanbans."

## Continuous Improvement

Just-in-Time relies on the concept of Continuous Improvement (or in Japanese, *kaizen*) to identify and eliminate nonvalue-adding activities, and Total Quality Control (TQC)* provides a set of tools to make Continuous Improvement work. Key among the TQC tools is a methodology to identify the root causes of problems so that permanent solutions can be developed and implemented.

JIT companies also use innovative management approaches to

---

* Note: TQC is referred to elsewhere in this book as Total Quality Management; see chapter IV–1).

**FIGURE 2. PRODUCT-INDEPENDENT KANBANS (6 PRODUCTS)**

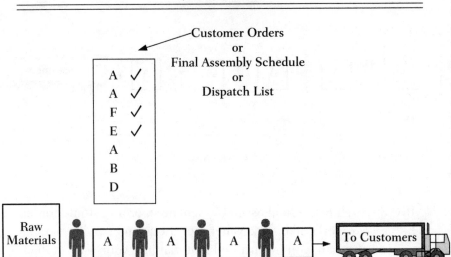

achieve dramatic and significant reductions in changeover times. A process developed by Shigeo Shingo called Single Minute Exchange of Dies (SMED), for example, is often used to analyze changeover activities to determine areas where improvements are practical.

The phrase "single minute exchange" refers to making changeovers in less than ten minutes. In his book *A Revolution in Manufacturing: The SMED System*, Shingo cites numerous examples of companies that reduced their setup times from hours to less than ten minutes. The results are not limited to merely saving money on shorter changeovers; they include shorter runs, less inventory, more responsiveness to customers, and higher utilization of capacity.

## *Benefits*

Just-in-Time, when correctly implemented, creates simultaneous benefits in quality, delivery responsiveness, and cost. Companies implementing JIT have achieved the following improvements:

- 30 to 70 percent reduction in inventory levels
- 40 to 90 percent reduction in throughput times
- 40 to 70 percent reduction in floor-space requirements
- 50 to 90 percent reduction in cost of quality
- 70 to 90 percent reduction in changeover times

In three to seven years, the company that successfully implements JIT can reasonably expect to achieve a four- to tenfold improvement in overall quality and inventory turns. Imagine the competitive advantage this would give to your company—and imagine what would happen if your competitors did this and you did not!

Costs for a JIT program are eclipsed by the magnitude of the results. A typical company with sales of $25 million to $100 million can expect to spend less than $50,000 to $75,000 for a four- to six-month pilot operation. In eighteen to twenty-four months, the entire plant could be converted to JIT and achieve the kinds of results cited above.

## *The Continuous Improvement Process in Action*

Companies begin their Just-in-Time journey of Continuous Improvement by learning how to economically produce smaller and smaller lot sizes. For example, if a company has a process that requires a lot size of 200, and the process works well and economically, it should try a lot size of 190. It will probably find that everything still works well and that the process is still economical. So what will it be like at 180 or 170? As it gradually reduces the lot size, it will eventually expose a problem. Something, some constraint, will prevent it from making additional reductions.

The constraint might be equipment changeover, material handling, output quality, or even paperwork. Whichever, the process of progressively stressing the system exposes the barriers to continued improvement. Once exposed, the Total Quality Control problem-solving tools can help the company determine the root cause of the problem and implement a permanent solution. Once the problem is eliminated, the process again works economically, and the company can continue to gradually reduce the lot size, exposing and eliminating subsequent problems. This process moves its user toward the ability to produce exactly what the customer wants in terms of delivery and quality, and away from making everything in batches with minimum purchase and manufacturing quantities (lot sizes).

## *Implementation*

Many traditional attitudes and behaviors must be changed for successful JIT implementation:

- The idea of inventory, traditionally counted as an asset, must be seen as a liability
- Lead times, often a focus of complaints, must be seen as a challenge to be systematically reduced
- The production process must be reoriented from production push to demand pull
- Scrap must become a mark of failure—something to be eliminated
- Good-enough quality must give way to the concept of 100 percent quality
- Supplier relationships must become cooperative arrangements
- Shop-floor personnel must become totally involved in the design and execution of the work

Bending the production process to the philosophy of Just-in-Time also requires certain physical changes to both plant and equipment:

- Equipment must accommodate minimal changeover times
- Housekeeping must be neat and clean, with a place for everything
- Manufacturing processes must move from functional to cellular (see chapter V–5)
- Material must be stored at point of use
- Material kitting and staging need to be eliminated

A decision to implement Just-in-Time is more than a decision to do things differently—it is a decision to change the way people think about how the company should operate and the way individuals should do their jobs. For this reason, it is important to start with a small pilot and not to try to implement JIT throughout the entire company at one time. A preferred approach is to identify a pilot area that would represent 10 to 30 percent of the employees and/or 10 to 20 percent of the cost of sales. Do it there. Learn what works well and what doesn't. Then use what you have learned to repeat the process elsewhere, until the entire company is operating in a JIT mode. The implementation process involves the following steps:

1. Appoint a senior management champion.
2. Select the implementation team.
3. Create an education plan for the implementation team.
4. Identify the pilot area.
5. Establish JIT measurement criteria.
6. Start up the pilot under kanban control (no work orders).
7. After the new process is under control, begin gradually reducing the number of kanbans.
8. Initiate the TQC problem-solving process to resolve key problems.
9. Measure and display performance results.
10. Select the next candidate area for JIT and repeat steps 4 through 9.
11. Develop a formal JIT/TQC education program for the company, suppliers, customers, union, etc.
12. Write a vision statement showing how the company will be operating in a full JIT environment.

## KEY CONCEPTS

**Champion**: In the context of Just-in-Time, a charismatic senior manager who identifies himself or herself with the success of the program.

**Change-over**: All those activities involved in moving from the last value-added activity of the previous job or batch to the first value-added activity of the next job or batch.

**Continuous Improvement**: An integral component of JIT that reflects a never-ending determination to eliminate the root cause of problems.

**Demand pull**: Production in which a customer, either internal or external, pulls product from a supplier.

**Employee involvement**: The concept of using the intelligence of all workers by treating them with dignity, trust, and respect; by communicating frequently; and by requesting their input in their areas of experience.

**Just-in-Time (JIT)**: An approach to manufacturing based on planned elimination of all waste and Continuous Improvements in productivity. JIT encompasses the successful execution of all manufacturing activities required to produce a final product from design engineering to delivery, including all stages of conversation from raw material onward. In the broad sense, it applies to all forms of manufacturing: job shop, process, as well as repetitive. Also known as stockless production, zero inventories, short-cycle manufacturing.

**Kanban**: A Japanese term that, literally translated, means card or signal. JIT uses kanban (rhymes with "bonbon") as a visual technique for authorizing the movement or the production of material, based on consumption.

**Kaizen**: A Japanese term referring to Continuous Improvement.

**Order push**: Production, in which a work order or a purchase order authorizes the supplier to deliver to the customer at a predetermined rate.

**Product-dependent kanban**: A visual system for signaling the need to replenish another of the same kind.

**Product-independent kanban**: A visual system for signaling that it is time to move on or to produce another item that may, or may not, be the same as the one consumed.

**Single Minute Exchange of Dies (SMED)**: A process developed by Shigeo Shingo to analyze changeover activities and determine areas where improvements are practical, then cause improvements to happen. The long-term goal is to complete changeovers in less than ten minutes.

**Total Quality Control (TQC)**: A system for integrating the quality development, quality maintenance, and quality improvement efforts within an organization with the goal of providing production and service at the most economical levels to provide full customer satisfaction.

**TQC problem-solving tools**: Seven basic problem-solving tools are used to determine the root cause of a problem: check sheets; control charts; flowcharts; histograms; Ishikawa diagrams; Pareto charts; and scatter diagrams. (See chapter IV–2.)

**Waste**: Any activity done or resource consumed in the production of the product that does not add value for the customer.

## ACTION STEPS

- Enlist top managers to serve as champions for change to JIT.
- Look at every process in terms of this question: Does this activity add value for the customer?
- Stop thinking in traditional terms: Inventory is no longer an asset, but a liability. Products and processes are no longer good, but things to be made better.
- Make everyone in the organization—down to the lowest level—part of the JIT program.

## PROBLEM-SOLVING

*"It's not practical for us to issue many orders for small quantities. The additional paperwork would kill us."*

Work orders are the basis for an informational-based material control system. This means lots of paperwork and lots of transactions. Stop issuing work orders and replace them with kanbans. Kanbans are an important means of reducing waste—in this instance, the waste of writing, issuing, checking, and recording work orders. None of these activities add value for your customer.

*"It's not economical for us to produce smaller quantities more often. The additional changeover times would be prohibitive."*

Reduce changeover times by 50 to 75 percent without spending a lot of money—use the SMED process to determine areas where improvements are practical, and then cause improvements to happen.

*"I know that it's important to eliminate wasteful activities, but how do I go about exposing areas for improvement and how do I assign the priorities of what to work on?"*

A continual and gradual reduction of inventory will sooner or later expose the wasteful practices that the inventory was put in place to hide: high setup costs, machine breakdowns, unreliable supplier deliveries, inconsistent process yields, inaccurate forecasts, etc. As these practices are exposed, they should be addressed (improved or eliminated) in the same sequence in which they were exposed.

*"How do you expect to create a work place in which employees freely share ideas if those ideas will lead to improvements that eliminate jobs?"*

The person closest to the work knows the most about how his or her work processes can be simplified or eliminated. But no one will commit employment suicide. So how can we get workers to share what they know? Two steps are required to motivate employees to share their ideas:

1. Help workers make the distinction between *job* security and *employment* security. In a JIT environment, jobs will change and jobs will be eliminated, but employment will remain because the com-

pany will become more productive and more competitive in the marketplace.

2. Senior management must communicate to all employees a position statement to the effect that no one will lose employment as a result of productivity improvements. We all know and understand that you cannot guarantee employment. You can, however, guarantee that no employee will be "productivity improved" into the unemployment line. This statement must be sincere, and it must be backed up with action. How you follow through on your employment statement will speak louder than any words you may use.

## SUMMARY

- Just-in-Time is not simply a theoretical approach to eliminating waste; it has a very practical side that you can apply for measurable benefits.
- Quantum improvements come not from simply working harder or smarter at the same old things, but from figuring out how to eliminate the *need* to do the same old things.
- The person closest to the work knows best how that activity can be simplified or eliminated altogether. The challenge is to create an environment that energizes and stimulates workers to share their ideas, even if it means their own job will be eliminated.
- The Japanese word *kanban* literally translated means card or signal. JIT uses kanban as a visual technique for authorizing the movement of material or for authorizing production to begin by signaling to the proceeding operations that the succeeding operation is ready to receive work. Kanban enables demand-pull production in which a customer, either internal or external, pulls product from a supplier—again, either internal or external. It contrasts with order-push production, in which a work order or a purchase order authorizes the supplier to deliver to the customer at a predetermined rate.
- Drastic and significant reductions in changeover times can be achieved using a process developed by Shigeo Shingo called Single Minute Exchange of Dies (SMED). This is a scientific process used

to analyze changeover activities, to determine areas where improvements are practical, and then to cause improvements to happen.

## INFORMATION RESOURCES

*APICS Dictionary*, 7th edition, American Production and Inventory Control Society, 1992.
*APICS CPIM 1993 Study Guide*, American Production and Inventory Control Society.
*Just-in-Time: Making It Happen*, William A. Sandras, Jr., Oliver Wight Publications, 1989.
*Attaining Manufacturing Excellence*, Robert W. Hall, Business One Irwin, 1987.
*Japanese Manufacturing Techniques*, Richard J. Schonberger, The Free Press, 1982.
*A Revolution in Manufacturing: The SMED System*, Shigeo Shingo, Productivity Press, 1985.
*Just-in-Time for America*, Kenneth A. Wantuck, KWA Media, 1989.

## INTERNAL CROSS-REFERENCE

Your understanding of this topic may be enhanced by the following chapters:

 I–6. Resource Planning: For Manufacturing, the Business, and the Enterprise

 IV–1. Total Quality Management (TQM)

 IV–2. Tools for Total Quality Management (TQM)

## About the Author

William M. Boyst, Jr. (III), CFPIM - CPMM, is an American Just-in-Time/Total Quality Control pioneer, active in the field since the 1970s. He is a principal of the Oliver Wight Companies and president of W. M. Boyst & Associates of Raleigh, North Carolina, an international management development and consulting firm specializing in Just-in-Time, Total Quality Control, and Manufacturing Resource Planning. Prior to forming his firm, Mr. Boyst was director of materials management at Northern Telecom's INS Switching Division.

# The Malcolm Baldrige National Quality Award Program
## Stephen George

### IN A NUTSHELL

The Malcolm Baldrige National Quality Award program was established by Congress in 1987 to increase awareness of quality, promote an understanding of the requirements for quality excellence, and encourage information sharing about successful quality strategies and their benefits. The program meets these objectives through a public-private partnership designed to:

- Increase awareness of quality: the Baldrige Award is given annually to companies judged to be world class role models for American business.
- Promote an understanding of the requirements for quality excellence: judging is based on criteria that define the essential elements in a total quality system.

- Encourage information sharing: Nearly a quarter million copies of the criteria are distributed annually for little or no charge. Companies that win the Baldrige Award share their quality strategies through written materials, speeches, and seminars.

Manufacturers can apply for the Baldrige Award in either the manufacturing category (500 or more employees) or the small business category (fewer than 500 employees).

A manufacturing subsidiary of a company may apply in the manufacturing category. Application forms and booklets describing the criteria, evaluation process, and the dates for key events are available from the National Institute of Standards and Technology (NIST), which administers the Baldrige program. The application takes the form of a company's written response to the award criteria, and must be submitted to NIST by the application deadline (usually in early April).

Nineteen companies received Baldrige Awards in the first six years of the program; fifteen have been manufacturing companies or subsidiaries, including in the manufacturing category Motorola, Westinghouse Commercial Nuclear Fuel, Milliken & Company, Xerox Business Products and Systems, Cadillac, IBM Rochester, Solectron, Zytec, AT&T Network Systems Group, Texas Instruments Defense Systems & Electronics Group, and Eastman Chemical, and in the small business category Globe Metallurgical, Marlow Industries, Granite Rock Company and Ames Rubber. Most of these companies will provide information about their award-winning applications upon request (see Information Resources at the end of this chapter).

### *The Baldrige Criteria*

The Baldrige Award has seven categories of criteria:

- Leadership
- Information and Analysis
- Strategic Quality Planning
- Human Resource Development and Management

- Management of Process Quality
- Quality and Operational Results
- Customer Focus and Satisfaction

Each category is subdivided into items. For example, the Leadership category is divided into three items: Senior Executive Leadership; Management for Quality; and Public Responsibility and Corporate Citizenship. Each item is subdivided into areas to address. Senior Executive Leadership, for example, consists of four areas that ask for details about senior executive leadership, a summary of the company's customer focus and quality values, how these values are communicated, and how the senior executives evaluate and improve their effectiveness as leaders.

Companies respond to these criteria by identifying how their organizations achieve them. Their responses fit one or more of three evaluation dimensions: approach; deployment; and results. By understanding these dimensions and evaluating their responses, or by having members of the Board of Examiners evaluate their responses (done when a company applies for the award), they gain a clearer picture of their strengths and weaknesses. They also gain a much better understanding of how their management system functions.

The management model defined by the Baldrige criteria works as a system. The key elements of the system—the categories in the criteria—are interconnected as shown in Figure 1.

The Baldrige model is driven by customer requirements and works toward customer satisfaction. Leadership and information affect every part of the organization: leadership commits everyone in the organization to meeting customer requirements through Continuous Improvement; information is gathered from all critical points to evaluate and improve ongoing operations and to help people make decisions that are based on facts. The planning process involves everyone—managers, employees, customers, and suppliers—in charting a course that every department, team, and employee can translate into actions. People are at the center of the new model, involved in planning, managing, improving processes, and serving customers.

**FIGURE 1. THE BALDRIGE MANAGEMENT MODEL**

Requirements — YOUR CUSTOMERS — Satisfaction

- Leadership
- Information
- Planning
- Results
- People
- Processes

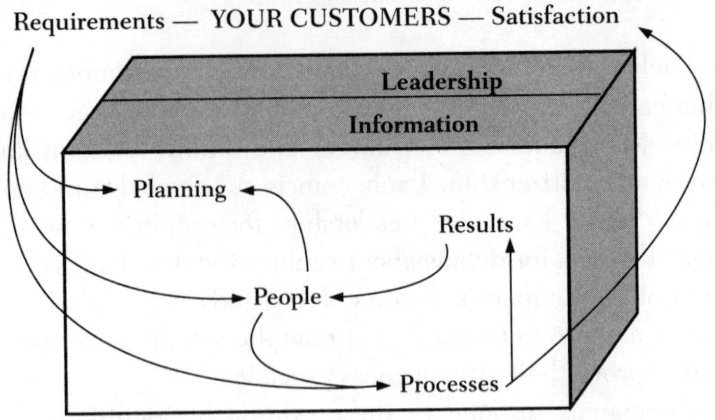

From Total *Quality Management: Strategies* and *Techniques Proven at Today's Most Successful Companies*, by Stephen George and Arnold Weimerskirch, John Wiley & Sons, Inc., 1993.

The Baldrige management model is aimed, first and foremost, at meeting customer requirements. And the measure of success, whether of processes, products, services, or performance, is then to develop or modify plans, improve processes, and predict customer satisfaction.

This new management model is built on a set of core values that include customer-driven quality, leadership, Continuous Improvement, employee participation and development, fast response, design quality and prevention, long-range outlook, management by fact, partnership development, and corporate responsibility and citizenship.

## *Benefits*

The criteria are the key to the Baldrige Award program; any serious discussion of the benefits of the program begins with them. Manufacturing companies of all types and sizes around the world are using these criteria to understand, assess, control, and improve their organizations. As applicant companies interpret the criteria and respond to them, they begin to understand how their organization works to meet customer requirements and where it must improve. They become systems thinkers. No other self-assessment tool provides such a holistic perspective.

Of the hundreds of companies that use the criteria to assess their organizations, only a few actually apply for the Baldrige Award. The majority create an application to assess their own operational health, a critical step in the process of systematically improving management systems.

The benefits of the Baldrige criteria, then, come from a self-assessment that:

- Involves and motivates people throughout the organization
- Provides a proven quality system
- Focuses that system on the customer
- Assesses quality
- Demands data
- Provides feedback
- Encourages sharing with quality leaders
- Stimulates change
- Builds financial success

## KEY CONCEPTS

**Approach**: How a company achieves the requirements in the Baldrige criteria. A world class approach is sound, systematic, fully integrated, and regularly refined.

**Board of Examiners**: Volunteer quality experts, primarily from the private sector, who are selected by NIST to evaluate Baldrige Award applications, prepare feedback reports, and make award recommendations to the director of NIST.

**Continuous Improvement (Baldrige core value)**: Holds that a focus on incremental and "breakthrough" improvement needs to be part of all operations and work activities of a company.

**Corporate responsibility and citizenship (Baldrige core value)**: Stretches the company's quality system objectives to include business ethics, protection of public health and safety, and leadership and support of publicly important purposes.

**Customer-driven quality (Baldrige core value)**: States that "all product and service attributes that contribute value to the customer and lead to customer satisfaction and preference must be the foundation for a company's quality system."

**Customer focus and satisfaction (seventh Baldrige category)**: Examines the company's relationships with its customers, its knowledge of customer requirements, its methods of determining customer satisfaction, and its trends and levels of customer satisfaction.

**Deployment**: The extent to which a company has applied an approach to all relevant areas of its organization. World class deployment means an approach is fully deployed without weaknesses or gaps in any areas.

**Design quality and prevention (Baldrige core value)**: Encourages problem and waste prevention, Continuous Improvement, and corrective action "upstream," at the early stages in processes.

**Employee participation and development (Baldrige core value)**: Recognizes the link between employee satisfaction and customer satisfaction and encourages the improvement of the skills and dedication of the entire work force.

**Fast response (Baldrige core value)**: States that "faster and more flexible response to customers is now a more critical requirement of business management."

**Human resource development and management (fourth Baldrige category)**: Examines how the workforce is empowered to pursue the company's objectives.

**Information and analysis (second Baldrige category)**: Looks at how the company uses data and information to drive quality excellence, improve performance, and meet customer requirements.

**Leadership (first Baldrige category and Baldrige core value)**: Examines how senior executives personally create and sustain a customer focus and quality values, and how those values are integrated into the company's management system.

**Long-range outlook (Baldrige core value)**: States that achieving leadership "requires a company to have a strong future orientation and a willingness to make long-term commitments to customers, employees, suppliers, stockholders, and the community."

**Management by fact (Baldrige core value)**: Holds that process management must be based on reliable information, data, and analysis.

**Management of Process quality (fifth Baldrige category)**: Assesses the processes the company uses in all parts of the organization to pursue its objectives.

**Partnership development (Baldrige core value)**: Encourages companies to build internal and external partnerships to reach their goals.

**Quality and operational results (sixth Baldrige category)**: Looks at the company's quality levels and improvement trends, and how those levels and trends compare to the competition's.

**Results**: The quantifiable effectiveness of a company's approach and deployment. World class results show excellent improvement trends and levels that lead the industry or other benchmarks.

**Strategic quality planning (third Baldrige category)**: Explores the company's planning process and how all key quality requirements are integrated into the company's Business Plan.

## ACTION STEPS

The best way to get the full value of the Baldrige Award program is to complete an application that responds to the criteria. Only by wrestling with the criteria can a company understand them, and only by writing down what it is doing in each area can it truly understand the condition of its quality system.

The steps to follow in the application are as follows:

- Involve senior management. The more involved they are in the assessment process, the better they will understand their own system and how to improve it.
- Establish Baldrige teams. Teams share the workload, bring individual insights and ideas to the process, and become valuable resources as they develop their "systems thinking."
- Train the team members to understand the criteria and the application process.
- Assign responsibilities. Key responsibilities include who will lead the effort, who will be responsible for the final written responses, and who will be in charge of layout and graphics.
- Collect data and information. Team members need to identify what they must find out and who has the necessary data and information, interview the subject experts, and organize their data.
- Identify areas for improvement. As the team members collect data, they will discover holes in their responses—places where the company lacks a systematic approach, full deployment, or positive results. This is the most valuable result of the application process.
- Communicate needs, ideas, and information. Team members need to establish continuous formal and informal methods of communication to produce the best possible application.
- Write the first draft. Most companies assign this task to several writers, usually the category leaders.
- Begin the layout, including graphics. Organize and present your information clearly to communicate it effectively.
- Evaluate the first draft. This can be done internally or by outside experts.
- Write subsequent drafts.
- Coordinate writing and graphics. Team members need to pull the responses and graphics together into a unified application.
- Produce the final draft.
- Print and deliver the application. Printing quality and distribu-

tion depend on whether you are submitting the application for the Baldrige Award and how widely you wish to communicate it within your company.

## PROBLEM-SOLVING

> "We understand that we need to improve quality to compete, and we've elevated the stature of our quality department, but interest in quality seems to be declining. How can we get people who are already very busy to focus on quality?"

Companies new to Total Quality Management and the Baldrige criteria often view quality as distinct from the rest of their operation. They put quality in a slot next to sales and marketing, legal, accounting, and other functional departments. The most successful companies understand that quality is not a department, nor can it be separated from any of the processes that allow a manufacturer to produce its goods. Quality *is* the system. The best description of this system is found in the Baldrige criteria.

> "We've studied all the quality gurus and applied what we've learned, but we always slip back into our old ways of doing business. How can we make Continuous Improvement part of our corporate culture?"

Every business wants to operate more efficiently. Manufacturers that make this a top priority often turn to quality programs as a way of identifying inefficient processes and activities and initiating improvements. Too often, however, this "quality program of the month" approach attacks the symptoms and not the causes, resulting in a return to the old methods as soon as the program ends.

The Baldrige criteria help leaders get their arms around their organizations. Through the self-assessment process, companies can identify the major areas of inefficiency and how they affect customer satisfaction and business performance. They can then apply quality tools and techniques to solving the problems. Subsequent assessments use the criteria as progress reports. Faced with the task of making their organizations more efficient, most people do not know where to start. An assessment using the Baldrige criteria will tell them.

> *"Quality improvement sounds good, but we're a 'bottom-line-oriented' company. If Total Quality Management doesn't improve profits, we're not going to do it. Is there a connection that will convince senior management to lead the quality effort?"*

Financial success is a measure of the effectiveness of a company's entire system. In the management model defined by the Baldrige criteria, the goal is not profits but customer satisfaction, with the understanding that financial success derives from quality improvement. Quality leaders have shown that a systematic quality improvement process results in less waste and greater productivity. Quality products also increase the number of customers willing to buy from your company. The collective result is lower cost, better margins and asset utilization, and greater revenues. These enhance profitability.

## SUMMARY

- The objectives of the Malcolm Baldrige National Quality Award are to increase awareness of quality, promote an understanding of the requirements of quality excellence, and encourage information sharing about quality strategies.
- Manufacturing companies or subsidiaries apply for the Baldrige Award through a written application that responds to the Baldrige criteria.
- The criteria are the key to the Baldrige Award program. Manufacturers of all types and sizes are using the criteria to understand, assess, control, and improve their organizations.
- The criteria are built on a set of core values and concepts that are embodied in the seven Baldrige categories.
- The new business management model defined by the Baldrige criteria is driven by customer requirements and directed toward customer satisfaction.

## INFORMATION RESOURCES

*Baldrige Award-Winning Quality: How to Interpret the Malcolm Baldrige Award Criteria*, 3rd Edition, Mark Graham Brown, Quality Resources, 1993.

*The Baldrige Quality System: The Do-It-Yourself Way to Transform Your Business*, Stephen George, John Wiley & Sons, Inc., 1992.

*Managing the Total Quality Transformation*, Thomas H. Berry, McGraw-Hill, 1991.

*Total Quality Management: Strategies and Techniques Proven at Today's Most Successful Companies*, Stephen George and Arnold Weimerskirch, John Wiley & Sons, Inc., 1994.

## INTERNAL CROSS-REFERENCE

Your understanding of this topic may be enhanced by the following chapters:

    IV–6.  ISO 9000: The International Quality Standard

    VII–1.  Measuring Customer Satisfaction

    VII–2.  Performance Measures That Support World Class Manufacturing

### About the Author

Stephen George is the author of two books on the Baldrige Award program and the co-author of *Corporate Realities and Environmental Truths*. He has consulted with twelve companies that have applied for the Baldrige Award and/or state quality awards, ten have been finalists for the awards and three have won. Mr. George is currently helping businesses use the Baldrige criteria and assessment process to better understand their management systems and to implement Continuous Improvement.

# ISO 9000: The International Quality Standard

*Robert L. Jones and Joseph R. Tunner*

**IN A NUTSHELL**

ISO 9000 is a series of internationally accepted quality standards that describe the elements of a solid quality assurance system. The series includes ISO 9000, ISO 9001, ISO 9002, ISO 9003, and ISO 9004.

The ISO 9000 series was written by the ISO/Technical Committee (TC) 176, a worldwide body made up of several standards committees and subgroups. Five national associations—Association Française de Normalisation (AFNOR), American National Standards Institute (ANSI), British Standards Institute (BSI), Nederlands Normalisatie Instituut (NNI), and Standards Council of Canada (SCC) participate in ISO/TC 176. Other member countries are represented by their respective national standards bodies.

Prior to development of the ISO series, many countries had developed their own quality systems standards; so had many branches of their governments, industries, and corporations. At best this situation was confusing; at worst it has been expensive and counterproductive.

The ISO 9000 series replaces this web of existing and conflicting quality systems standards with a single, universally accepted framework. As of late 1993, more than ninety-five national bodies have adopted the ISO 9000 series, including all major European countries, Japan, South Korea, the People's Republic of China, and the United States.

## *Functional Description*

Each country generally rewrites the ISO 9000 series into its native language, usually with very few structural changes, and assigns its own series documentation numbers. The ANSI/ASQC Q90 series is the United States' version of ISO 9000. Q90 corresponds to ISO 9000, Q91 to ISO 9001, etc.

Although the government of a country can subscribe to the ISO 9000 series, it cannot mandate compliance. Rather, individual companies must decide if and how they will apply the standard—both internally and as a demand on their suppliers.

Of the five documents in the ISO 9000 series, three are the actual standards and serve as models of quality assurance systems, while the remaining two are supporting documents (see Figure 1).

Depending on the scope of its organization, a company can opt to follow one of three registration options that most closely matches its activities. The first, ISO 9001, is the most demanding and is designed for organizations that cover a broad range of activities, from product design through manufacturing, testing, installation, and postsale service. The last, ISO 9003, is the simplest and is geared for companies that depend mainly on testing and inspection systems to control quality; in practice it is used mainly by internal departments of larger organization or by distributors rather than manufacturers. The middle registration option, ISO 9002, is the one most organizations pursue, and falls between the others in complexity.

Figure 2 shows the major paragraphs and subject areas for each of the quality systems models. It illustrates that quality systems models increase in complexity from 9003 to 9001 to match the specific situa-

## Figure 1. The ISO 9000 Series

**ISO 9000**

> A road map on how to use the other four documents in the series.

**ISO 9004**

> An explanatory guide to the requirements contained in ISO 9001 through 9003.

**ISO 9003** (12 requirements)

> The quality model for companies requiring final inspection and testing — for example, a jobber, installer, or distributor. It is the least rigorous and least applied for certification.

**ISO 9002** (18 requirements)

> The quality model for companies manufacturing and/or offering a service to a published catalog or to a customer's specification. It incorporates 9003 and is the most commonly pursued certification.

**ISO 9003** (20 requirements)

> The quality model for companies that design, develop, manufacture, install, and service their products. It incorporates ISO 9003 and 9002. Also, it is the most demanding and second most commonly pursued certification.

*VERTICAL INTEGRATION*

tion of the company seeking registration. Figure 2 is adapted from the current version (1987) of ISO 9000. Several changes to the current version are presently being circulated for approval, and they will generally increase the requirements of each of the standards. While no new major paragraphs have been added in the revision, most have been strengthened. In addition, several of the paragraphs that do not apply to the present version of ISO 9003 are included in the proposed revision.

**FIGURE 2. ISO 9001, 9002, 9003 CROSS-REFERENCE**

|  | 9001 | 9002 | 9003 |
|---|---|---|---|
| Management Responsibility | 4.1 | 4.1a | 4.1b |
| Quality System | 4.2 | 4.2 | 4.2a |
| Contract Review | 4.3 | 4.3 | * |
| Design Control | 4.4 | * | * |
| Document Control | 4.5 | 4.4 | 4.3a |
| Purchasing | 4.6 | 4.5 | * |
| Purchaser Supplier Product | 4.7 | 4.6 | * |
| Product Identification and Traceability | 4.8 | 4.7 | 4.4a |
| Process Control | 4.9 | 4.8 | * |
| Inspection and Testing | 4.10 | 4.9 | 4.5a |
| Inspection, Measuring, and Test Equipment | 4.11 | 4.10 | 4.6a |
| Inspection and Test Status | 4.12 | 4.11 | 4.7a |
| Control of Nonconforming Product | 4.13 | 4.12 | 4.8a |
| Corrective Action | 4.14 | 4.13 | * |
| Handling, Storage, Packaging, and Delivery | 4.15 | 4.14 | 4.9a |
| Quality Records | 4.16 | 4.15 | 4.10a |
| Internal Quality Audits | 4.17 | 4.16a | * |
| Training | 4.18 | 4.17a | 4.11b |
| Servicing | 4.19 | * | * |
| Statistical Techniques | 4.20 | 4.18 | 4.12a |

a Less stringent than 9001
b Less stringent than 9002
* Element not present
*Source:* James L. Lamprecht.

The bottom line of ISO registration is to contract with a registrar to perform a formal audit, a prerequisite to becoming registered. In the United States, registrars are licensed by the Registration Accreditation Board, an arm of the American Society for Quality Control; they are licensed by similar bodies in other countries.

A number of steps should be taken in preparation for an audit, steps that often require six to eighteen months of effort (see Action Steps). These preparatory steps can be done independently, with the aid of an appropriate consulting firm, or with the help of a registrar.

Once registered, a firm can advertise its compliance to ISO 9000.

The registrar will continue to conduct periodic surveillance to ensure that the applicable standards continue to be met.

ISO 9000 is now seen as a true win-win-win standard for any manufacturing or service organization. The first, and in the long run the largest win, is the big return on investment that derives from having a strong internal quality assurance system—waste, rework, downtime, and complaints decrease, while profits climb.

The second win lies in being able to satisfy the quality systems requirements of many different customers by showing compliance to one standard. No longer will a company need to be audited by numerous customers. Maintenance of a current ISO 9000 certification is proof that the company maintains an approved quality system.

The third win is being able to select good suppliers without having to audit them yourself. You will know that any supplier who is registered to one of the ISO 9000 standards has already satisfied a rigorous audit process and must continue to show compliance in the future.

In addition, ISO 9000 focuses employees on customer-centered improvements, identifies internal improvement opportunities, and serves as a benchmark of performance.

## KEY CONCEPTS

**First-party audit**: An audit done by an organization on itself.

**First-tier documentation**: The quality manual.

**ISO 9000**: An international standard describing sound quality principles.

**ISO/Technical Committee 176**: The worldwide committee that wrote the standard.

**Major discrepancy**: A significant violation of an element of the standard found by an auditor. This would be cause for failing an audit.

**Minor discrepancy**: A nonconformity to the standard found by an auditor that does not appear to seriously compromise quality and can be easily corrected.

**Reciprocity**: Agreement among registering bodies (e.g., standards organizations of different nations) to accept registration done by one of their counterparts.

**Quality manual**: The core document that defines a quality system.

**Registering body**: The organization empowered to select and approve registrars.

**Registrar**: A group authorized to register an organization to one of the standards.

**Second-party audit**: An audit done by an organization on its suppliers.

**Second-tier documentation**: Practices and procedures referenced in the quality manual.

**Surveillance audits**: Periodic audits to verify that a registered organization continues to satisfy the requirements of the standard.

**Third-party audit**: An audit done by a disinterested party.

**Third-tier documentation**: Records of specific events such as test tickets.

## ACTION STEPS

Figure 3 details a six-phased approach to achieving ISO 9000 registration. The process frequently takes six to eighteen months for many companies, depending on their starting point. The action plan in Figure 3 shows fourteen months.

*Phase I. Awareness—Management Overview and Commitment*
ISO registration involves commitment to a long-term operating strategy. Management needs to understand the reasons for registration, what is involved, and that it has a major and continuing

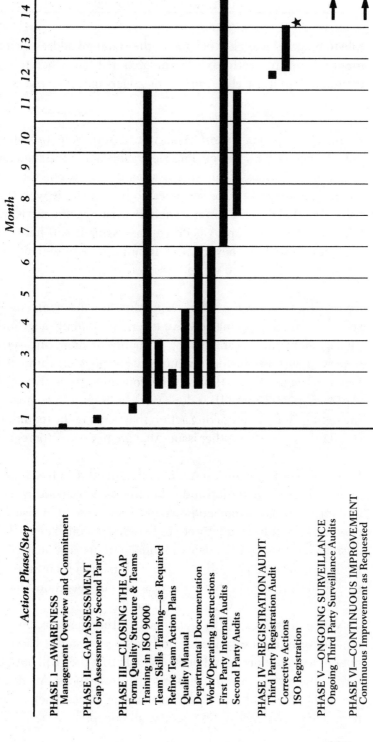

FIGURE 3. ACTION PLAN FOR OBTAINING ISO 9000 REGISTRATION

role to play. In fact, a key portion of the standard addresses management responsibility; this is often an area that fails when the audit is conducted, so it is well to apprise managers of their part early in the process.

*Phase II. Gap Assessment* A survey of your activities should be done by people who are very knowledgeable about the standards and the auditing process. This survey should identify the gap between where you are and where you need to be to comply with the standard. The assessment can also define what specific steps must be taken to close the gap. A good gap assessment can help pinpoint opportunities to go beyond the minimum requirements of ISO registration and lead to world class performance.

*Phase III. Closing the Gap* Depending on the company's initial state, closing the gap may involve extensive training, a rethinking of management's role, establishing a quality manual, and setting up improved systems for documenting what goes on throughout the facility. Because Phase III is so time-consuming, it is critical that the gap assessment (Phase II) is done well. Otherwise, a company could waste time and money taking action that is not really required by the standard and overlook other issues that are necessary for registration.

*Phase IV. The Registration Audit* If the first three phases have been done well, the registration audit should proceed smoothly. Typically, a team of three or four auditors from an accredited registrar will conduct the audit over a three- to five-day period. They will ask for an advance copy of the quality manual and use it to help plan their audit. Following a kick-off meeting with management, the auditing team will conduct an extensive review of your operations, looking for evidence that you do what you say you do.

Nonconformities will be classified as either major or minor. Major nonconformities are cause for not passing the audit. If only minor nonconformities are found, it is probable that they will not be cause for failure, although you will need to correct them. At the close of the audit, the team will indicate whether or not they are recommending you for registration, review all nonconformities, and follow up later with a detailed written report. Should you not pass, the team will arrange for another visit during which it will review the changes you have made to comply with the standard.

*Phase V. Ongoing Surveillance* Once registered, you must agree to have the registrar back on a regularly scheduled basis to confirm that you are still in compliance with the standard. These surveillance audits are normally much less comprehensive than the initial audit, and often focus on areas where earlier nonconformities had been noted (although they will spot check other areas, too).

Registrars decide the frequency of surveillance audits; a typical pattern would involve a partial audit every six months, with perhaps a more thorough audit every three years. Should major problems surface during a surveillance audit, the registrar can revoke your certification.

*Phase VI. Continuous Improvement* ISO 9000 helps companies discover opportunities for improvement. You can build upon what was learned through the ISO registration process to move your company toward world class performance. As noted earlier, some of this may begin during Phase III, as an outcome of the gap assessment, but improvement is an ongoing process. This phase is not a required part of the ISO registration process, but is highly recommended.

## PROBLEM-SOLVING

> "Our company is being audited to death. It seems that most of our current and prospective customers want to perform individual audits of our operations, and every customer has a different format. The workload required to complete these audits is killing us."

The ISO 9000 registration process audits your company against internationally accepted standards that describe the elements of a solid quality assurance system. Being ISO 9000 registered will answer many of your customers' concerns and leave your company with more time to focus on improvements, rather than escorting team after team on quality audits.

*"We've got a great quality system in place, but nobody else seems to know about it."*

Once you have become registered with ISO 9000, you can advertise your registration and it will be listed, by your registrar, in a book of ISO 9000–registered companies.

*"I'm not sure whether our company's quality and operating procedures are valid, and if so, whether they are being followed."*

An ISO third-party audit is an unbiased outsider evaluation as to whether your company's quality manual meets established international standards. The auditors will take a sampling of your quality processes to ascertain whether your company is complying with your quality manual, your operating procedures, and the international standard. You will be given a verbal and written report detailing their specific findings.

*"We need to focus our company on meeting our customers' needs and expectations."*

ISO 9000, while not directly providing a process to initially uncover your customers' needs, is intensely focused on determining whether you have a quality process in place that allows you to achieve agreed-upon customer needs through your stated quality procedures and instructions. The audit process uses the following priority sequence in auditing your quality system:

1. Customer/legal contractual requirements
2. Quality manuals, procedures, and instructions
3. The appropriate ISO 9000 quality assurance standard

## SUMMARY

- The ISO 9000 series is an internationally accepted quality standard that describes the elements of a solid quality assurance system.
- Registration is obtained by contracting with an approved regis-

trar to conduct a rigorous third-party audit of your facility and certify that you are in compliance with the applicable standard.

- In the United States, registrars are licensed by the Registration Accreditation Board—an arm of the American Society of Quality Control.
- A company will register against one of three standards, depending upon the scope of its organization: ISO 9001, ISO 9002, or ISO 9003.
- Benefits of registration include a reduced need for audits from your customers, identification on internal improvement opportunities, employee participation on increasing performance, and a benchmark for evaluating and selecting suppliers.

## INFORMATION RESOURCES

*ISO 9000: Preparing for Registration*, James L. Lamprecht, ASQC Quality Press, 1992.
*American National Standard—ANSI/ASQC Q90 Series*, ASQC 1987.
"Updating the ISO 9000 Standards: Responding to Marketplace Needs," Ian Durand, Donald Marquardt, Robert Peach, and James Pile, *Quality Progress*, July 1993.

## INTERNAL CROSS-REFERENCE

Your understanding of this topic may be enhanced by the following chapters:

IV–5. The Malcolm Baldrige National Quality Award Program

IV–7. Discovering Improvement Opportunities Through Quality Auditing

## About the Authors

Robert L. Jones is an international educator and consultant in the areas of MRP II, TQM, and ISO 9000. He has more than twenty-five years of managerial and consulting experience and is a senior partner in the firm of R. Reed & Associates, Downers Grove, Illinois. Mr. Jones is a fellow in APICS and a senior member of ASQC.

Joseph R. Tunner is an independent consultant with broad experience in quality engineering and quality management, including thirty-two years with Eastman Kodak. A fellow of the American Society for Quality Control, he is the author of *A Quality Technology Primer for Managers* and of many papers on quality-related issues.

# IV-7

# Discovering Improvement Opportunities Through Quality Auditing

### Greg Hutchins

**IN A NUTSHELL**

The American Society of Quality Control (ASQC) describes quality auditing as "a systematic examination of the acts and decisions by people with respect to quality, in order to independently verify or evaluate and report compliance to the operational requirements of the quality program or the specification or contract requirement of the product or service."

This definition highlights some important aspects of quality auditing and the people who do it. The auditor must be systematic and follow a logical sequence of activities to reach a decision in terms of planning, conducting, and reporting audit results. And the auditor must evaluate independently, and not be tied to any group that could bias or cloud his or her judgment or create the appearance of a conflict of interest.

## Purposes of Quality Auditing

Quality auditing is a method of verifying a producer's compliance with a customer's quality requirements. Here, the auditor verifies whether the auditee, or the activity being audited, is complying with requirements spelled out in a contract, policy standard, specification, regulatory standard, engineering print, procedure, or other document.

Audits are also useful in establishing quality baselines, measuring improvements, benchmarking competitors, and for other purposes, which include:

- Selecting, monitoring, and improving suppliers
- Assessing quality processes and systems
- Measuring customer satisfaction
- Monitoring operational efficiency, effectiveness, and economy

An auditor may conduct one of several types of audits: a compliance audit, a performance audit, or a risk-assessment audit. In ISO 9000 auditing, the quality auditor evaluates compliance or conformance to the quality system requirements of the standard. In a performance audit, the quality auditor assesses the efficient, effective, and economic utilization of internal resources. In a risk assessment, the quality auditor evaluates whether internal controls are minimizing risk of product or system failure. These audits can be conducted in any business—large or small, in the public or private sector, either internally or externally.

## Corrective Action Requests

In a case where the audit determines that quality requirements are not being met, the auditor may issue a Corrective Action Request (CAR), sometimes called a deficiency finding. To satisfy the requirements of the CAR, the auditee is responsible for determining the true cause of the deficiency, not only the symptom, and eliminate the root cause of the problem so that it doesn't recur. The auditor is usually not responsible for indicating how a deficiency is to be resolved.

As noted above, there is more to a quality system than simply high-quality output. There should be an internal control system for correcting errors when they occur. Quality auditors look for such a system.

Typical questions found in a questionnaire for evaluating corrective action include:

- Is there an effective corrective action system?
- Is corrective action audited after implementation?
- If quality deficiencies recur, are they resolved quickly and efficiently?
- Is the goal of corrective action to resolve the symptom and eliminate the root cause?
- Is company-wide Continuous Improvement pursued?
- Is a written correction action plan with implementation and timing criteria developed?

## *The Quality Audit Process*

Quality auditing follows a three-part process: Planning, Conducting, and Reporting.

*1. Planning* Experienced quality auditors plan the audit so as to minimize disruptions to the auditee's operations. The auditor's objective is to obtain the required evidence and issue an opinion as quickly and cost effectively as possible. The professional auditor does not waste time reviewing paperwork at the auditee's facility that could have been done before the audit. During this phase, the auditor develops a program, process, and system-specific questionnaire to use as an audit guide. Planning steps include the following:

- Understand customer expectations and requirements
- Notify the auditee of impending audit
- Understand auditee's operations and quality systems
- Identify audit constraints and requirements
- Prepare the audit plan and audit questionnaire

2. *Conducting* In this part of the process—sometimes called implementation or field work—the auditor gathers, arranges, and evaluates evidence in order to evaluate the auditee's quality systems or whatever is required by the customer. The auditor may test products, evaluate documentation, perform calculations, evaluate work standards, or conduct other tests. Conducting steps include:

- Determine compliance with customer requirements
- Identify internal quality controls
- Determine if processes are in control, capable, and improving
- Test the effectiveness of internal controls
- Evaluate audit evidence
- Issue an opinion

3. *Reporting* The auditor communicates results in a quality report. The reports include background information, findings, opinions, and corrective action requests. It's critical that the report is clear and objective. If it contains recommendations, they should be workable actions. The report should also address and satisfy customer requirements. Typical elements in an audit report are:

- Executive summary
- Introduction
- Opinion
- Findings
- Corrective action requests
- Background information

## A New Profession

Quality auditing is a relatively new profession. It is not as developed as its brethren, financial auditing and operational auditing, which have well-developed methodologies and reporting mechanisms. Quality auditing is just becoming understood, accepted, and valued in the marketplace.

Quality auditing originated with the need to ensure that suppliers and contractors provide consistent quality of products and services.

Traditionally, incoming material inspection provided this assurance. Inspection, though, was expensive, ineffective, and took responsibility for quality away from the supplier. The inspection method had the same shortcomings as traditional quality assurance programs: it focused on products after they were built, and tried to "inspect in" quality instead of focusing on the processes that built them.

With quality auditing the goal is for the supplier to prevent deficiencies from occurring by controlling the processes that produced products or provided services. The customer was assured quality by auditing the supplier's control systems and processes.

As it develops visibility, credibility, and trust, quality auditing is developing into a profession. And like any profession, its practitioners must meet certain high standards, in this case:

- Professional proficiency
- Sufficient skills and knowledge
- Communication skills
- Analytical skills
- Diligence
- Critical attitude
- Honesty
- Flexibility

## KEY CONCEPTS

**Assessment**: Similar to an audit.

**Audit team**: Group of professionals conducting an audit.

**Client**: The customer, the person authorizing or requesting the audit.

**Compliance**: Same as conformance; an indication that requirements have been satisfied.

**Compliance audit**: Yes/no, complying/not-complying with requirements type of quality audit; ISO 9000 is a compliance audit.

**Corrective action**: Action to eliminate the symptom and root cause of a deficiency.

**Deficiency**: Same as defect, discrepancy, or nonconformity; an activity, product, or service characteristic that does not conform to requirements.

**Internal control**: Systems, such as training or documentation, that prevent deficiencies from occurring.

**Lead auditor**: Person responsible for directing the audit and reporting its results.

**Product audit**: Examination or test of a product's quality characteristics or performance.

**Quality auditing**: Independent, objective, and systematic quality evaluation.

**Report**: Formal communication of audit results.

**System audit**: Assessment of a set of activities to determine compliance with quality requirements.

## PROBLEM-SOLVING

*"We manufacture a health and safety product and want to minimize the risk of a product failure."*

Periodic internal audits of quality documentation, training, and processes would indicate if deficiencies currently exist or if they may occur. High-risk products require equally high levels of assurance through extensive and intensive quality auditing.

*"We procure about 80 percent of our manufacturing materials from outside suppliers. We want to integrate suppliers into our operations and treat internal and external suppliers similarly. How do we do this?"*

Quality, cost, technology, delivery, and service requirements are spelled out in supplier certification documents. Internal and external suppliers often have to comply with similar requirements. Quality audits can be used to select, monitor, and improve suppliers and to determine compliance to customer standards.

> *"We still inspect incoming supplier shipments. We know this is not quality prevention. We also know that quality responsibility rests with the supplier, not with our inspectors. If we stop our own inspections, how can we assure the quality of our suppliers?"*

The goal is to move upstream from inspection at the loading dock to prevention at the supplier's facility. Quality auditing assesses the supplier's processes and systems to determine their capability to provide products and services that satisfy your requirements.

## SUMMARY

- Quality auditing is an independent, objective, and systematic quality evaluation.
- Quality auditing is used to determine compliance, evaluate risks and controls, and assess internal efficiencies and supplier effectiveness.
- Quality audits are used to verify compliance with customer requirements, establish quality baselines, and measure improvements.
- Quality auditing follows a structured format of planning, conducting, and reporting.

## INFORMATION RESOURCES

*Quality Auditing*, Greg Hutchins, Prentice-Hall, 1992.
"Quality Certifications," Giovanni Grossi, *Internal Auditor*, October 1992, pp. 33–35.
"Dynamic Auditing of Quality Assurance: Concepts and Methods," Walter Willborn, *International Journal of Quality & Reliability Management*, 1990, pp. 35–42.
"Evaluate Standards and Improve Performance with a Quality Audit," Dennis Arter, *Quality Progress*, September 1989, pp. 41–43.

## INTERNAL CROSS-REFERENCE

Your understanding of this topic may be enhanced by the following chapters:

IV–2. Tools for Total Quality Management (TQM)

IV–6. ISO 9000: The International Quality Standard

### About the Author

Greg Hutchins is a principal of Quality Plus Engineering in Portland, Oregon. He is the author of *ISO 9000*, *The ISO 9000 Implementation Manual*, *Quality Auditing*, and *Purchasing Strategies for Total Quality*.

# PART V
# INFRASTRUCTURE AND TECHNOLOGY

**1. Automation**
*Wayne Ralph*

**2. Information Technology in Manufacturing**
*Gyanendra (Jerry) Singh*

**3. The Focused Factory**
*Thomas L. Niehaus*

**4. Manufacturing Process Choice**
*Peter T. Ward*

**5. Converting to Just-in-Time Production Flow**
*Alfred W. Webber*

**6. Plant Scheduling for High Customer Service**
*Ray Reed*

**P**HYSICAL THINGS ARE important also. Plants and distribution centers, equipment, tooling, computers, robots—all of these make up the "brick and mortar" portion of manufacturing excellence; they're the muscle and the bone. Neglect them at your peril, for they play an important role in the world class manufacturing enterprise.

Part V begins with an examination by Wayne Ralph of the Delta group, of how **Automation** fits into the overall excellence picture. Next, Jerry Singh, formerly chief information officer for Procter & Gamble Japan, discusses **Information Technology in Manufacturing**.

The next three chapters deal with how manufacturing facilities are organized. First we take a tour of **The Focused Factory**, courtesy of Tom Niehaus of OPW/Dover. Peter Ward from Ohio State discusses the broad range of plant layouts available in **Manufacturing Process Choice**, and Al Webber makes the case for flow manufacturing **in Converting to Just-in-Time Production Flow**. Part V closes with Ray Reed's article on **Plant Scheduling for High Customer Service**.

# Automation
## *Wayne Ralph, P.E.*

**IN A NUTSHELL**

Automation is the automatic operation of a system by mechanical or electronic devices that takes the place of human observation, decision making, and action.

Automation makes it possible to free people from tasks related to the production, testing, and handling of products, components, and raw materials—as well as data collection. People—being what they are—often introduce variability into routine, repetitive tasks and this can be a significant source of defects and error. For this reason, many consider automation to be a key component of an overall quality initiative within a manufacturing enterprise.

The effective use of automation has been shown to:

- Increase quality
- Reduce labor costs
- Decrease scrap and rework
- Improve testing of finished products
- Enhance manufacturing flexibility
- Feed data directly to the manufacturing information systems

Therefore it's often the case that automation is at the heart of major improvement initiatives, particularly in large-scale operations.

Automation has benefited dramatically from microelectronics technology over the last twenty years. While the overall costs of doing business have been steadily increasing, the cost of automation has actually decreased. In addition, major new capabilities have been developed. Robotics, expert systems, bar coding, systems to enhance vision, and smart transmitters are examples of this ongoing pattern of more automation performance for each dollar invested. Any manufacturing strategy that ignores these kinds of capabilities is almost certainly at risk.

## *Origins*

Automation developed from the need to relieve people of tedious tasks that required constant attention and quick response. Watt's application of the flyball governor to the steam engine in 1787 is the first well-defined application of a feedback control system. Early systems were self-contained mechanical systems that evolved into pneumatic systems. Pneumatic systems have since been largely replaced with electronic or microprocessor-based systems.

Today most new manufacturing facilities allocate about 20 percent of manufacturing capital expenditures to automation.

## *Benefits*

Direct benefits from automation include labor savings, improved yields or efficiency, consistent quality, higher and more stable production rates, and a single source of fundamental data for information systems.

Many automation projects provide significant benefits that were not anticipated. Common indirect benefits are:

- *Process Improvements.* While defining automation requirements, people often identify process problems and can develop solutions resulting in a more stable, controllable process. The data from the automated system also allows for continuous improvement, improved process models, and better process troubleshooting.
- *Improved Flexibility.* Automation systems are programmable

and can be readily modified to reformulate or implement process improvements. People-based systems normally require more training and consensus building for successful change. This can be the major benefit for businesses that require quick response for rolling out product innovations or reducing the time-to-market for new initiatives.

In addition to new facilities, existing manufacturing operations are also candidates for automation projects. With a proper strategic automation plan, the cost for a significant automation project can frequently be readily justified by projected savings from the project itself.

There are several different approaches to automation that can lead to highly competitive operations and larger bottom-line results, including:

1. Invest minimum capital and develop an organization that functions well with basic technology tools. A well-run, fundamentally sound organization can be very competitive without extensive amounts of automation.

2. Invest substantial capital to selectively take full advantage of available automation technology.

The latter approach, along with highly effective people development processes, can result in an organization where "the whole is greater than the sum of the parts"—world class people operating world class equipment.

## *Elements of Automation*

The different forms of automation systems include automated test equipment, robotics systems such as welders or painters, numerically controlled machine tools, automated materials handling equipment, and cell controllers for assembly. While these have very different characteristics, they are actually specialized applications of the basic automation concept. Automation requires three fundamental functions:

1. *Sensing.* The ability to sense or measure is critical. Transmitters analyzers, vision systems, and automated test equipment are typical devices used as inputs to automation systems replacing human observation.
2. *Decision Making.* Decision making has evolved from go/no-go and algorithmic decision making to fuzzy logic, and even "expert" systems for decision making. Most common are feedback control algorithms for the process industry and ladder logic or sequential function charts for the discrete manufacturing sector.
3. *Action.* The ability to reject a bad part, vary a flow rate, and start or stop a motor are typical automation actions.

The two basic automation system platforms are the distributed control system (DCS) used largely by the process industries and the programmable logic controller (PLC) used largely by the discrete manufacturing and packaging industry. The operator interface for DCSs have been custom-programmed, CRT-based workstations. PLC-based systems have used a wide range of operator interfaces, including dedicated field devices, local operator stations, central control panels, electronic displays, and CRT-based systems.

There is a tendency toward using personal computers with specialized software to replace DCSs, PLCs, and operator interfaces. Continued evolution is inevitable. Major technical improvements to automation system hardware at the sensor and actuator levels are anticipated from implementation of Fieldbus—a network linking field devices to the automation system. Major improvements for overall systems integration and data access will result from open systems and client/server technology standards.

## *Implementation Issues*

Clear, focused management direction on how these technologies will be utilized can avoid much waste and frustration, while speeding up the implementation process.

The most common barriers to the successful implementation of automation are lack of direction, lack of resources, and pursuing the wrong strategy. Lack of direction often results from Top Management—and the people advising them—not having a handle on how to assess potential benefits from automation and thus being unable to charter the development of an effective automation strategy. Lack of resources almost always results from lack of direction and support from the people at the top.

Pursuing the wrong strategy can result in massive expenditures of money for little, or no, or even negative results. A well-documented example is that of General Motors which, under the leadership of Roger B. Smith during the 1980s, pumped billions of dollars into factory automation. In so doing they did not lower their costs but rather *raised* them. An underlying implicit part of GM's strategy seemed to be that workers were detrimental to the production process, and that automation should be used to eliminate workers wherever possible. This is not the case; rather, workers are essential to the production process. Automation is a tool to enhance the abilities of workers, to make them more productive, and to make their jobs safer. Therefore GM's strategy, based on a faulty premise, was doomed to failure.

## KEY CONCEPTS

**Automated material handling**: These approaches are normally PLC- or computer-based. They can include the automated functions of delivering materials to the production process and—for finished products—palletizing, shrink wrapping, and moving to a warehousing or shipping operation.

**Automated Storage/Retrieval Systems (AS/RS)**: These systems grew out of the need to maintain, store, and retrieve material with high efficiency and accuracy. They use stacker cranes or indexing retrieval systems depending on the physical size and unit load size of the goods. By automating these processes, it's possible to maintain highly accurate inventory data, and to easily use a first-in, first-out distribution scheme.

Today's AS/RS tend to be computer-based with bar code scanner input from a hard-wired or radio-frequency link.

**Automated test equipment**: Applies the principles of automation to the testing of products and materials, including such diverse applications as electronics, pulp and paper, and the wet chemistry testing of fine chemicals.

**Automated warehousing**: *See* **Automated Storage/Retrieval systems.**

**Automation**: The automatic operation of a system by mechanical or electronic devices that take the place of human observation, decision making, and action.

**Distributed Control System (DCS)**: Developed out of the need of the process industries for a reliable, small, integrated, configurable replacement for loop controllers, recorders, and control panels. First introduced in 1975, the breakthrough was the integration of feedback control loops, with supervisory computers and CRT-based operator displays via a digital communications bus. Operators could monitor and change setpoints for a whole plant from one operating console.

Today's DCS often includes PLCs in the hardware configuration as well as smart transmitters that can be validated and recalibrated from the system console. These consoles have evolved to represent "multiple personalities" such as operator, engineer, and maintenance technician. *See* **Programmable Logic Controller (PLC).**

**Fieldbus**: A standard currently in development which will allow automation systems to cable directly to sensors, actuators, and other control devices from different manufacturers. The intent is to develop an open interconnect network for automation system field inputs and outputs.

**Microelectronics technology**: Integrated circuitry that has progressed to the large-scale integration present in today's industrial and consumer electronics. This term is often used to include the total microcomputer technology breakthrough, including software, networking, and communications.

**Numerical controls (NC/CNC)**: Developed out of the need of the metalworking industries to be able to program machines to perform machining/metalworking operations.

Numerical controls predate both DCSs and PLCs; they were applied to lathes and turret punches in the 1950s. Today's systems are computer-based (computer numerical-controlled CNCs) and are most common on machine tools and machining centers. *See* **Distributed Control System (DCS); Programmable Logic Controller (PLC).**

**Programmable Logic Controller (PLC)**: Introduced in 1969, PLCs developed out of the needs of the automotive industry for a reliable, inexpensive, small, and programmable replacement for relay cabinets and hard-wired panels.

Today they are computer-based tools designed to operate on the factory floor and to be programmed and maintained by plant electricians or technicians. PLC applications may vary in size from $100 units with less than a dozen inputs/outputs to million dollar networked PLC systems with thousands of inputs/outputs. *See* **Distributed Control System (DCS).**

**Robotics**: The application of artificial intelligence using intelligent, programmable, multi-purpose devices (robots) for assembly, welding, painting, and other manipulative operations. This technology is in its infancy.

## ACTION STEPS

The key action steps for automating a manufacturing operation include:

- Identify the expected business benefits from automation and estimate the savings that would result from successful automation. What are the implementation costs and what organizational barriers exist? Are the responsible key people committed to developing an automation strategy?
- Define the process that will be used to develop an automation strategy. Identify the management sponsor, the available technical resources, available consultant help, funding plan, timetable, who is responsible, and who participates in the development of the plan.

- Identify the best available technology and installations of world class technology. Using vendor and trade organization contacts, arrange visits to benchmark the technology and benefits.
- Develop the system architecture, implementation plan, justification, and funding plan.
- Implement the plan and begin to monitor the automation system performance. An ongoing program to increase business results from the automation system should be part of the program.

## *PROBLEM-SOLVING*

*"We have installed automation and control systems that don't work. We need to deal with these systems before we can make additional investments in automation."*

First recognize that these systems are just tools. Using a commonsense, hard-nosed approach, define the plan to make them work or tear them out. Ineffective systems give a clear message to the organization that it is okay to have things that don't work. Behavior really defines standards. It's important to define why a system does not work and what can be done to fix it, and make a sound business decision to allocate resources to fix it or to write it off. Learn from these systems and take measures to not repeat mistakes.

*"We want to implement a manufacturing information system but our processes are manually operated. Do we have to automate the operation? What about just a data acquisition system?"*

You need a plan that defines how to implement your system and the system benefits. Do not make any major commitment without this plan. The old phrase, "If you don't know where you're going, any road will take you there," does not go far enough. Indeed, if you don't define where you're going, it's likely that no road can lead to good results (even without time and budget constraints).

The most practical approach to implementing these systems is from the ground up, with the automation system as the foundation for the manufacturing information system. Beware of a plan that builds from the top down. It needs to be examined closely because it runs counter to common practice and common sense.

> "We want to implement integrated manufacturing automation/information systems projects, but we can't seem to agree on where to start."

If you have not yet developed a plan, start here. Develop one.

If you have developed a plan, it should have identified key quick-payback showcase projects to demonstrate the value of this program to the organization. If you are really committed, move ahead with the plan even if you start on a small scale. Success is empowering. These projects should have strong organizational support, strong resource support, and strong budgetary support. Don't start on a shoestring budget with little organizational support; instead, keep working to build support.

> "We have developed an automation plan and are ready to begin the first of our planned sequence of projects. The organization that runs the operation is reluctant and seems to be setting up roadblocks for the project. Should we push ahead or select a different project with another organization?"

Do not proceed with a reluctant manufacturing organization partner. An early failure is likely to kill the whole program. Consider asking a top manager to sponsor the first project and help emphasize the importance of the pilot project to the future of the overall organization.

From personal experience, I can testify to the importance of the commitment of the people operating the system: It's the single most important factor in the entire process. We had developed a plan to upgrade twelve plants by installing new automation equipment. The plan was to install the system in one plant, quickly verify the benefits, and roll the system out to the other eleven plants. The management team selected the plant to receive the first installation, but the plant response was not enthusiastic. Let's call it "Plant A." Another plant (Plant B) was very interested in this project, and actually lobbied management to let them get started.

The equipment was installed at both plants. It was installed more quickly and with less cost at Plant B, which was able to show a three-month payback for the new equipment. On that basis, the automation equipment was successfully installed in the other ten plants. Plant A struggled for three years, and finally admitted grudgingly that the equipment did work.

The message: Consider the people, the organization, and other intangible factors carefully when making decisions on early technology installations.

## SUMMARY

- Automation makes it possible to free people from boring, repetitive, physically difficult, and potentially hazardous tasks while improving quality, reducing scrap and rework, enhancing flexibility, and providing a direct data link to manufacturing information systems.
- Automation technology today delivers "more bang for the buck"—it provides greater results for fewer dollars than just a few years ago.
- Management should set the technology strategy for the organization with an automation plan and implementation program.
- Major implementation problems arise from having faulty or nonexistent strategies, and from a lack of a consistent approach over time.
- The success of automation projects is almost always determined by the commitment and support of the organization receiving the technology. An unused tool, however good, is of little value. The right tools, used by people who are dedicated and well trained in their use, makes for a winning combination.

## INFORMATION RESOURCES

*A Reference Model for Computer-Integrated Manufacturing*, T. J. Williams, Instrument Society of America, 1989.

*CIM in the Process Industries*, J. W. Bernard, Instrument Society of America, 1989.

*Industrial Robots: A Handbook of Automated Systems Design*, K. Stonecipher, Hayden Book Company, 1985.

*Real-Time Control Networks*, D. T. Miklovic, Instrument Society of America, 1993.

*Understanding Distributed Process Control—Revised*, S. M. Herb and J. A. Moore, Instrument Society of America, 1987.

## INTERNAL CROSS-REFERENCE

Your understanding of this topic may be enhanced by the following chapters:

- III–1. Building a Learning Organization
- III–3. Energizing Your Workforce With High Performance Teams
- IV–1. Total Quality Management (TQM)
- V–2. Information Technology
- V–3. The Focused Factory
- V–4. Manufacturing Process Choice
- V–5. Converting to Just-in-Time Production Flow

### About the Author

Wayne Ralph, P.E., is president of The Delta Group, an engineering company focused on manufacturing automation/systems integration. He has held his current position for nine years. Prior experience includes twenty years in charge of control systems engineering for Shell and Procter & Gamble. He holds B.S. and M.S. degrees in engineering from the University of South Florida, Tampa.

# V-2

# Information Technology in Manufacturing
*Gyanendra (Jerry) Singh*

**IN A NUTSHELL**

Adding value to raw materials to create a product requires people, equipment, and information. Thus, every product has an information content, and information processing today is as important a value-adding activity in manufacturing as the processing of materials.

The extent to which information processing adds value depends on the sophistication of the product and processes, ranging from the Jacquard loom of the nineteenth century, in which punched cards were used to produce different designs, to the computer-aided design (CAD) technology used to produce the Boeing 777.

Information technology enables business processes to add value. Integrated, enterprise-wide information systems deliver the right information to the right people at the right time, and in the right format. In manufacturing, the appropriate use of information can lead to improvements in customer service, quality, yield and efficiencies, cost, flexibility, and time-to-market. Exploiting the benefits of information technology requires the design and successful implementation of a manufacturing systems architecture that spans the entire product supply chain. This architecture consists of customer-oriented manufacturing systems, Manufacturing Execution Systems, and process control systems.

Impediments to successful implementation are often due to legacy systems implemented with different technologies that are difficult to integrate, lack of standardization, and organizational issues between management information systems (MIS) and factory automation resources.

## Benefits of Information Technology in Manufacturing

Investments in information technology must be related to the critical success factors or the business drivers. The business drivers in manufacturing are customer service, quality, yields, costs, flexibility, and time-to-market. Information technology can impact these business drivers in the following ways:

1. *Improved Customer Service.* Customer service is essential to differentiation between manufacturers, and competition is based on value-added services customized to individual customer needs. These may range from special packaging, labeling, and consolidated ordering and shipment of product to Electronic Data Interchange (EDI) transactions and Continuous Replenishment Planning (CRP). The information systems required to meet these demands require sophisticated order fulfillment systems, integrated logistics systems, and system integration across the organizational boundaries of manufacturers and distributors.

2. *Quality.* Information technology can facilitate a more rapid and objective analysis of production process problems, leading to improved product quality and reduced scrap. Other quality-related benefits include:

- Support for Continuous Improvement through better understanding and modeling of production processes.
- Support for quality assurance and regulatory compliance processes.

3. *Improved yields and efficiencies.* The key to improving product yields and process efficiencies is assessing what happens during the production process and determining the appropriate response. In many plants, process control equipment aids in collecting data and can provide quick analyses and responses to steps in the process. Plant measurements also report overall yields and efficiencies. Substantial cost savings are possible if cause-and-effect relationships between product quality and process variables are better understood. Understanding how the individual characteristics of a material or process affects product quality or production costs requires high volumes of data and appropriate information technology applications.

4. *Lower costs.* When applied to demand forecasting, warehouse management, Distribution Requirements Planning, Production Planning and Scheduling, and Material Requirements Planning, information systems can reduce product supply chain costs. Integrated logistics systems, along with Automated Storage and Retrieval Systems (ASRS) can significantly lower distribution costs.

5. *Flexibility.* Computer control/robotics applications have dramatically lowered the economies of scale for manufacturing. Information technology makes it possible to achieve the production flexibility that delivers mass production efficiencies in lots of one. Thus, companies can economically manufacture products that meet the unique requirements of customers.

6. *Time-to-market.* Information technology is making Concurrent Engineering possible by distributed multifunctional teams across computer networks. Product development design and manufacturing do not have to be done sequentially. They can be done in parallel, cutting product development cycles by a factor of three or more. Computer-aided design (CAD) applications are a key factor in reducing the time-to-market across a wide variety of industries.

## *Implementation Issues*

Managers and operators need easy, flexible, and timely access to data from each layer of the manufacturing systems. This can be accomplished only through the use of consistent data definitions and the development and use of a shared manufacturing data model.

The technology needed to support these requirements in a cost-effective manner includes a Wide Area Network (WAN), Value Added Network (VAN), Local Area Network (LAN), data-centered client-server architecture, distributed relational database management systems, user-friendly access tools, and graphical user interfaces.

It is possible to achieve integration of the control layer by linking control systems networks with the plant local area networks and using client/server, open systems, and shared data model standards. The integration of Manufacturing Execution Systems for multiplant organizations, and between manufacturing execution and customer oriented systems, can be accomplished using wide area networks or through value-added networks.

Data can be passed across layers in one of three ways:

1. Storing the data in a single common relational database residing on a generally accessible network
2. Obtaining standard packets (or transaction sets) from another application
3. Developing a system of distributed databases with controlled redundancy

Implementation challenges arise due to both technical and organizational factors. The technical factors are as follows:

- Typically, the Customer-Oriented Manufacturing Management Systems (COMMS) applications are mainframe based, whereas the Manufacturing Execution Systems (MES) applications reside on midrange computers. The software and data bases differ between these two computer platforms.
- The Process Control Systems (PCS) applications have real-time operating systems and require integration with process instrumentation and programmable controllers. The computing platforms are typically distributed control system vendors versus mainstream computer vendors.
- While open systems standards are evolving, today's reality is that of legacy systems; both within management information and

control systems. This makes it difficult to integrate across layers with easy exchange of information across levels.

The organizational challenges arise from the fact that each of these three layers has traditionally been the domain of different organizations. The COMMS layer has been managed by corporate MIS, the MES by plant MIS (sometimes managed by and/or controlled by corporate MIS), and the PCS layer by control engineers (generally part of the engineering function). This typically results in lack of focus, coordination, and speed in the deployment of manufacturing systems.

## KEY CONCEPTS

**Architecture of Manufacturing Systems**: An "architecture" is defined as a cohesive framework of highly configurable elements, interfaces, and services that allow the creation of highly customized and integrated systems.

Achieving the full potential of information technology in manufacturing requires a manufacturing systems architecture that integrates across business processes throughout the product supply chain: from order fulfillment to manufacturing execution and process control to procurement. Often the data required for analysis comes from a variety of sources. Unless the discipline of a data architecture is employed, with common and consistent data definitions, the data may not be suitable for analysis.

The current "best practice" manufacturing systems architecture is based on a model developed by Advanced Manufacturing Research (AMR) in consultation with several manufacturing companies. This model provides a conceptual framework for information systems and the manufacturing processes they support; and it has received wide acceptance in the industry. The manufacturing systems architecture based on the AMR model is shown in Figure 1.

The purpose of this architecture is to provide an integrating framework for manufacturing systems, tying together systems all the way down from plant floor computing and process control systems to plant planning, and all the way up to division/corporate systems.

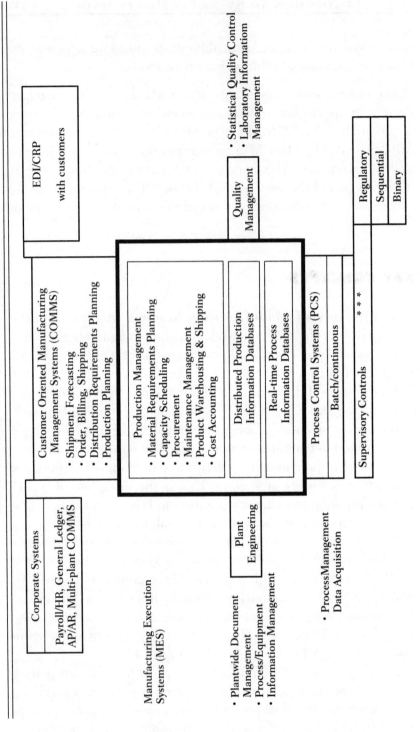

FIGURE 1. MANUFACTURING SYSTEMS ARCHITECTURE

The AMR model provides a coherent, cross-functional systems strategy with three levels. Each level has a different focus. Enterprise-wide Customer Oriented Manufacturing Management Systems (COMMS) focus on customer-related business processes and is planning oriented. It encompasses the entire supply chain, from raw material acquisition to delivery of product to customers. Plant-wide Manufacturing Execution Systems (MES) focus on the actual manufacture of the product. Process Control Systems (PCS) are centered on the manufacturing process, and require separate process-oriented real-time databases and networks.

All levels should support one another and need to be integrated for maximum effectiveness and efficiency. The model recognizes the importance of breaking through the functional silos that have traditionally dominated manufacturing enterprises, and the importance of a common database for multifunctional use.

**Customer-Oriented Manufacturing Management Systems (COMMS)**: The characteristics of these systems include:

- Multiplant capabilities
- Supply chain integration
- R&D/engineering integration
- Sales and Operations Planning integration

These applications include shipment forecasting; orders, billing and shipping; Distribution Requirements Planning (DRP); and Production Planning for both multiplant and single-plant manufacturing organizations. Effective deployment of these systems calls for an enterprise-wide planning and management system that unites a manufacturer's functions and suppliers around its customers. These systems also provide the basis for Continuous Improvement in cost, quality, responsiveness, regulatory compliance, and customer satisfaction.

**Manufacturing Execution Systems (MES)**: An integrated Manufacturing Execution System addresses the need for cross-functional integration within the plant. MES has been defined by Advanced Manufacturing Research as "plant management systems designed to provide operators and managers with current views of all manufacturing resources." The key MES applications are Material Requirements Planning, capacity scheduling, cost accounting, procurement, quality management, maintenance management, warehousing and shipping, and manufacturing/process engineering.

Historically the systems servicing different functions within a plant have addressed their particular department's needs, but have not been integrated with other applications. As a result, communication of information between functions has been limited by communications through the people networks within the organization.

As the demands and complexity of manufacturing operations have increased, and information technology costs have decreased, it is no longer cost effective to rely on the organization structure to support the need for cross-functional information. Therefore, integrated MES, within a single plant and common MES across all plants within a division or strategic business unit, are essential for effective and efficient manufacturing systems.

Plant-wide information systems unite the various factors of production around the product. In contrast to departmental or production cell solutions, they:

- Manage a plant's standard operating procedures
- Offer applications covering more than a single function's needs
- Integrate their own and partner applications via an industry-standard database management system

**Process Control Systems (PCS)**: The traditional controls focus has been on process/machine control of the process equipment or production/packaging lines. Instrumentation and data acquisition systems were seldom designed with the overall production control needs of the plant, let alone the information needs of the enterprise in mind. However, the process control systems level has a key role to play as a provider and user of manufacturing information.

Additionally, today's business requirements need controls systems designed to allow sharing of information between business functions. Therefore, the controls applications should be integrated with the Manufacturing Execution Systems. These applications consist of:

- Binary or on/off control of process equipment
- Regulating process variables to the desired set point
- Operating equipment in a predefined or calculated sequence
- Supervisory control or calculation of the set point targets for the process variables
- Real-time and historical databases for monitoring processes by events or for process analysis and simulation

## ACTION STEPS

The key action steps for creating an information infrastructure for manufacturing include:

- Identify critical success factors or key drivers for manufacturing, and estimate the business benefits of the appropriate use of information technology. As part of this exercise, it may be necessary to benchmark the critical success factors or the drivers versus world class performance.
- Develop a manufacturing systems architecture, as a blueprint for implementation. This should be done either jointly by MIS and Engineering or through an integrated manufacturing systems organization comprising all of the necessary resources.
- Implement the blueprint, using rapid application development methodologies now available. Execution accountability should reside within a single organization.
- Continuously monitor and improve the manufacturing systems to ensure their evolution with the changing needs and expectations of the business.

## PROBLEM-SOLVING

*"Our company wants to implement integrated manufacturing systems, but we're having a difficult time reaching agreement among our functional units on how to prioritize the projects."*

The product supply or operations function head and the MIS function head should be held accountable for giving you direction. They should commission a team to develop the architecture and implementation plan within a reasonable time. This activity should not take more than three to six months with a focused approach, provided all of the stakeholders are involved.

*"We have a blueprint for manufacturing systems, but implementation progress is extremely slow."*

You should first look for organizational barriers. If the projects are not being managed by an integrated organization, then putting a single organization in place should be first priority. Next, look for technical barriers. Are technical standards in place? Are they being followed? Does the organization have the necessary execution skills?

Today's technologies, application development methodologies, and training techniques make rapid application feasible. No information systems project should take more than nine to twelve months if things have been done right.

*"In spite of considerable investment in factory automation/ information systems, our business results are below expectations."*

The work system and business processes need to be reengineered to fit with new technology. Insist on every systems project being preceded by business process redesign. Doing this does not increase implementation time; on the contrary, it can shorten the implementation cycle by eliminating rework. It almost always increases the payout.

*"We would like to implement single-vendor solutions for enterprise-wide manufacturing systems; is this feasible?"*

No. Today it is not feasible to implement single-vendor-enterprise-wide solutions due to differences in technologies, business processes and production processes; across industries, within the same industry, or even within the same enterprise. Integrated software packages for each of the three layers in the manufacturing systems architecture are the current state of the art. For example, integrated logistics, manufacturing management and distributed plant-wide control systems applications software is available. However, even their successful implementation cannot be ensured unless the business/production process maps to the software package.

*"We are not sure if we should be implementing systems customized to our needs or software packages."*

It depends on whether the business/production processes offer proprietary advantages, and the extent of the standardization within the industry. There may be situations where proprietary considerations may require a custom solution, or where the business/production processes may not be sufficiently standardized. Examples of these are: a production process requiring a proprietary control systems application or order, billing and shipping software customized for a manufacturer's distribution system, product mix, pricing and promotion policies, etc.

In the absence of standard processes, enhancements and/or modifications can negate much of the benefits from the use of software packages.

## SUMMARY

- Information technology adds value to products and processes. Effective and efficient deployment of manufacturing systems is a key objective of companies with world class status.
- The business benefits from information technology on the critical success factors or the key drivers in manufacturing should be estimated and a manufacturing systems architecture developed.
- The manufacturing system architecture consists of customer-oriented, manufacturing-execution, and process-control systems.
- Implementation issues arise primarily due to dissimilar technologies implemented by different organizations.
- Successful execution is possible through an integrated organization held accountable for rapid implementation of the architecture.

## INFORMATION RESOURCES

*Corporate Information Systems Management: The Issues Facing Senior Executives*, F. Warren McFarlan and James McKinney, Richard D. Irwin, Inc., 1983.

*Enterprise Computing*, Alan R. Simon, Bantam Books, 1992.

*Client/Server Computing*, Dawna Travis Dewire, McGraw-Hill, 1993.

*Process Innovation: Reengineering Work Through Information Technology*, Thomas H. Davenport, Harvard Business School Press, 1993.

*The Corporation of the 1990s: Information Technology and Organizational Transformation*, Michael S. Scott Morton, Ed., Oxford University Press, 1991.

*Competing in World Class Manufacturing: America's Twenty-First Century Challenge*, National Center for Manufacturing Services, Richard D. Irwin, 1990.

*The AMR Source Book on COMMS*, Advanced Manufacturing Research, Inc., 1993.

## INTERNAL CROSS-REFERENCE

Your understanding of this topic may be enhanced by the following chapters:

I–6. Resource Planning: for Manufacturing, the Business, and the Enterprise

V–1. Automation

VI–1. Enterprise Logistics Management (ELM)

## About the Author

Jerry Singh is currently managing partner responsible for information technology with The Partnering Group, a consulting company focused on partnering between manufacturers and retailers in support of the Efficient Consumer Response (ECR) initiatives. Prior to this, Mr. Singh had twenty-three years of business experience with Procter & Gamble in a variety of product development, marketing, and management systems assignments in the United States and Japan. He holds M.S. and M.B.A. degrees from the University of Illinois, Urbana-Champaign.

# The Focused Factory
## *Thomas L. Niehaus*

### IN A NUTSHELL

Over twenty years ago, manufacturing expert Wickham Skinner complained in his seminal 1974 *Harvard Business Review* article that "the conventional factory attempts to do too many conflicting production tasks within an inconsistent set of manufacturing policies," whereas "a factory that focuses on a narrow product mix for a particular market niche will outperform the conventional plant."

Skinner's remarks, written long before our experience with flexible manufacturing, demand pull systems, and other manufacturing improvements, was farsighted. Indeed, anyone who has worked in both conventional and focused factories can appreciate how the latter creates a more competitive manufacturing operation.

### *The Unfocused Factory*

The unfocused factory typically results from the lack of effective strategic planning for manufacturing. As new products are developed, they are assigned to a given plant without regard for the plant's current mission and capabilities. Often, the decision criterion has been as simple as "Which plant has enough space to take the new product?" or "Which plant will give us the lowest freight costs?" The result is often a plant which manufactures many different products for a wide variety of customers and markets.

The problem is that most plants can't be all things to all people. They can't be good at everything. Often the things at which the plant originally excelled are not important to the customers for the new products, and, conversely, the plant can't do well the things that are important to them. To quote Wickham Skinner again: "The result more often than not is a hodge-podge of compromises, high overhead, and a manufacturing organization that is constantly in hot water with Top Management, marketing management, the controller, and customers."

## *The Focused Factory*

The focused factory is set up to deal with a specific range of products and customer markets. Machinery, assembly, and support functions are grouped in terms of the end products and the customers who buy them. Machinery is designed for rapid changeovers to accommodate variety within a product family. Machines are located to minimize materials handling, minimize work-in-process inventory, improve quality, and maximize customer service. The design of this factory begins with the needs of the customer and the manufacturing specifications of the product; it creates the physical layout and support services that will best satisfy those customer needs. It is focused specifically on those customers whom the plant is chartered to serve.

## *The Factory-Within-a-Factory*

The focused factory can be an entire facility dedicated to a single product family, or it can be what's called a "factory-within-a-factory." (These are actually more common in most industries.) Some companies have three or four discrete manufacturing operations under one roof, each dedicated to a single product family. Each may have its own inventory, receiving, and production control staff. Each tracks its own data. Many world class companies identify their focused operations through color-coded equipment and different personnel uniforms. In effect, each factory-within-a-factory is a stand-alone operation. Certain functions, such as computer services, finance, and plant administration are shared in common.

## *Beyond Manufacturing*

More and more we're seeing companies focusing not only within manufacturing. People from both manufacturing and nonmanufacturing areas are being integrated into operational units focused by customer group and/or product. In some companies, people from a variety of departments—order entry, customer service, design, shipping—have been co-located into the manufacturing areas along with the production people. This has resulted in dramatic reductions in cycle time and comparable increases in customer service.

The primary goal, of course, is to enable the people inside the company to get closer to the people outside the company who buy the product: to better serve them with faster deliveries and with products that meet and exceed their expectations.

## *Benefits*

The benefits of the focused factory are many, and vary from company to company. The author's plant is representative of what can be accomplished with focused people and equipment. It experienced the following benefits in its conversion from a conventional to a focused operation (which included many of the Just-in-Time and total quality processes referenced elsewhere in this book).

This plant now makes and ships every product every day, making customer service highly effective. Work-in-process inventories are minuscule when compared to previous levels, as are the numbers of personnel dedicated to controlling those inventories. The amount of time and effort devoted to moving materials from one work station to another—which adds nothing to customer value—has been slashed by some eighteen times.

Another benefit has to do with smallness. As plants focus, and

|  | Conventional | Focused |
|---|---|---|
| Units shipped/year | 150,000 | 180,000 |
| Inventory turns/year | 2 | 40+ |
| Lot sizes | 10,000 | 500 |
| Service level | poor | 100% |
| Throughput | 6 months+ | 2.3 days |
| Production/control specialists | 36 | 6 |
| WIP tracking system | complex | simple |
| Total distance traveled in plant | 3.9 miles | 300 feet |

factories-within-a-factory are created, the individual units become smaller. With fewer people in a given unit, it's easier to get teamwork, cooperation, and a shared set of objectives. As Tom Wallace has pointed out, "Small *is* beautiful when dealing with people, and that's what plants are mostly about—people."

## *Implementation*

Many companies experience an intermediate step in the evolution from conventional to focused factory: the use of manufacturing cells. Manufacturing cells are a rearrangement of machines to make certain types of components, but not the entire product. They may, for example, group all the equipment needed to cut, mill, and polish shafts. They arrange the equipment to make these shafts in a focused way, but stop short of doing the same for the entire product. The use of manufacturing cells represents the stage to which many companies have progressed—but most have stopped there. Fully focused companies integrate these cells into the complete production process.

Implementation of factory focus typically brings a company face-to-face with a number of managerial issues:

- Adopting demand pull. Conventional factories typically schedule work at workstations on the basis of machine capacity. Focused factories often use a demand pull, or kanban, scheduling system. As actual customer demand comes to the factory, materials are drawn through the production process. Rapid throughput, small lot sizes, and personnel trained in rapid changeovers make this possible.

- Personnel issues. People who have spent their lives trying to maximize machine utilization often experience a high degree of discomfort with the demand pull nature of the focused factory. Without mountains of work-in-process piled up at their workstations, some operators get nervous about having enough work to keep their jobs. Demand pull has almost no work-in-process. There is no obvious backlog of work, and short periods of slack are typical. Personnel need to be reassured that this is not job threatening, and that slack time is to be spent in light maintenance and in finding ways to improve processes. Job classifications usually need broadening.
- The conversion challenge. The multiproduct factory can rarely move to full implementation without causing tremendous disruption. Most authorities suggest moving just one product family at a time to the focused approach. Experience indicates that this first experiment with focus implementation may take three to six months, but that subsequent implementations will be much shorter. Thus, prudence suggests that the first product family converted to a focused approach not be the most critical product to the company.
- Some companies need to invest in added equipment as they make the conversion. This equipment need not be faster, but it should be capable of faster changeovers. In fact, rapid changeover is a critical implementation issue.

## KEY CONCEPTS

**Changeover**: The process of converting a piece of equipment or a manufacturing line to work on a different product. In the days of mass production of thousands of standard parts or products, a changeover could take days or weeks. In the modern environment of small lot sizes and high product variety, the ability to effect changeovers in minutes or hours is a critical capability.

**Conventional factory**: A manufacturing facility that organizes work by function in the making of many products for different customer markets.

**Demand pull**: A method for Just-in-Time operations in which demand—beginning with shipping orders—pulls materials through the production process. For example, demand to ship a product creates a demand for packaging a finished product, which in turn creates demand back through the operation to make a product. This is the essence of the Japanese kanban system, in which a visible signal (kanban) authorizes work at each lower level.

**Factory-within-a-factory**: A number of separate manufacturing units within the same four walls of the overall plant.

**Focused factory**: A manufacturing facility that organizes work by product and customer requirements. This factory is set up to deal with a range of products and customer markets.

**Kanban**: *See* **Demand pull**.

**Throughput**: The start-to-finish time to manufacture a product.

## ACTION STEPS

- Begin by securing the support and commitment of senior management. They must see the focused factory as an extension of their larger strategy for creating and serving customers.
- Give the job of converting from a conventional to a focused factory to a champion—a person who is totally committed to the conversion, and who has the authority and resources to act. Normally, this person comes out of operations, and has experience with the equipment and the people who run them.
- Train personnel in the principles of demand pull. A demand pull operation represents a culture change for workers who have traditionally had very narrowly defined jobs, and whose performance has been measured in terms of machine utilization. The focused factory tends to broaden job responsibilities and downplay machine utilization.
- Make a passion out of Continuous Improvements in changeover time. Rapid changeovers are essential to the ongoing success of the focused factory.

## PROBLEM-SOLVING

*"Our conventional factory is doing fine. In fact, we are working overtime. Why should be change to a focused factory format?"*

One reason might be the elimination of overtime. Overtime is as much a symptom of inefficiency as a mark of a company that has as much demand as it can handle. Secondly, your business might be doing well now, but if your competitors focus their operation, and if they achieve the performance benefits noted earlier, you will be the high-cost producer, the company that requires long lead times, and inferior on most dimensions of customer service. Make the change *before* your competitors force it upon you.

*"We already operate with manufacturing cells. What are the issues in moving from cells to the focused factory?"*

Very few. Cells normally operate from demand pull. To make the full transition, think beyond the component level served by your cells to the whole product served by the focused factory.

## SUMMARY

- Unfocused factories are tasked with trying to be all things to all people. Very few plants can excel at everything.
- The concept of focused factories deals with a limited range of products and customers. Thus it's able to concentrate on doing best what's important to those specific customers.
- Moving to focused factories does not normally require building new plants. Rather, the factory-within-a-factory approach can be taken, where distinct units can be formed within the larger plant.
- Manufacturing cells are an intermediate step between conventional and focused factory.
- Focused operations depend upon demand pull and the ability to make rapid equipment changeovers.

## INFORMATION RESOURCES

*Customer-Driven Strategy: Winning Through Excellence,* Thomas F. Wallace, Oliver Wight Publications, 1992.

*Japanese Manufacturing Techniques,* Richard J. Schonberger, The Free Press, 1982.

*Operations Management,* 5th edition, Richard J. Schonberger and Edward M. Knod, Irwin, 1993.

"The Focused Factory," Wickham Skinner, *Harvard Business Review,* January–February 1971.

*World Class Manufacturing Casebook,* Richard J. Schonberger, The Free Press, 1987.

## INTERNAL CROSS-REFERENCE

Your understanding of this topic may be enhanced by the following chapters:

III–3. Energizing Your Workforce with High Performance Teams

IV–4. Just-in-Time: Driver for Continuous Improvement

V–4. Manufacturing Process Choice

V–5. Converting to Just-in-Time Production Flow

### About the Author

Thomas L. Niehaus is president of OPW Engineered Systems, a division of Dover Resources, located in Cincinnati, Ohio. Mr. Niehaus holds a degree in industrial management from the University of Cincinnati and was selected to participate in the Japan Study Program for International Executives. He is a frequent speaker at national and regional manufacturing conferences.

# Manufacturing Process Choice

*Peter T. Ward*

---

## IN A NUTSHELL

The most fundamental decision in manufacturing strategy is the choice of process. Choice of process is important because it influences and constrains other strategic choices available to a manufacturer. In essence, process choice involves an implicit tradeoff between producing one-of-a-kind products in small quantities at relatively high cost or producing standardized products in high volume at relatively low cost. The tradeoff exists because of difficulty in producing both customized and standardized products in the same plant while satisfying customer expectations with respect to price, quality, and delivery performance. Also, process choice implicitly constrains other important decisions, such as whether to use special or general purpose equipment, the relative level of investment in production processes, capacity level, and key technical and managerial roles.

## Types of Production Processes

Process choice is played out on a continuum of production technologies ranging from job shop to line-flow processes. This chapter also discusses a midrange process choice, batch or decoupled line flow, which represents the most common process choice made by manufacturers. One way to visualize the differences along the continuum is to consider the equipment layout in the factory that each choice suggests. Figure 1 contrasts the facility layout implied by the three types of processes, using equipment found in a machine shop for illustration.

*Job shop (jumbled flow)* Job shops are used by firms that produce single units or small batches of a large number of different products, most of which require a different set or sequence of processing steps. Process equipment is organized by function rather than dedicated to a particular product type. This process type provides maximum flexibility with respect to product changes.

The functional layout of the job shop is illustrated in Figure 1a, in which similar equipment is grouped together without regard to product flow. Functional layout makes sense when the types and quantities of products ordered are so variable that a predominant flow through the factory cannot be identified. In this situation, some semblance of order is achieved by placing equipment near other equipment of the same type, thus allowing managers to shift workers and orders around the plant to break bottlenecks and achieve priorities. Note that orders move from machine to machine through the factory in what appears to be random fashion. Customers of job shops require nonstandard products and expect to pay a premium.

*Batch (decoupled line flow)* Batch processes are used by producers with a relatively stable line of products, each of which is manufactured periodically in "batches." In a batch process, which is a hybrid between a job shop and a line process, products typically follow the same predominant flow pattern within the factory, although there are often exceptions. Batch processes seek to achieve some of the flexibility of the job shop at a somewhat lower average cost. Small

**FIGURE 1. ILLUSTRATION OF LAYOUTS SUGGESTED BY PROCESS CHOICE**

(a) Job shop (Jumbled flow)

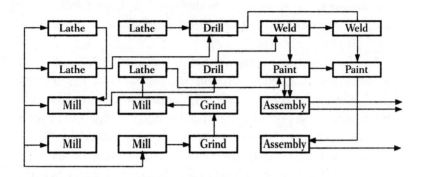

(b) Batch (Decoupled line flow)

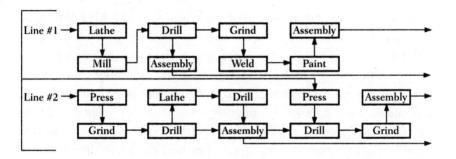

(c) Line (Connected line flow)

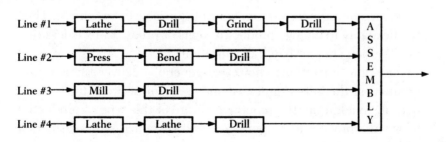

SOURCE: Drawings are taken from J. A. Tompkins, and J. A. White, *Facilities Planning*, John Wiley & Sons, Inc., 1984, p. 228.

batch operations (few units produced per run and many different production runs) resemble job shops, while large batch operations (long production runs of a limited number of product lines) are similar to line processes.

As illustrated in Figure 1b, batch factories may be divided into cells or lines designed to manufacture similar products in sequence. The batch layout is inherently simpler than job shop and results in a smoother flow, less confusion, and less need to expedite to get orders out of the factory. Note that the products depicted in each of the cells of the batch process in Figure 1 follow more or less the same sequence. The factory illustrated contains two cells because the products manufactured in that factory can be categorized into two separate groups, each having its own predominant flow through the factory.

*Line (connected line flow and continuous flow)* Line-flow processes (Figure 1c) are used by firms to produce a small group of highly similar products. Workstations are laid out in sequence and the product passes through a series of steps at a predetermined and controlled rate. Line processes usually involve large capital investments and are generally economic only when few changeovers or setups for different products are required. Thus, line production yields low unit manufacturing costs as long as the volume for each product is high and changes are minimal.

Standardized products and commodities are generally made in sufficiently high volumes to warrant dedicated manufacturing lines. Changing products in such an environment requires expensive and time-consuming setups or retooling of specialized equipment. Thus, the flexibility to change product designs or product mix is less than in either job shop or batch organizations.

Line-flow operations, however, generally deliver standardized products at the lowest unit cost and at the most predictable rate of output. In addition, the repetitive nature of this type of production allows the process to be perfected and sustained more easily than with batch processes.

Process choice has clear implications for both flexibility and unit cost: Job shops permit maximum flexibility at relatively high product costs while line processes are relatively inflexible but with lower unit costs. In addition to flexibility and cost, a factory's position on the continuum from job shop to line suggests numerous other characteristics. For example, we expect capital intensity to be low in job shops relative to line factories, which are typically highly mechanized and specialized. We also expect that batch operations, with their typically moderate unit volumes, will fall somewhere in between the two extremes. Figure 2 characterizes a number of key attributes along the process choice continuum. As Figure 2 illustrates, process choice reveals a good deal about what is important to a manufacturer.

## *Products, Customers, and Processes*

Top managers often delegate process choice decisions along with decisions about other, more technical factory specifications to the company's manufacturing experts. This is a mistake because process

**FIGURE 2. CHARACTERISTICS THAT VARY WITH PROCESS CHOICE**

| Characteristic | Job Shop | Line |
| --- | --- | --- |
| Order size | Small | Large |
| Cost per unit | High | Low |
| Volume | Low | High |
| Plant size | Small | Large |
| Scale economics | Unimportant | Important |
| Capital intensity | Low | High |
| Output per hour | Low | High |
| Bottlenecks | Many | Few |
| Number of setups | Many | Few |
| Labor: skill, training, wage | High | Low |
| Compensation scheme | Incentive-based | Hourly |
| Material requirements | Unpredictable | Predictable |
| Frequency of schedule changes | High | Low |
| Number of different products | High | Low |
| Inventory, raw material | Low | High |
| Inventory, work-in-process | High | Low |
| Inventory, finished goods | Low | High |

choice is intimately connected with strategic decisions about the kinds of products the company offers and the kinds of customers it can best serve.

The product-process matrix introduced by Robert Hayes and Steven Wheelwright is one way to illustrate the nature of correspondence between manufacturing process type and various product/market attributes. Figure 3 shows an adaptation of the product-process matrix. The product characteristics captured by this matrix are (unit) volume and degree of standardization, and the range of process types is as we discussed earlier (from job shop to line).

The diagonal in Figure 3 illustrates the inherent correspondence

**FIGURE 3. PRODUCT-PROCESS MATRIX**

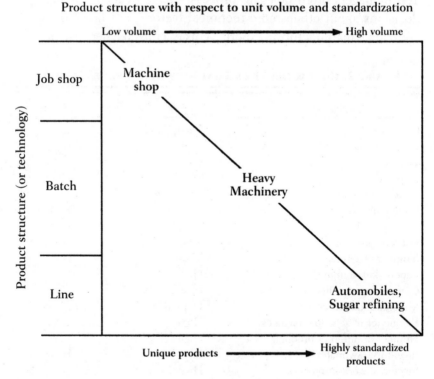

SOURCE: Adapted from Robert H. Hayes and Steven C. Wheelwright, *Restoring Our Competitive Edge*, John Wiley & Sons, Inc., 1984, p. 209.

between product and process characteristics. Consider, for example, the typical machine shop that produces many different machined products requiring a range of production processes. In order to accommodate the necessary product and process variety, the typical machine shop chooses to organize its production facility by function and is thus classified as a job shop. Since the typical machine shop manufactures a great variety of product, the particular processes required to fill any order are relatively unpredictable. The job shop's functional layout has generally afforded machine shops the flexibility needed to deal with the variability inherent in their business.

Similarly, heavy equipment manufacturers typically choose to adopt decoupled line-flow (or batch) technologies to produce multiple product lines with relatively low unit volumes. Producers of products with higher unit volumes (e.g., auto assembly and sugar refining) typically exploit the lack of product and process variety by adopting less flexible but more efficient connected line flow (or assembly line) or continuous flow process technologies.

The diagonal of the product-process matrix describes the range of positions occupied by typical firms in their industries. Not all firms in an industry choose a position on the diagonal. Some firms, either by accident or design, operate above or below the diagonal occupied by their typical competitors. For example, a machine shop could make the strategic choice to specialize and configure its process equipment to produce a particular type of order economically, say titanium brackets for aerospace customers. The machine shop choosing this strategy would be able to provide good service at a relatively low price to aerospace bracket buyers but would be at a disadvantage for other kinds of machined metal orders. This machine shop's position on the product-process matrix would be below and to the right of the typical machine shop's location on the diagonal.

## *Advanced Manufacturing Technologies*

Advanced manufacturing technologies and concepts challenge traditional wisdom about what is possible in various production environments. It is therefore important to explore how technologies such as Flexible Manufacturing Systems, Computer-Aided Design and

Manufacturing, MRP II, and others might change the interpretation of the product-process matrix and strategic configurations.

In general, advanced manufacturing technologies are an exception to the process life-cycle progression (from job shop to line manufacturing—see chapter V–5) suggested by the product-process matrix. Specifically, these technologies allow line producers to be more flexible than previously possible, thus allowing more product diversity with little sacrifice on other dimensions. Similarly, the new manufacturing technologies enable batch producers to become more efficient at setups, thus freeing them to pursue line economies.

The best manufacturing companies have, generally, become adept at maintaining the required flexibility and finding ways to organize their factories so that product flows smoothly. This usually results in better performance across the dimensions of cost, quality, delivery, and inventory. Such achievements are made possible by judicious and appropriate applications of advanced manufacturing technologies and concepts such as Group Technology, lean production, and facilities focus along with investments in people.

## *KEY CONCEPTS*

**Batch (decoupled line flow)**: Used by firms with a relatively stable line of products, each of which is produced in periodic batches. In a batch process, products typically follow the same basic flow pattern within the factory, although there are often exceptions. Batch processes are the most common industrial arrangement and seek to achieve some of the flexibility of the job shop at a somewhat lower average cost.

Batch processes are hybrids between job shop and line processes. Small batch operations (few units produced per run and many different production runs) resemble job shops and large batch operations (long production runs of a limited number of product lines) and are similar to line processes.

**Bottleneck**: A resource (machine, workstation, etc.) that limits flow through the factory. This occurs when the resource has less capacity than the demand placed on it requires.

**Computer-Aided Design/Computer-Aided Manufacturing (CAD/CAM)**: Interactive computer graphics systems used for product design and documentation and to create a manufacturing database.

**Connected line flow**: Also referred to as an assembly line, connected line flow is used to produce a group of highly similar products. Workstations are laid out in sequence and the product passes through a series of steps at a prespecified and controlled rate.

**Continuous-flow processes**: Used for manufacturing products in very high volumes with very few changeovers and fixed, predetermined process flow. Continuous processes are highly capital intensive. Products made in continuous-flow processes are often commodities and are frequently dimensional products, i.e., sold by weight or volume rather than by unit. Paper mills and sugar refineries are examples of continuous processes.

**Facilities focus**: Concept that when a relatively narrow range of demands is placed on a facility, the resulting concentration of effort will lead to superior results.

**Flexible Manufacturing Systems (FMS)**: A configuration of computer-controlled machines, interconnected by an automated material handling system, and controlled by an integrated computer system.

**Group Technology (GT)**: An approach that identifies and catalogues families of parts based on physical attributes. Applications of GT concepts can result in great economies in design and in manufacturing.

**Job shop (jumbled flow)**: Used by firms that produce single units or small batches of a large number of different products, most of which require a different set or sequence of processing steps. Process equipment is organized by function rather than dedicated to a particular product type. This process type provides maximum flexibility to accommodate product changes.

**Lean production**: The "Toyota style of manufacturing" in which all assets are used frugally, thus allowing little slack in the system and resulting in opportunities to improve the system continuously. Just-in-Time inventory concepts are an integral part of lean production.

**Line flow (connected line flow and continuous flow)**: Used by firms to produce a group of highly similar products. Workstations are laid out in sequence and the product passes through a series of steps at a prespecified and controlled rate. Line processes involve large capital investments and are generally economic only when few new product setups are required. Thus, line production yields low unit manufacturing costs as long as volume is high and changes are minimal.

**MRP II (Manufacturing Resources Planning)**: A fully integrated system in which material requirements in materials, manufacturing, and engineering elements are linked with the company financial system.

## ACTION STEPS

Process choice requires that the Top Management team weigh product technology, market, and manufacturing choices simultaneously:

- Determine the plant charter. For what specifically is the plant responsible? Which products will be made in the plant? Which components will be purchased or produced in other facilities? Which markets will be served by the plant? What order sizes are typical for each product/market?
- Consider your customers and what you must do to attract and keep them. For example, long production runs tend to keep production costs down but often require customers to tolerate long production lead times.
- Consider the current and projected volumes of each product to be produced in the plant. What capacity is needed? How many setups are implied? Low unit volumes and numerous setups suggest a position toward the upper left of the product-process matrix.
- Consider the life cycle of the product. How likely are major

changes in product design? Volatility in product design suggests a position toward the upper left of the product-process matrix.
- Consider the product mix and the volatility and seasonality of the mix. Do changes in mix imply radically different levels of equipment utilization and routings in the factory? Positive answers also suggest an upper left position on the product-process matrix.

## *PROBLEM-SOLVING*

> "We've seen reasonable profits but limited growth opportunities in our major business, custom built equipment. For this reason, and because we have some excess capacity, we have been trying to market some lower priced, standard products. There appears to be plenty of this business available, but we just can't seem to make money on our new line."

Although there are many possible reasons why the new line is not profitable, one likely suspect is process choice. Utilizing the custom product plant to manufacture standard products suggests that the same job shop process is being used to make both types of products. It is difficult to capture scale economies in a job shop. The company should consider separating the new line into its own section of the factory and organizing the required people and equipment to form a line-flow process. In so doing, both margins and quality should increase, while inventory is reduced.

> "Customer surveys tell us that our reputation for quality is the best in our industry. High quality has helped us to enjoy steady growth and a dominant share of the market. In recent years, however, more and more of our customers have asked for special formulations or packaging, and we are losing a disturbing percentage of this business to smaller competitors."

The high-volume line process implied in this situation was the right choice when it was made and is still the right choice for most customers. The growing business in special orders, however, suggests that the company should consider adding a more flexible batch operation to its current capacity to enable it to better accommodate those customers or risk losing the growth part of its business.

## SUMMARY

- Process choice needs to be a key element of a company's manufacturing strategy.
- Process choice takes place along a continuum of production technologies ranging from the job shop on one extreme to line-flow processes on the other extreme.
- Job shops are suited to firms that produce single units or small batches of many different products.
- Line-flow or continuous-flow processes support high-volume production of standardized products.
- Batch production is a hybrid of job and batch production.
- Choice of production process is the responsibility of Top Management.

## INFORMATION RESOURCES

"Plan for Economies of Scope," Joel D. Goldhar and M. Jelinek, *Harvard Business Review*, 61, 1983, pp. 141–148.

*Restoring Our Competitive Edge*, Robert H. Hayes and Steven C. Wheelright, John Wiley & Sons, Inc., 1984.

*Manufacturing Strategy: Text and Cases*, Terry J. Hill, Irwin, 1994.

*Managing the Dynamics of New Technology: Issues in Manufacturing Management*, H. Noori, Prentice-Hall, 1989.

*Production/Operations Management*, 3rd ed., Roger Schmenner, SRA, Inc., 1987.

## INTERNAL CROSS-REFERENCE

Your understanding of this topic may be enhanced by the following chapters:

V–3. The Focused Factory

V–5. Converting to Just-in-Time Production Flow

---

### *About the Author*

Peter T. Ward joined the faculty at Ohio State University upon completing his doctorate at Boston University in 1988. Prior to his academic career, he was a manufacturing engineering manager in the computer industry and, prior to that, an economist specializing in manufacturing industries. Dr. Ward's teaching and research interests are focused on operations strategy, specifically on how companies can gain a competitive advantage through manufacturing.

# Converting to Just-in-Time Production Flow
## *Alfred W. Webber*

### IN A NUTSHELL

Production flow is a simple form of Just-in-Time (JIT) manufacturing in which the resources required for making a product are grouped into a separate manufacturing cell by their sequence in the manufacturing process. Products or components can then move through the manufacturing cell in a continuous manner. Companies that have converted from job shops to manufacturing cells achieve a number of important results, including improved product quality, shorter lead times, less work-in-process, and greater employee involvement.

### *Manufacturing Layouts*

Broadly speaking, there are two basic approaches to arranging manufacturing facilities: job shop and flow shop. In a job shop, like machines are grouped together (see Figure 1). Materials to make a product are generally brought to the machine groups in large lots.

## FIGURE 1. JOB SHOP

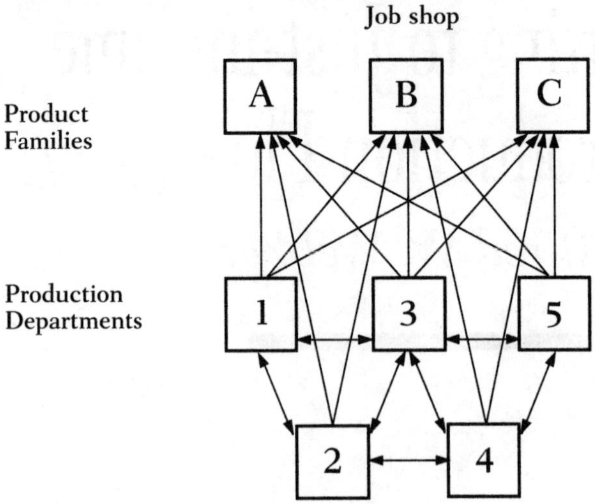

Job shop

Product Families: A, B, C

Production Departments: 1, 2, 3, 4, 5

SOURCE: Thomas F. Wallace, *Customer-Driven Strategy: Winning Through Operational Excellence*, Oliver Wight Publications, 1992.

Many times, these materials are moved into and out of an inventory stockroom between manufacturing operations, or are stored in queues in front of the next manufacturing operation. Control of these materials, while in manufacturing, is usually accomplished through the use of a shop packet containing information about routing, materials, processing, and any other special instructions needed to make the product.

In a flow shop, only the machines necessary to make a product or product family are grouped together (see Figure 2), and kanbans are usually used to control the movement of materials.

## Job Shop to JIT Conversion

The key to converting from a job shop to a JIT flow shop is the creation of manufacturing cells (also known as flow lines, demand pull lines, U-lines, and kanban lines). These manufacturing cells must be designed to contain one of each machine type required to

## Figure 2. Flow Shop

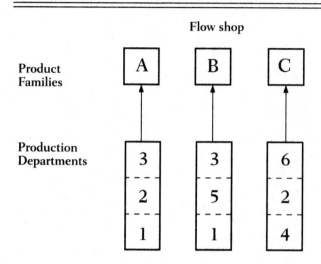

SOURCE: Thomas F. Wallace, *Customer-Driven Strategy: Winning Through Operational Excellence*, Oliver Wight Publications, 1992.

completely process an item. The machines must also be sequenced in the order that the process operations are performed.

To establish manufacturing cells, the following steps are required:

1. Industrial engineers first conduct a Pareto analysis on the most common routes of manufacture through the factory.
2. A given routing is then selected that may cover only 1 to 2 percent of the products made, but account for 5 to 10 percent of the factory throughput.
3. The various pieces of equipment needed from the job shop to make the products identified are placed in the sequence defined in the product routing.

The top of Figure 3 is a simplified schematic of a job shop with all similar machines grouped together. The bottom part of the figure shows what a manufacturing cell would look like after its creation. Note how very different pieces of equipment are now located side by side.

**FIGURE 3. CONVERSION FROM JOB SHOP TO CELL**

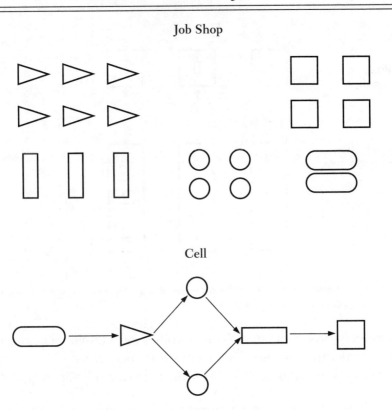

SOURCE: Thomas F. Wallace, *Customer-Driven Strategy: Winning Through Operational Excellence*, Oliver Wight Publications, 1992.

Materials enter the front end of a manufacturing cell and come out the back end as finished items. Items produced in a manufacturing cell flow continuously from one operation to the next, either one at a time or several at a time. The kanban technique is usually used to control the movement of material between operations as well as between different manufacturing cells and from the stockroom or suppliers.

Manufacturing cells allow us to minimize the levels of both safety stocks of completed items and of inbound queues of waiting materials. As a result, the inbound/outbound storage areas of the cell are also minimized.

A manufacturing cell often has fewer operators than machines because the machines are located close enough to each other that one operator can attend several machines at one time. This configuration eliminates wasted operator time and motion.

Frequently, manufacturing cells are U-shaped. The purpose of the arrangement is to further reduce the travel distance of operators and to minimize space requirements (see Figure 4).

Because they cluster workers in close proximity to each other, U-shaped cells improve communication among machine operators. Greater communication leads to improved teamwork and lays the foundation for the empowerment programs that allow operator teams to successfully manage their own manufacturing cells.

## *Implementation*

Control of machine setup and downtimes is a prerequisite for successful JIT manufacturing cells. This control is necessary because materials must move through flow lines in quantities of one or a few,

**FIGURE 4. U-LINE LAYOUT**

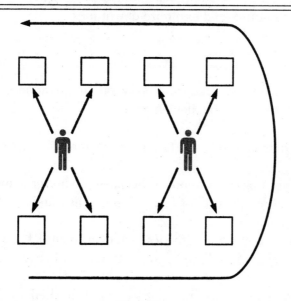

Work Flow

and in a continuous manner. Long setup times, which require large lot sizes, and machine downtime, which stops the flow, must both be brought under control before attempting to start up manufacturing cells.

Production flow using JIT manufacturing cells can be successfully implemented in almost every type of manufacturing operation. Large and complex operations, as well as small operations, should use a pilot line approach to implementation in which only a small but significant part of the operation is converted from job shop to a JIT flow manufacturing cell. Once this has been successfully implemented, successive JIT manufacturing cells can be started up until the entire operation has been changed over.

Companies that have control over their setup times and machine downtimes need two to four months to start up their first manufacturing cell. Subsequent cells usually take less time to implement, because the methodology required to identify and setup cells was learned during the first cell startup, and the creation of most cells only involves the movement and realignment of existing equipment. Those companies that have long setup times or excessive machine downtime will need additional time to put programs in place to reduce setup times and minimize downtimes.

## *Benefits*

Dramatic savings can be achieved when an operation is converted from a job shop to a JIT flow operation:

- Products can be made faster for greater customer responsiveness.
- All inventories are reduced because of shorter manufacturing lead times, improved performance to schedules, and the elimination of queues.
- Non-value-adding activities, such as material handling, are greatly reduced overall and nearly eliminated between processing steps.
- Reductions in stockroom, queue, and finished-goods inventories free up floor space for other activities.

- Manufacturing costs decrease and product quality increases because of reduced scrap and rework, elimination of nonvalue-adding activities, and increased operator efficiencies.

The costs of converting from a job shop to a JIT flow operation are rarely significant. Most costs are associated with moving utilities, minor facility modifications, workstation and/or equipment modification and relocation, and outside education. In instances when JIT cells are being created throughout the entire operation, additional equipment may be required to fill in all of the cells needed. This new equipment, however, is often lower-cost, single-purpose machinery.

## KEY CONCEPTS

**Flow shop**: A form of manufacturing organization in which machines and operators handle a standard, usually uninterrupted material flow. Operators generally perform the same operations for each production run. Each product, though variable in material specification, uses the same flow pattern through the shop. Production is usually set at a given rate.

**Job shop**: A form of manufacturing organization in which the productive resources are organized according to function. The jobs pass through the functional departments in lots and each lot may have a different routing.

**Just-in-Time (JIT)**: In the narrow sense, a method of execution designed to result in minimum inventory by having material arrive at each operation just as it is needed. In the broad sense, JIT refers to all of the activities of manufacturing and purchasing that make the JIT movement of material possible, with the ultimate goal being elimination of waste.

**Kanban**: A method for Just-in-Time production in which consuming (downstream) operations pull from feeding (upstream) operations. Feeding operations are authorized to produce only after receiving a kanban card (or other signal) from the consuming operation.

**Manufacturing cell**: A manufacturing process that produces families of parts within a single line or U-shaped cell of machines run by operators who work only within the line or cell.

**Pilot line**: A manufacturing cell setup with the necessary resources to test the effectiveness of a production flow line in the manufacture of a product or product family.

**Production flow**: A form of Just-in-Time manufacturing organization in which the people and equipment required for making the product are aligned by their sequence in the manufacturing process. Material flows from one operation to another in a continuous manner.

**Queue**: In manufacturing, the jobs at a given work center waiting to be processed. As queues increase, so do average queue time and work-in-process inventory.

**Total Quality Management (TQM)**: The group of techniques that companies use to improve the quality of their products to their customers and to involve employees in manufacturing issues.

**U-shaped cell**: Production flow lines shaped like the letter *U*; they allow workers to easily perform several different tasks with greatly reduced walk time. U-shaped cells promote better communication among operators in the cell.

## ACTION STEPS

- Learn about production flow, manufacturing cells, kanban, and other Just-in-Time manufacturing techniques and how they lead to better manufacturing performance.
- Evaluate your company with respect to its readiness for the transition to production flow, manufacturing cells, and kanbans.
- Develop detailed plans for implementing manufacturing cells, to include the establishment of task forces, training and the scheduling of the implementation process.

- Select a product line to start in a pilot manufacturing cell.
- Train the implementation team members and start up the pilot manufacturing cell.
- Fine-tune your manufacturing cell implementation process.
- Train new implementation team members and start up more manufacturing cells.

## PROBLEM-SOLVING

*"We want to start manufacturing cells but don't know where to begin. We're thinking of setting up a cell for our highest-volume product first, then duplicating it in other product lines."*

Before attempting any new improvement program, learn about the concepts first from someone with experience. Someone well versed in JIT manufacturing can guide you in the application of those concepts to your operations. Once you've learned about JIT and manufacturing cells, you will have the knowledge and skills to identify the product, or product families, that would be a good choice for your first manufacturing cell. Using lessons learned from that first cell, you'll be ready to identify and initiate your next cell.

*"We have a very large and complex job shop with machines and people all over the place. Manufacturing cells just won't work for us."*

JIT and manufacturing cells are applicable to almost every manufacturing operation. Larger operations offer two challenges. The first is the identification and configuration of the individual cells to support the operation. The skills to accomplish this are learned during your workshops on JIT and manufacturing cells. The second, and more difficult, is the layout of all of the individual cells in your operation; it must allow for the smooth and efficient flow of materials between cells as well as the flow to and from raw material and finished-goods inventories. This is best accomplished with the help of a person experienced in creating manufacturing cells.

*"We tried to implement manufacturing cells in the past but they failed. We wound up with large lot sizes, excessive inventories, and long lead times."*

There are two main reasons why manufacturing cells fail, and neither has anything to do with the configuration or operation of the cells themselves. The first reason is long setup times. When setup times are long, the first reaction is to go to larger lots of material to spread the cost of the setup over more materials. Of course, this returns you to the job shop approach, only now all your machinery is arranged in a straight line or U-shaped configuration. The second reason for unsuccessful manufacturing cells is excessive machine downtime. In a manufacturing cell, when one machine is down, the whole cell is down. You could add backup machines, but before you know it, your factory will once again resemble a job shop. As you can see, the source of your manufacturing cell failure was not the cell itself, but an inability to control setup times and machine downtime. Programs to reduce excessive setup times and machine downtimes must either precede or, at worst, be implemented in conjunction with your manufacturing cells.

## SUMMARY

- Many companies are converting from job shops to Just-in-Time flow shops to achieve total quality results.
- The key to converting from job shop to flow shop is the creation of manufacturing cells.
- Creation of a manufacturing cell often requires only the movement of the equipment, utilities, and personnel needed to run the new cell.
- Manufacturing cells complement a Total Quality Management program by improving product quality, increasing responsiveness to customer needs, and involving employees in manufacturing issues. In addition, they offer the benefits of lower inventories, less material handling, and reduced floor-space requirements.
- Control of machine setup times and machine downtimes is a prerequisite of successfully JIT manufacturing cells.

## INFORMATION RESOURCES

*World Class Manufacturing: The Lessons of Simplicity Applied*, Richard J. Schonberger, The Free Press, 1986.

*Just-in-Time: Making It Happen*, William A. Sandras, Jr., Oliver Wight Publications, 1989.

*Customer-Driven Strategy: Winning Through Operational Excellence*, Thomas F. Wallace, Oliver Wight Publications, 1992.

*Reinventing the Factory: Productivity Breakthroughs in Manufacturing Today*, Roy L. Harmon and Leroy D. Peterson, The Free Press, 1990.

*Dynamic Manufacturing: Creating the Learning Organization*, Robert H. Hayes, Steven C. Wheelwright, and Kim B. Clark, The Free Press, 1988.

*Attaining Manufacturing Excellence*, Robert W. Hall, Dow Jones–Irwin, 1987.

*APICS Dictionary*, 7th edition, American Production and Inventory Control Society, 1992.

## INTERNAL CROSS-REFERENCE

Your understanding of this topic may be enhanced by the following chapters:

IV–4. Just-in-Time: Driver for Continuous Improvement

V–3. The Focused Factory

V–4. Manufacturing Process Choice

## About the Author

Alfred W. Webber is a senior associate with R. Reed & Associates located in Carmel, Indiana. He has provided businesses with quality solutions, education, and advice for more than twenty years. His broad business background includes management responsibilities in manufacturing, sales/marketing, engineering, systems, and distribution with Corning Incorporated, Cabot Corporation, and the Wickes Companies. He is the author of numerous articles on various manufacturing management topics.

## V-6

# Plant Scheduling for High Customer Service
### Ray Reed

### IN A NUTSHELL

The purpose of scheduling in a manufacturing company is to communicate priorities regarding what work should be done and when it should be performed. Properly executed, scheduling provides the vital link between managerial plans and the efficient use of manufacturing resources. This fulfills a fundamental business goal: supplying customers with what they want, when they want it.

If a company had only one customer and made only one product, communicating priorities would be simple. The vast majority of companies, however, supply many products to a large customer base and have traditionally established their priorities through expediting, a procedure in which urgent orders are placed on lists and communicated to plant supervisors by expediters. In plants producing thousands of different components and/or end products, expediters can realistically follow only a small percentage of these items. The nonexpedited items are somehow expected to make it through the process and be available as needed.

The application of computers to manufacturing, beginning in the early 1960s, created tremendous opportunities for new and far more effective methods of establishing, communicating, and maintaining production priorities. Computers and software of the 1990s allow for instantaneous updating of manufacturing priorities and contribute significantly to Continuous Improvement efforts.

The primary purpose of scheduling is to communicate work priorities in a timely and accurate fashio. Timely means that changes in priorities are communicated rapidly through a tightly controlled process. Accurate means that all relevant data is correct (e.g., quantity, due date, order number, current location, etc.).

This tightly controlled process begins with a Master Schedule. The purpose of the Master Schedule is to balance demands with resources, ensuring that sales plans, production rates, and inventory/backlog planned levels are synchronized (see page 61). The word "master" has definite implications for scheduling. One dictionary defines it as "a device or mechanism that controls the operation of another mechanism." In this context, Master Scheduling is analogous to the function of mission control in NASA. All communications to and from the spacecraft are through mission control. The primary purpose is to ensure that the crew does not get conflicting messages on what to do and when do it. One can only imagine the potential for chaos if many people could communicate directly with the crew, each offering instructions for them to follow. This same potential for chaos exists within manufacturing companies. In the absence of a Master Schedule, production supervisors would be inundated with schedule change requests or edicts from most, if not all, functional areas within the company.

Once in place, the Master Schedule becomes the driver for material planning, Capacity Planning, and plant scheduling.

The communication of the priorities established by the Master Schedule is generally accomplished by one or more of the following three methodologies:

*1. A "Work-to" List* As the name implies, this list shows the sequence in which work should be performed and when. This list may in fact be a computer screen. In a totally integrated system, changes to the Master Schedule are updated automatically at each terminal, thereby communicating current priorities.

These work-to lists are typically generated for each individual line or work center. For process manufacturing, the detailed schedules are most often derived directly from the Master Production Schedule. In a job shop, these schedules—often called a dispatch list—are normally the results of a process known as back scheduling, which calculates the setup time, run time, move time, and queue time for each operation to be performed on the job.

*2. A "Pull" System (e.g., Kanban)* This method of communicating priorities is quite simple. A production area maintains a small amount of inventory of the components or products it makes repetitively. Its signal, or "schedule," to produce more of an item is triggered when a quantity of that inventory is "pulled" by the next production area, or by the customer in the case of finished products.

*3. Finite Scheduling* This is an advanced form of the scheduling process, which assigns jobs to resources and sequences them to arrive at an optimal or near-optimal schedule. In some environments—for example, flow shops and process manufacturing—Finite Scheduling has yielded significant benefits.

Finite scheduling works best when it's used as a simulator, and many of today's Finite Scheduling software packages do just that. They're highly interactive and graphical, displaying to the scheduling person the results of the trial schedule, including changeover costs, inventory carrying costs, stockout/late shipment costs, etc. It's then the scheduler's job to accept the schedule as generated, or to tell the software to try another solution by varying one or more of the scheduling parameters. For example, the system's first solution may have carried an unacceptably high stockout rate. The scheduler could tell the system to reduce the number of stockouts to x or less. The system would then generate another schedule, reflecting the scheduler's input.

Many companies integrate Finite Scheduling with their MRP II system. They'll download the Master Schedule from MRP II into the finite schedule (which often runs on a personal computer), do the simulations, select the best solution, and then upload it back into the Master Schedule so that it can be executed. The characteristics of the manufacturing process ultimately determine which of these systems is most suitable.

## Benefits

When plant scheduling is an integral part of an integrated planning and execution process, the benefits can be outstanding. Examples of quantifiable benefits include:

- Increases in on-time delivery to customers, resulting in increased sales
- 50 to 100 percent improvements in inventory turnover
- Operating cost reductions of 15 to 30 percent
- Dramatic reductions in new product introduction time

A nonquantifiable but significant benefit of good scheduling is improved quality of work life in the form of improved communications, the elimination of conflicting priorities and "hot lists," and the satisfaction of being able to get the job done to the delight of the customers.

Costs for scheduling systems can range from $20,000 to $400,000, depending on the size and complexity of the company and the quality of the entire planning/execution process.

## Implementation Issues and Time Frame

A totally integrated planning process, managed by the executive team (see Sales and Operations Planning, chapter I–5), is a prerequisite to effective scheduling. With this in place, and the required software installed, the scheduling systems can be made operable in two to three months. These scheduling methodologies may change over time as a result of Continuous Improvement efforts.

All too often, certain traditional performance measures constrain the implementation of scheduling systems that would otherwise greatly facilitate Continuous Improvement and customer delight. For example, measures that focus on efficiency and deployment of people and equipment may satisfy performance criteria at the expense of Master Schedule–driven priorities. Likewise, piecework systems, when used as a method of determining compensation, focus on volume of output, often at the expense of customer service and/or quality.

## KEY CONCEPTS

**Dispatch list:** *See* **Work-to-list**

**Expediting**: A process for communicating priorities, usually verbally and followed up frequently. Typically only a small percentage of items purchased or procured can be prioritized in this manner. A well-managed, totally integrated planning and scheduling process eliminates the need for expediting.

**Finite scheduling**: A rigorous approach to fitting demand into available capacity. One primary consideration is to "level" or balance loads on all resources involved, but other factors—order due dates, changeovers, inventories—can be factored into the process.

**Integrated planning, scheduling, and execution system**: A business process in which the executive team takes ownership and develops, at least monthly, a set of Sales and Operations Plans for a minimum twelve-month rolling horizon. These plans are used to develop Master Schedules, which in turn drive all material and Capacity Planning and all schedule requirements. This business process is referred to as Manufacturing Resource Planning (MRP II).

**Kanban system**: A method of communicating priorities in which a production operation is authorized to produce only when a visual signal is received from its customer (next operation). This visual signal is often in the form of a card (kanban).

**Master Scheduling**: The function that serves as mission control in that all detail schedules by department and operation are derivatives of the Master Schedule. All requests for schedule changes, from every functional area and individual in the company, are directed to Master Scheduling, nowhere else.

**Schedule**: A statement of priorities indicating what should be produced next and when. Schedules are communicated in a variety of ways, ranging from printed lists and human directives to computer terminals and kanban systems.

**Work-to list**: A listing (either hard copy or on a computer terminal) of the specific jobs to be performed at a certain work center.

## ACTION STEPS

- Ensure that work centers are properly defined.
- Ensure that routing or process steps are defined in the current sequence.
- Develop the basic data required for a plant scheduling system, such as queue times, lead time offsets, move time, setup and changeover times, and run times. The software package will identify and define the required data elements.
- Identify work centers where a work-to list (dispatch list) will be used to communicate scheduling priorities versus those where a kanban-type of system would be appropriate.
- Ensure that work-in-process information is accurate. This includes job number, quantity, location, and status.
- Before implementing a scheduling system, ensure that Sales and Operations Planning, Master Scheduling, and material planning are functioning properly. These are excellent scheduling tools, but they will be of little value if the higher-level processes are not managed properly.

## PROBLEM-SOLVING

*"Schedules in our company are not worth the paper they are written on. By the time the factory receives them, they are obsolete."*

Schedules need to be timely and accurate. There are excellent systems available that facilitate timely communication of valid priorities.

*"In our company, everybody schedules. It seems that everyone from the president on down has an opinion on what should be worked on next and when it should be done."*

This is a common symptom of the lack of control over production priorities, and it results in chaos. A formal plant scheduling process is needed so that there is one source from which all scheduling information is derived.

*"We can't agree on which scheduling method to use. Some people feel that a formal scheduling system using work-to lists or computer terminals at workstations is too cumbersome and expensive. They're pushing for a kanban-type of approach that's simple and does not require lists or computers. Others argue that we are not ready for a kanban-type of system."*

A kanban-type of scheduling system is definitely simple and efficient, and it works best in repetitive manufacturing environments. The scheduling system must support the underlying operations. If the current environment is more of a job shop and material moves through many departments and multiple locations, then a kanban system will probably create more problems than it solves. There is often a need to use both of these approaches within the same production facility because certain operations are repetitive and others are not.

*"We feel that we have a very good integrated planning and scheduling system, including Master Scheduling. But we frequently find operations that produce more than what was scheduled and work on jobs out of sequence from the schedule."*

You will probably find that performance measurements that focus on elements like direct labor efficiency and equipment utilization are given a higher priority by management than schedule conformance. There needs to be an equivalent emphasis on schedule conformance. When a shared vision is in place and continuous improvement is a company policy, these measurements can exist together and actually facilitate excellence.

## SUMMARY

- Scheduling in a large percentage of manufacturing companies is a constraint to Continuous Improvement and customer service.
- The primary purpose of scheduling is to perpetually answer the questions, What do we make next? When must we make it?
- Human expediting of important or critical items has been the most common method of establishing priorities.
- Systems capabilities today allow for instantaneous updating of priorities on all items being produced, at every point in the production process.
- Schedules need to be established by a Master Scheduling process that is part of a well-managed, totally integrated planning and execution process.
- A dynamic, flexible scheduling environment offers enormous potential for quantifiable and nonquantifiable benefits.
- The critical path to dynamic, flexible scheduling starts with education and understanding, followed by commitment on the part of key executives and managers to Continuous Improvement and customer delight.

## INFORMATION RESOURCES

*Gaining Control: Capacity Management and Scheduling,* James G. Correll and Norris W. Edson, Oliver Wight Publications, 1990.

*Master Scheduling,* John Proud, Oliver Wight Publications, 1994.

## INTERNAL CROSS-REFERENCE

Your understanding of this topic may be enhanced by the following chapters:

- I–6. Resource Planning: For Manufacturing, the Business, and the Enterprise
- II–3. Efficient Consumer Response
- V–2. Information Technology in Manufacturing
- VI–1. Enterprise Logistics Management (ELM)
- VI–3. Supplier Scheduling: Linking Suppliers with Customers

### About the Author

Ray Reed has extensive experience in helping U.S. and multinational companies change their operating cultures. His broad experience includes management responsibility for marketing, engineering, materials, manufacturing, and finance. In 1981, prior to founding R. Reed & Associates, Inc., in Downers Grove, Illinois, he was executive vice president and general manager for Goodman Equipment Corporation, and president of its wholly owned subsidiary, Improved Plastics Machinery. He holds a B.S. in engineering and finance from the University of Scranton in Pennsylvania. He currently serves as a director of Moore Products Company and SDTV Inc.

# PART VI
# SUPPLY CHAIN

**1. Enterprise Logistics Management (ELM)**
*Thomas G. Gunn*

**2. Supplier Quality Management (SQM)**
*Kenneth J. Stork*

**3. Supplier Scheduling: Linking Suppliers with Customers**
*Alfred W. Webber*

**A** COMPANY'S SUPPLIERS, subcontractors, and carriers comprise a critically important part of its total resources. It's not good enough for a company to be excellent at taking care of its internal infrastructure; these external resources need care, nurturing, encouragement and support to become world class partners.

Part VI opens with a global view of this topic, in **Enterprise Logistics Management (ELM)** by Tom Gunn. In the next chapter, Ken Stork calls on his years of experience in materials at Motorola and focuses on **Supplier Quality Management (SQM)**. Lastly, Al Webber returns for a discussion of **Supplier Scheduling: Linking Suppliers With Customers.**

# VI-1

# Enterprise Logistics Management (ELM)

*Thomas G. Gunn*

### IN A NUTSHELL

Enterprise Logistics Management (ELM) is an umbrella strategy for effective management in a fast-paced and highly competitive global marketplace.

"Enterprise," as used in ELM, means the entire manufacturing company or corporation. The term "Logistics" indicates that ELM deals with materials management and production-scheduling activities throughout the value-added pipeline—from final customer all the way back to the supplier of the rawest material. ELM is thus concerned with the sourcing and distribution, movement, and storage of materials and products—from earliest supplier right through to end user. ELM extends as well to service or replacement parts, and even to demanufacturing/reclamation activities. The "Management" component of ELM conveys that the approach is concerned both with planning and execution.

The concept of integration is implicit to ELM. ELM spans the entire value-added pipeline of the enterprise, regardless of organizational boundaries.

TABLE 1. CHARACTERISTICS OF ELM

| | Each Plant Autonomous | With Enterprise Logistics Management |
|---|---|---|
| MRP | Each plant has its own. | All plants, materials, and management/logistics systems integrated in one common system. |
| DRP | Option; seldom used. | DRP part of integrated system for distribution-intensive products. |
| Information to and from corporate | P&L summary only to corporate from plants. | All plant, supplier, customer information flow available electronically to corporate. All order entry and scheduling information flows from corporate to plants. |
| Logistics staff | Full complement needed at each plant, including purchasing, staffing and training with little or no regard for corporate welfare. | Minimal staffing at plants, main strength at corporate level; all staffing and training done with a consistent approach and to maximize corporate strength. |
| Suppliers | Each supplier supplies each plant separately, thus has to deal with a number of customers in the corporation. | Suppliers deal with corporate on aggregated major product purchases, lesser buying done locally; suppliers have to deal with fewer customers and can be more effective for the corporation. |
| Material tracking in the logistics pipeline | Each plant does its own in different ways to a different extent. | All material movement tracked fully on a common computer system, including use of EDI, through the logistics pipeline. |

| | | |
|---|---|---|
| Capacity management | Each plant does its own with little or no regard for corporate performance. | Performed centrally (first) with regard to maximizing corporate performance, then plant performance. |
| Inventory management | Each plant does its own with little or no regard for corporate performance. | Performed centrally (first) with regard to maximizing corporate performance, then plant performance. |
| Customers | Managed by each plant separately and to varying degrees of customer satisfaction, with little or no regard for overall corporate priorities. | Managed with regard to corporate strategic and operational priorities. |
| Information systems | Each plant has its own. Electronic communications between plants difficult, costly, and usually nonexistent; plant to corporate telecommunication usually primitive. Even aggregation of data from separate plant systems difficult due to different definitions, MRP system use, and timing cutoffs. | Corporate systems use standard data dictionary, database management systems, operating system, application system (ELP), and telecommunication system to create and effectively use management information. |
| Ability to exchange design data between plants | Limited to none. Each plant may have its own CAD system. Plant-to-plant telecommunications usually nonexistent or primitive. | Full corporate engineering network with sufficient graphics capacity running standard CAD/CAE applications available at all plants. |

## Origins

ELM brings together ideas that originated in different parts of the manufacturing business. MRP and DRP provide a solid base for tying together dependent demand throughout the value-added pipeline. Just-in-Time and, on a broader front, Business Process Reengineering (BPR), form the basis for minimizing lead times, inventory, and waste. Customer satisfaction represents an underlying theme of ELM. A focus on customer demand pull instead of the traditional producer's push is also a modern concept that finds a home in ELM. Modern information systems—computerized networks that make real-time integration of customer, enterprise, and supplier on a real-time basis—are also integral to ELM.

Figure 1 reveals some of the functional characteristics of ELM by contrasting them to today's typical autonomous MRP/MRP II systems.

## The ELM Organization

ELM global manufacturing environments tend to be highly complex. Typically, there are several layers of organizational hierarchy. Also, most plants draw some of their supplies from external sources; some plants are established to provide output to other plants in the same organization. Taken together, these form the enterprise linkages in the supplier-to-customer value-added pipeline. In many organizations, this picture is complicated by the existence of a network of distribution centers.

ELM thus deals with an extremely complex network of organizational, geographic, material flow, and scheduling dynamics. That we can begin to even think about it as one integrated operating system is due to the progress made in information technology, product design, inventory management, and customer service over the last decade.

## Benefits

ELM offers a number of significant benefits to companies that adopt it as an approach to global business management. First, the ability to perform ELM on a real-time basis takes days and weeks out of most planning and execution cycles, making ELM-based companies more responsive to their customers. ELM firms need less inventory, and less inventory means fewer dollars tied up in working capital. These funds can be directed to value-adding activities such as R&D, capital equipment, information system investments, employee education and training, and the like. Shorter lead times also allow ELM companies to reduce the forecast lead time, which automatically improves the accuracy of the forecast.

## KEY CONCEPTS

**Enterprise**: A corporate umbrella that embodies all business units and business processes of the company.

**Global**: An enterprise whose business practices span worldwide markets.

**Integrated**: A seamless continuum of business processes that utilize the minimum possible set of data to complete business transactions.

**Logistics management**: The total spectrum of materials management and operations scheduling that begins with global suppliers and links with the global customer; in short, managing the entire value-added pipeline.

**"Real-time" information**: Information that can be accessed, manipulated, analyzed, and displayed in a matter of seconds or minutes, rather than hours, days, or weeks. Real time in this context is relative to the normal length of time required to run MRP replanning (typically thirty hours) and other lengthy functions.

## ACTION STEPS

- Understand the vision of Enterprise Logistics Management and create a version of this vision that is tailored to your corporation or industry.

- On a corporate basis, analyze the current mix of information systems, software packages, and operating policies used to manage your company's entire logistics process.
- Develop a strategy to integrate and reengineer the two logistics business processes: the customer order-to-delivery and the materials management/operations scheduling.
- Develop a plan to upgrade your company's information systems to provide more real-time information, especially in planning and in material tracking.
- Educate and train personnel, from users through senior management, as to the benefits (financial and strategic) of the company's new ELM approach.
- Incrementally pursue the implementation of your company's ELM vision through new business practices and processes, more advanced software applications, and more real-time information systems.

## *PROBLEM-SOLVING*

*"Our planning process has too much waste—it takes a week or a month to create a Master Production Schedule for a product that we can build and ship in forty-eight hours."*

Many large companies have concentrated on improving execution at the expense of planning. The first step in reducing planning time is to regard planning as a business process, subject to the same principles of reengineering as other processes. The second step is to actually apply the principles of reengineering—i.e., document the total business process and understand it, eliminate the waste, and simplify the functions involved. Then use information systems to improve the speed, quality, productivity, and flexibility of the business process, and to integrate it with the firm's internal and external business partners.

*"We don't have the data or information we need to effectively plan our logistics."*

The information may already exist, but in many separate databases, or other information repositories (file cabinets, backs of napkins, foremen's heads, etc.). These are generally disconnected and not designed to work as a system. Many information repositories are geographically dispersed as well.

The solution is an integrated flow of data and information for the customer order delivery process—which is primarily outward and forward looking; and the materials management scheduling process—which looks inward to your own plants and backward up the industry supplier chain or value network.

> "Our planning process takes too long—particularly our manufacturing-resource-based planning. Our MRP II system requires thirty hours to process replanning. Because of this massive tie-up of computing power, we're lucky if we can obtain our MRP replanning run once a week over the weekends."

New software that works in conjunction with any MRP software package runs on high performance RISC-based computers. These allow you to carry out an MRP replanning run in a few minutes or less. Faster replanning allows you to run MRP II every day, making it possible for you to react more quickly to increasingly volatile business conditions. It also relieves your mainframe computer of a lot of processing and may avoid the need for a major computer upgrade.

In addition, the new software allows you to run MRP on a *comparative* basis and vary the Master Schedule, as well as lot sizes, routings, and other resources. You then have a simulation tool for modeling changes in the business with *actual* production data, rather than as an abstracted set of data that must be translated back into the real world. This provides you with very powerful Business Planning and management capabilities.

> "We don't have the necessary feedback mechanism to the planning process, i.e., the ability to track material on a real-time basis throughout the logistics pipeline."

You need some means of tracking materials electronically, such as bar coding, with the ability to update your database in real time.

Equally important, your systems must feed back to the planning system and close the loop. Using today's technology, it is both cost effective and feasible to track material on a global basis in real time.

## SUMMARY

- Enterprise Logistics Management is an approach to materials management and production scheduling throughout the value-added pipeline—from suppliers to final customers.
- As an integrative management approach, ELM ties together materials resource planning, distribution resource planning, Just-in-Time, and other planning and process improvement initiatives.

## INFORMATION RESOURCES

*21st Century Manufacturing: Creating Winning Business Performance,* Thomas G. Gunn, Oliver Wight Publications, 1993.

"Logistics Planning: Improving the 'Forgotten Business Process,'" *OR/MS Today,* October 1992.

"Managing Supply Chain Inventory: Pitfalls and Opportunities," Hau Lee and Cory Billing, *Sloan Management Review,* Spring 1992.

## INTERNAL CROSS-REFERENCE

Your understanding of this topic may be enhanced by the following chapters:

I–6. Resource Planning: For Manufacturing, the Business, and the Enterprise

II–3. Efficient Consumer Response (ECR)

IV–4. Just-in-Time: Driver for Continuous Improvement

## About the Author

Thomas G. Gunn is president of Gunn Associates, Inc. He has more than fifteen years of management consulting experience, and he specializes in manufacturing strategies and performance improvement programs. Mr. Gunn is a frequent speaker at conferences and executive programs throughout North America and Europe, and is the author of several books, including *21st Century Manufacturing: Creating Winning Business Performance* and *In the Age of the Real-Time Enterprise*. His articles have appeared in *Scientific American, Production, CIM Review*, and other publications.

# VI-2

# Supplier Quality Management (SQM)
*Kenneth J. Stork*

## IN A NUTSHELL

While most North American manufacturers have made a commitment to one or another quality or operational improvement program, relatively few companies have committed themselves to improving the quality of their relationships with key suppliers. Those that do practice what is called Supplier Quality Management (SQM), which is, in essence, the application of Total Quality Management to the supply chain. SQM is a process of Continuous Improvement with external manufacturers devoted to quality, delivery, and cost that benefits all parties.

SQM requires a change in the traditional customer-supplier relationships, from the adversarial model that still prevails in most North American industry to one based upon long-term mutual benefit. SQM facilitates the building of mutual trust—the cornerstone of any relationship—between customer and supplier. A customer cannot maintain trust in a supplier when the quality of its products is not consistently reliable. Nor can suppliers trust customers who are generally unwilling to make major operational improvements of their own.

SQM, though a subset of larger quality efforts such as TQM, makes it possible for suppliers and customers to engage in win-win relationships.

## *Why SQM?*

SQM is a logical extension of Total Quality Management. The manufacturer that aims for world class performance quickly realizes that its business is not confined to the boundaries of the factory walls, but extends forward to customer distribution and backward along the supply chain. That supply chain is, in a very real sense, an extension of the manufacturer, and it must be operated to world class standards if the manufacturer is to attain its own performance goals. In a very real sense, a manufacturer is no better than its suppliers. If it hopes to raise itself up, the suppliers must raise themselves up as well.

Suppliers have every reason to cooperate in a program of SQM. Like their customers, they cannot operate in isolation, but are affected by the actions and performance standards of their customers, from whom they face ever-increasing demands—quality audits, supplier certification requirements, and different ways of measuring supplier performance, to name just a few.

Each of these demands is time-consuming and costly for the supplier, a source of confusion when shifting from one customer's order to another's, and a source of errors that result in scrap and rework. Many of the best suppliers are reacting to these demands by reducing their customer bases—maintaining those accounts that are most profitable and most straightforward with respect to specifications and performance standards, and dropping others as their capacity allows. On their part, the best companies are attempting to corner the limited output of these superior suppliers by becoming world class customers (see chapter II–1).

SQM programs are an important way of rationalizing the burdens on suppliers and help them raise their own performance.

## SQM's Underlying Requirements

Supplier Quality Management has three critical underlying requirements:

1. Visible support of senior management for SQM as a long-term proposition. Management leads the organization to select and retain suppliers on total cost/life-cycle cost rather than unit price alone. Senior management is willing to make long-term commitments to those suppliers that consistently meet its SQM objectives. Result: Trust develops between customer and supplier; both benefit from cost reductions and greater efficiencies.

2. A credible, visible leader of the process. Results tend to be better when this leader is the current head of purchasing/procurement or a strategic sourcing function. When this person is a quality zealot, the suppliers are much more quickly motivated to improve quality at a satisfactory rate.

3. Cross-function teaming. It is critical to deal with all suppliers of commodities important to the customer's business. And since these suppliers typically represent different technologies, cross-functional teams are needed to extend the supplier quality program to these suppliers. If plastic moldings and power supplies are two key areas or commodities, for example, an effective team would consist of the following functional experts: quality engineer, design/development engineer, purchasing buyer, and financial representative.

## Benefits

Whether they realize it or not, customers are competing for a share of the output of a limited number of world class suppliers. Creating productive relationships with high-quality suppliers is one way for a company to gain a significant competitive advantage. The quality, productivity, and overall competence of primary suppliers are subsumed into the overall quality and competence of the customer's own products.

The cost of an effective SQM process can run in a range of 1 to 3 percent of total purchases. This investment, however, is easily recovered through economic benefits that greatly exceed the upfront costs.

### *Implementation*

Successful SQM implementation requires:

- Multifunctional buy-in to a common process for working with suppliers.
- Appropriate ways of measuring supplier performance.
- Joint goal setting with primary suppliers on annual improvements.
- Awarding more business to the best-performing suppliers at the expense of poorer-performing competitors.
- Total cost rather than unit-price-purchase decision making.
- Attacking major SQM issues through improvement teams composed of customer and supplier personnel.
- SQM treated as a continuous process, not as a program.

## KEY CONCEPTS

**Commodity team**: A multifunctional team focused on a strategic or primary technology or service that is important to the customer. The team is chartered to obtain significant improvements in quality, delivery, and cost.

**Competing for supply**: A proactive approach designed to obtain significant shares of the output of best-in-class and world class suppliers.

**Supplier certification**: A widely used program that focuses on eliminating incoming inspection.

# Supplier Quality Management (SQM)

**Supplier Quality Management (SQM)**: A process of Continuous Improvement with external manufacturers devoted to quality, delivery, and cost that benefits all parties involved.

**Total cost of ownership**: Efforts to identify life cycle or all related costs in lieu of the prevalent focus on unit price to award business to a supplier.

**World class customer**: Strategic approach to cornering the supply from best-in-class and world class suppliers for competitive advantage.

## ACTION STEPS

Each of the following steps must be carried out by senior management and appropriate individuals and teams.

- Communicate the SQM process and related strategies, both internally and to key suppliers.
- Select leaders for the process.
- Select key indicators of supplier performance; refine them continually; measure progress monthly.
- Charter initial commodity teams.
- Disseminate results both internally and externally.
- Reward the winners—i.e., more business for best-performing suppliers, and promotions, money and recognition for your key employees.
- Reevaluate and improve your formal quality system, methods for developing and publishing engineering specifications, etc.

## PROBLEM-SOLVING

*"Our competitors are able to produce higher-quality products at lower-selling prices."*

Benchmark your supplier's approach to SQM. An easy place to start is to discuss with common suppliers the advantages and disadvantages to your approach, or lack thereof, to SQM.

*"When capacity and supply of critical purchased materials are tight, our purchasing department and suppliers shut our lines down too often. Premium costs to try to maintain supply are rising rapidly."*

A proactive approach to becoming a world class customer is appropriate. Work more closely and communicate future schedule needs more often.

*"Our competitors are able to beat us to market with new products. Frequently they contain new technology from a supplier that wasn't made known to us."*

Your key suppliers may be quietly working on phasing you out as a customer. Your CEO needs to personally revitalize your SQM program and entire process of managing its relationships with key suppliers.

*"Our quality, purchasing, and engineering directors are always blaming each other for operating problems."*

Appoint a strong, credible leader to successfully implement SQM. Results will come more quickly if the thrust is based on total cost of ownership progress and increased business awards to the best-in-class performers.

## *SUMMARY*

- Supplier Quality Management (SQM) is the application of Total Quality Management to the supply chain. It is an important element in strategic approach to mutually beneficial customer-supplier relationships.
- Senior management must be involved in establishing SQM and providing visible leadership.
- World class suppliers are quietly focusing their efforts on a few enlightened customers that offer potentially great profits in the future.
- Enlightened customers recognize that they are competing for the output of the best suppliers.

- The historic, adversarial model of customer-supplier relationships is still prevalent in industry and benefits neither party.

## INFORMATION RESOURCES

*On the Road to Manufacturing Excellence,* a video. Association for Manufacturing Excellence, 1989.

*Quality System Review Guidelines,* revised, Motorola Corporation, 1992.

*Strategic Supply Management,* Keki Bhote, AMACOM, 1989.

## INTERNAL CROSS-REFERENCE

Your understanding of this topic may be enhanced by the following chapters:

II–1. Being a World Class Customer

IV–1. Total Quality Management (TQM)

IV–7. Discovering Improvement Opportunities Through Quality Auditing

---

### About the Author

Kenneth J. Stork is president of Ken Stork & Associates, Inc., an independent educational and consulting firm that assists clients in achieving operational improvements. From 1978 to 1992, Mr. Stork served as corporate director of materials management and purchasing for Motorola, Inc. He is a co-founder and past president of the Association for Manufacturing, and is an instructor at the California Institute of Technology.

# Supplier Scheduling: Linking Suppliers with Customers
## Alfred W. Webber

### IN A NUTSHELL

Supplier scheduling is a process that provides your suppliers with information about future requirements for the goods or services you will need and when you will need them. It has been shown that companies that use supplier scheduling effectively consistently achieve better delivery performance, lower purchasing costs, lower inventories, shorter lead times, and reduced paperwork than companies that operate under traditional supplier arrangements.

### Traditional Arrangements

The traditional method used to procure goods or services from a supplier involves a purchase order (PO). A PO is a formal agreement between buyer and seller stating the quantity, description, price, payment terms, discounts, date of performance, transportation, and all other agreements pertinent to the purchase and its execution by the supplier.

Purchase orders are normally short term in nature, covering only the immediate needs of a buyer. Quantities ordered are usually large in scale so that the buyer can take advantage of volume discounts. Delivery lead times are dependent on the lead times available from the supplier at the time the purchase order is placed.

## A Better Way

Supplier scheduling separates the contractual business agreement in the purchase order from the actual schedule for the goods and services required. Under this approach, buyers are responsible for developing supplier agreements while a new position, supplier scheduler, is responsible for providing the supplier schedules within the context of the supplier agreement.

The need for supplier scheduling came about for two reasons: First, companies wanted to free up buyers from the ongoing pressures of expediting and paperwork and let them concentrate on sourcing, negotiations, contracting, and value analysis. With supplier scheduling, buyers work with vendors to develop supplier agreements. Second, there was a need to improve communication between the buyer's material planning people and the supplier's operations. Traditionally, communications went from the company planner to the company buyer to the supplier's salesperson, then on to the supplier's planner. Now, supplier schedulers work directly with the material planners or production people in the supplier's own plant.

The supplier scheduler communicates a schedule via priority mail, fax, or electronic data interface to the supplier on a routine basis, typically once a week. This schedule (see Figure 1) not only shows the immediate needs of the buying company but also its medium- and long-term requirements. These requirements can be defined as follows:

*Immediate requirements* This is a firm authorization from the buyer to the supplier to manufacture and deliver the week's goods or service as defined in the supplier schedule. It is also a commitment from the buyer to purchase the goods or services scheduled. The

**FIGURE 1. SUPPLIER SCHEDULE**

**Jones Company supplier schedule for: Smith, Inc.—week of 02/01/9X**   **Supplier #114**

**Supplier Scheduler: AB**  **Firm Zone: first 04 weeks**  **Material Zone: next 06 weeks**
**Buyer: CD**

················································· Requirements ·················································
FFFFFFFFFFFFFFFFFFFFFFFFFFFFFFFF MMMMMMMMMMMMMM

| Item # | Description | | Week 2/1 & previous | Week 2/8 | Week 2/15 | Week 2/22 | Week 3/01 | Week 3/08 | Next 04 Wks | Next 12 Wks |
|---|---|---|---|---|---|---|---|---|---|---|
| 13579 | Plate | Qty: |  | 100 |  |  |  | 100 | 100 | 300 |
| 24680 | Panel | Qty: | 20 | 20 | 20 | 20 | 20 | 20 | 80 | 340 |
| 42457 | Tube | Qty: | 300 |  |  | 200 |  |  | 1100 | 3500 |
| 77543 | Frame | Qty: |  |  | 40 |  | 40 |  |  |  |

*Source:* John E. Schorr, *Purchasing in the 21st Century: A Guide to State-of-the-Art Techniques and Strategies,* Oliver Wight Publications, 1992, p. 42.

time period covered is kept to a minimum to hold inventory levels low and allow the buyer the flexibility to determine what goods or services are needed.

*Intermediate requirements* This, too, is an authorization from the buyer to the supplier to purchase the materials needed to provide the goods or services as laid out in the schedule. It is not, however, an authorization to manufacture the goods or provide the service. It is a commitment, however, by the buyer to purchase any materials not used by the supplier due to a change in schedule made by the buyer. The time period covered by intermediate requirements is usually long enough to cover the procurement lead times of the supplier.

*Long-term requirements* This part of the schedule is informational only. It represents the buyer's current planning information for the time period covered. No authorization is given from the buyer to the supplier to either purchase materials or provide any goods or services. The supplier uses this information to replace its previous forecast information and as an aid to planning its future material and capacity requirements.

Supplier scheduling is also applicable in a Just-in-Time (JIT) environment. With JIT, the supplier schedule typically has smaller time periods—days instead of weeks—and a more repetitive pattern to the quantities. The time periods covered by the immediate-, intermediate-, and long-term requirements are also shorter, reflecting the greatly reduced lead times associated with JIT manufacturing. Kanban may also be used as the commitment to produce and deliver, while the supplier schedule is used for planning purposes only.

## *Benefits*

The benefits of supplier scheduling can be significant:

- Reduced inventories because the buyer receives only what is needed

- Lower prices because of longer-term agreements with suppliers
- Shorter lead times because suppliers commit capacity to the buyer's future requirements as well as immediate needs
- On-time delivery performance improvement because the suppliers have the right information to be more responsive to buyer needs
- Paperwork reductions owing to elimination of purchase orders

Costs to implement supplier scheduling range from $30,000 to $200,000 depending on the size of the supplier base, the programming required to generate a supplier schedule, and the amount of outside education and facilitation required.

## *Implementation*

A prerequisite of successful supplier scheduling is that the buyer firm have its own valid schedules and internal operations that are under control. After all, buyer schedules are used to generate the supplier schedules, and the buyer can maintain its own schedules only if internal operations are under control.

Most companies use Material Requirements Planning (MRP) to produce valid schedules and to control their manufacturing operations. Unfortunately, most MRP software packages do not have reports suitable for use with supplier scheduling. On the positive side, the information needed to produce good supplier schedules is usually readily available. All that needs to be done is to program the report.

Companies that have valid schedules and good control of their manufacturing operations typically need three to six months to implement supplier scheduling with their major suppliers. Companies with very large supplier bases naturally require more time. Still more time is necessary if the buyer firm must first bring its own schedules and operations under control.

## KEY CONCEPTS

**Buyer**: An individual whose functions may include supplier selection, negotiations, order placement, supplier follow-up, measurement and control of supplier performance, value analysis, and evaluation of new materials and processes. In companies that use supplier scheduling, the functions of order placement and supplier follow-up are handled by the supplier scheduler.

**Material planner**: The person normally responsible for managing the inventory levels, schedules, and availability of selected goods or services, either manufactured or purchased. When using a computerized planning package, this person is also responsible for reviewing and acting upon order release, action, and exception messages from the planning system.

**Material requirements**: The date and quantity of all goods and services required for the manufacture or assembly of a component or end item. Requirements are calculated using a bill of material, inventory data, and the production schedule for the materials to be purchased or produced.

**Planner/buyer**: *See* **Supplier scheduler**.

**Purchase order (PO)**: The purchaser's document used to formalize a purchase transaction with a supplier. A purchase order, when given to a supplier, should contain statements of the quantity, description, and price of the goods or services ordered; it also contains agreed-to terms as to payment, discounts, and transportation, and all other agreements pertinent to the purchase and its execution by the supplier.

**Supplier agreement**: A long-term contract between a buyer and a supplier for a fixed period of time, or for an open-ended period. Statements contained could include description of goods or services, price of the goods or services, agreed-to terms as to payment, discounts, and transportation, and all other agreements pertinent to the purchase and its execution by the supplier. Used in conjunction with a supplier scheduling.

**Supplier scheduler**: A person whose main job is working with suppliers regarding goods and services they will provide, and when they will deliver them. Supplier schedulers do material planning for the goods or services under their control, communicate the resultant schedules to their assigned suppliers, do follow-up, resolve problems, and advise other operations personnel when purchased goods or services will not arrive on time to support the schedule.

**Supplier scheduling**: A purchasing approach that provides suppliers with schedules instead of hard copy purchase orders. Normally, a supplier scheduling system will include a business agreement (contract) for each supplier, a weekly schedule for each supplier extending for some time into the future, and individuals called supplier schedulers.

## ACTION STEPS

The necessary steps to evaluate your needs for supplier scheduling, plan the implementation, and then implement supplier scheduling are as follows:

- Learn about supplier scheduling and how it can lead to better manufacturing performance.
- Assess your company's status with respect to supplier scheduling and determine what you must do to use supplier scheduling to achieve the most benefit.
- Develop the detailed plans for implementing supplier scheduling, to include:
    1. Identifying detailed task work
    2. Determining resource requirements
    3. Establishing a project management structure
    4. Completing a cost/benefit analysis

5. Developing training and education plans for your company and your suppliers
6. Providing a schedule for complete implementation

- Select one supplier with which you will initiate supplier scheduling.
- Train and implement supplier scheduling with the selected supplier.
- Fine-tune your supplier scheduling implementation program.
- Expand supplier scheduling to the rest of your suppliers.

## PROBLEM-SOLVING

*"We want to implement supplier scheduling but do not have the valid internal schedules to run our own operations. We have determined that implementing supplier scheduling is more important to us right now than improving our internal scheduling."*

Some companies assume that providing their suppliers with more information based on bad internal schedules will make the information better. Unfortunately, sending information based on inaccurate internal schedules only results in more inaccurate information. It is critical for a company to get its internal operations under control and learn how to schedule them properly first, because internal schedules generate purchase requirements. Only then should a company generate supplier schedules.

*"We currently have a good MRP system running on the computer and feel that we run our operations with very valid schedules. We would like to use the planning reports generated by our current system instead of developing new ones."*

Your planning reports will usually have the kind of information that you will want to include in a supplier schedule. The problem with using your current planning reports is that they contain extraneous information that might confuse your suppliers. Also, you may want to present the information to your suppliers using different time periods than you use in your internal planning reports.

*"As part of our Just-in-Time program, we are using kanban to schedule parts of our manufacturing process and many of our purchased materials. We want to use kanban for all of our purchased parts and eliminate the need for any schedule."*

While kanban is an excellent tool for providing information on immediate scheduling needs, it does nothing to help with future scheduling. You still need to develop and maintain valid internal schedules in order to plan your future material requirements with your suppliers; otherwise, they will not have the appropriate materials on hand to meet your requirements.

## *SUMMARY*

- Supplier scheduling is being used in companies to replace the traditional purchase order with a separate supplier agreement and a separate schedule communicated to the supplier on a routine basis.
- Buyers in companies with supplier scheduling are responsible for sourcing, negotiations, contracting, and value analysis. A new position, supplier scheduler, is responsible for providing schedules to suppliers via priority mail, fax, or electronic data interchange.
- Companies that use supplier scheduling consistently achieve improved delivery performance, reduced purchase costs, smaller inventories, reduced lead times, and reduced paperwork.
- Before implementing supplier scheduling, companies must have their internal operations under control and have valid schedules in place.
- Supplier scheduling is also applicable in Just-in-Time and kanban environments.

## INFORMATION RESOURCES

*Customer-Driven Strategy: Winning Through Operational Excellence,* Thomas F. Wallace, Oliver Wight Publications, 1992.

*Purchasing in the 21st Century: A Guide to State-of-the-Art Techniques and Strategies,* John E. Schorr, Oliver Wight Publications, 1992.

*World Class Production and Inventory Management,* Darryl V. Landvater, Oliver Wight Publications, 1993.

*Supplier Scheduling and Development: How to Build Successful Partnerships Class,* Richard L. Norman and Cecil E. Bradshaw, Oliver Wight Publications, 1993.

*APICS Dictionary,* 7th edition, American Production and Inventory Control Society, 1992.

## INTERNAL CROSS-REFERENCE

Your understanding of this topic may be enhanced by the following chapters:

I–6. Resource Planning: For Manufacturing, the Business, and the Enterprise

II–1. Being a World Class Customer

V–6. Plant Scheduling for High Customer Service

### About the Author

Alfred W. Webber is a senior associate with R. Reed & Associates located in Carmel, Indiana. He has provided businesses with quality solutions, education, and advice for more than twenty years. His broad business background includes management responsibilities in manufacturing, sales/marketing, engineering, systems, and distribution with Corning Incorporated, Cabot Corporation, and the Wickes Companies. He is the author of numerous articles on various manufacturing management topics.

# PART VII
# MEASUREMENTS

**1. Measuring Customer Satisfaction**
*Charles O'Neal*

**2. Performance Measurements That Support World Class Manufacturing**
*Thomas E. Vollmann*

**3. One Set of Numbers: Integrating Operating Data and Financial Systems**
*Jim Burlingame*

**4. Activity-Based Costing: Driver for World Class Performance**
*Peter B. B. Turney*

**M**EASUREMENTS ARE THE company's equivalent of pulse, heartbeat, blood count, EKG, etc. Healthy individuals take these kinds of measures periodically; healthy, world class companies track them constantly.

Since the customer is number one, Part VII opens appropriately with **Measuring Customer Satisfaction** by Charles O'Neal, formerly in industrial marketing with General Electric. Next, Tom Vollmann from the IMD Graduate Business School in Switzerland defines **Performance Measurements That Support World Class Manufacturing**.

In the following chapter, how to achieve **One Set of Numbers: Integrating Operating Data and Financial Systems** is described by Jim Burlingame, calling on his years of experience at Twin Disc. Part VII closes with **Activity-Based Costing: Driver for World Class Performance** by Peter B. B. Turney, a pioneer in the field of Activity-Based Costing and Management.

## VII-1

# Measuring Customer Satisfaction
### *Charles O'Neal*

**IN A NUTSHELL**

Customer satisfaction has become a primary objective of business organizations with world class aspirations. Generally, customer satisfaction is a function of how customers perceive a company's products and services relative to their expectations.

Like quality, Continuous Improvement, and other business process initiatives, customer satisfaction must be carefully measured before it can be managed or improved. Too often, performance measures are internally focused with the objective of satisfying the controller, design engineer, operations manager, or quality assurance specialist. Internal measures usually center on conformance quality—doing things right—using such indicators as defect rates, scrap, and rework as key measures. These are appropriate indicators of internal efficiency, but may have little bearing on customer satisfaction. When customer satisfaction is measured, it is often an assessment of current customers and designed to measure whether the customer is or is not satisfied. Neither approach addresses the issue of delivering improved value to the customer.

Competition has forced companies to find a better way of measuring and improving customer satisfaction. It has triggered a transition to an external customer focus that uses customer satisfaction/delight as a basic strategy and a primary measurement of business performance. This transition has been accelerated by the Malcolm Baldrige National Quality Award, which emphasizes customer satisfaction, customer retention, and market share gain as major organizational goals. (The latter two goals are also broad indicators of customer satisfaction.) The Baldrige program also provides an outstanding set of guidelines for absolute and comparative measures of quality and customer satisfaction.

## *Key Measurement Issues*

Three key questions must be addressed by customer satisfaction measures: Whom to measure? What to measure? and What standards to use?

In terms of whom to measure, the customer, is the obvious answer. *Which* customer is less apparent. Here we should measure customers in terms of their position in the value-delivery chain and their position in time.

The customer satisfaction process begins with the measurement of target external customers. The process continues upstream with intermediary customers (if applicable), and moves inside the organization to measure the satisfaction of internal customers/employees. Internal customer satisfaction must be considered as both a vertical and horizontal process, each with its own appropriate measures. The process then moves further upstream to key suppliers (reverse customers). The satisfaction level of each particular customer group is important since each has an impact on the other groups and on total business performance.

A customer's position in time—present, past, and future—also provides valuable insights for process improvement. Present customers are a source of knowing what is going right. Past customers can report on what is going or what went wrong. Future (external) customers can tell you what important product or service features are missing.

What to measure must also focus first on the ultimate external customers, focusing on those quality attributes they perceive to be important in satisfying their needs and expectations. Their response sets the agenda for measuring all the upstream value-generating processes (suppliers).

Whom to measure and what to measure provide a basis for obtaining absolute measures of customer satisfaction but provide no standard for comparison. Comparison is critical if performance improvement is the goal. Bases of comparison include:

- Similar prior periods (trends)
- Key competitor(s)
- Industry average
- World class levels

These provide a set of important customer-focused indicators: customer satisfaction, market satisfaction, and market-perceived quality, the final measure being an acid-test indicator of marketplace quality and competitiveness.

## *Implementation*

Developing and implementing successful measures of customer satisfaction require:

- A customer-focused organizational culture without boundaries between functions
- Senior management commitment
- An orientation to serving internal customers (employees)
- A process-team approach with team members from each key value activity
- A close relationship with internal and external customers reflected by openness, honesty, and integrity in sharing needs/expectations and performance data
- Resources sufficient to ensuring the development and Continuous Improvement of the measurement process

## Benefits

Customer satisfaction pays significant dividends. Customer delight, the perception of unanticipated quality attributes by customers, holds even greater rewards for firms. There is a strong relationship between customer satisfaction, customer retention, and profitability. To the extent that measurement systems built to support this strategy focus on the right customers, measure the right things, and communicate measurement results quickly to key value-delivery units, they help management to set priorities on value activities that ensure customer satisfaction.

## KEY CONCEPTS

**Comparative quality measures**: A comparison of quality levels of key product and service features, such as on-time delivery, with important standards as shown in Figure 1.

Comparative quality measures become predictors of customer satisfaction and quality in use. The chart in Figure 1 is considered a

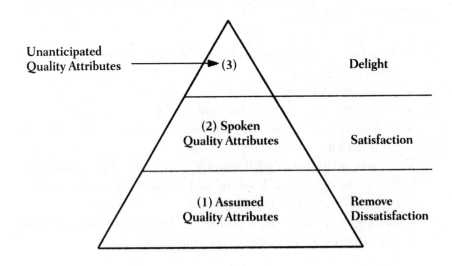

**FIGURE 1. LEVELS OF QUALITY ATTRIBUTES DELIVERED AND DEGREE OF CUSTOMER SATISFACTION**

model approach to charting quality measures by the Baldrige guidelines and would receive a 100 percent score in the results category because it demonstrates:

- An excellent improvement trend
- Results being evaluated against relevant comparisons and benchmarks
- That current performance is excellent
- Strong evidence of industry leadership

**Customer**: The focus and recipient of all the value activity of the organization. The four categories of customers are the downstream target external customers, the upstream key suppliers (reverse marketing), internal customers as served by management (vertical marketing), and internal customers as served by internal suppliers (horizontal marketing).

**Customer satisfaction**: The measure, based on important quality attributes, that compares customers' expectations with their perceptions of the actual purchase experience. It may be measured by a satisfaction scale with a range of possible outcomes, depending on the level of quality attributes delivered as perceived by the customer (see Figure 2).

Certain important quality attributes are not stated/spoken by the customer but are assumed to be provided. If not, the customer will be dissatisfied; if the quality attributes are subsequently delivered, the dissatisfaction will be removed, but the change will not result in customer satisfaction. Customer satisfaction results from the delivery of spoken attributes—quality characteristics expressed when customers indicate what they would like in the product or service. If these characteristics are delivered at the expected level, the customer is satisfied. Customer delight results when the quality delivered exceeds expectations and/or when unanticipated quality attributes are delivered.

**Customer Value (CV)**: The customer's perception of the quality delivered (Q), compared to the price paid (P), as expressed by the

**FIGURE 2. IMPORTANCE—PERFORMANCE MEASUREMENT GRID**

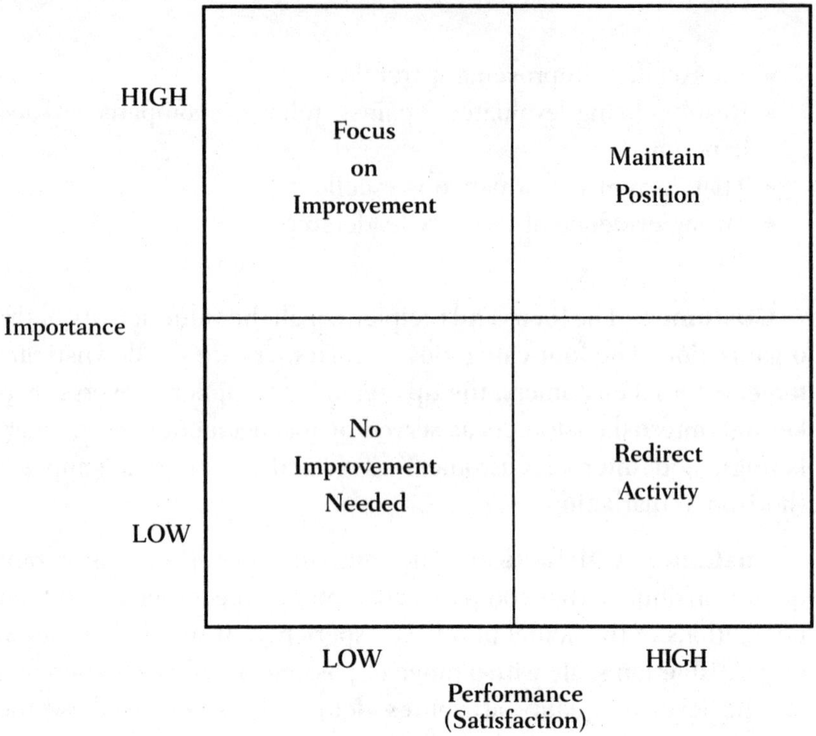

|  | LOW Performance (Satisfaction) | HIGH Performance (Satisfaction) |
|---|---|---|
| **HIGH Importance** | Focus on Improvement | Maintain Position |
| **LOW Importance** | No Improvement Needed | Redirect Activity |

simple mathematical equation: CV = Q/P where Q represents all of the nonprice quality attributes.

**Market-perceived quality and value**: The measurement of a company's performance compared to that of its key competitor(s), as perceived by it customers and by customers of competitors (lost customers and potential customers). This is the most meaningful measure of quality and competitiveness. An index of market-perceived quality may be calculated as shown in Table 1.

The index becomes the sum ($\Sigma$) of the weighted differences between a company's ratings and its competitors' ratings, divided by the total weight (100), as shown at the bottom of the rating differential column. The index provides an excellent measure for tracking quality and value if it is calculated regularly.

**TABLE 1. CALCULATING THE INDEX OF MARKET-PERCEIVED QUALITY**

| Key Quality Attributes | Relative Weights | Customers Rating of Your Company | Customers Rating of Competitor Company | Rating Differential |
|---|---|---|---|---|
| 1 | $W_1$ | $P_1$ | $C_1$ | $(W_1)(P_1 - C_1)$ |
| 2 | $W_2$ | $P_2$ | $C_2$ | $(W_2)(P_2 - C_2)$ |
| 3 | $W_3$ | $P_3$ | $C_3$ | $(W_3)(P_3 - C_3)$ |
| etc. | etc. | etc. | etc. | etc. |
| Total | 100 | (Scale = 1-10) | | (differentials) 100 |

**Market satisfaction**: The measurement of company performance based on the perception of its customers and customers of its competitors. This is a more meaningful measure than customer satisfaction.

**Prioritizing quality attributes**: Determining those attributes that become the primary focus of process-improvement activities. This is achieved by gathering performance and important measures on a wide range of attributes and charting the results on a grid as in Figure 3. The position (quadrant) in which they are positioned suggests the appropriate action.

The performance (satisfaction) measurement may be an absolute value (e.g., scaled 1–10) or a relative measure that compares performance with customer expectation or key competitors. The latter approaches permit gap analysis.

**FIGURE 3. COMPARATIVE QUALITY MEASURES**

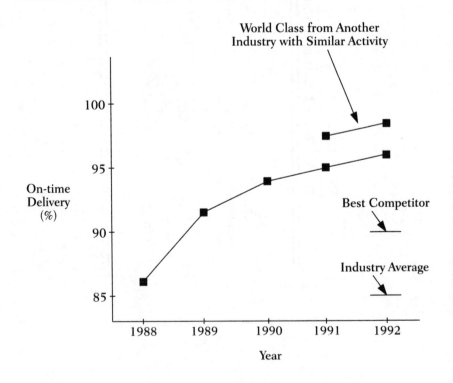

**Quality attributes measured**: These include both product (tangible) and service (soft) attributes perceived by the customer as important in the purchase decision. The following set of attributes has been developed from extensive research:

1. Core/product/service attributes

    - Tangibles/aesthetics. How does it look/feel?
    - Conformance. Does it meet the specification?
    - Features. What will it do?
    - Performance. How well will it do it?
    - Durability. How long will it continue doing it?
    - Serviceability. How easy is it to maintain and repair?

2. Product/service provider attributes
    - Responsiveness. How willing is the company to provide helpful, prompt service?
    - Assurance. How knowledgeable and courteous are employees and do they convey trust and confidence?
    - Empathy. How understanding, caring, and attentive is the company?

## ACTION STEPS

- Identify the external target customers (segments) to be measured.
- Determine key influencers of the purchase decision within these target customers.
- Learn the "whats" from the purchase influencers—what quality attributes they expect to be delivered—including those that are assumed but not usually expressed; what importance they place on each attribute; and what level they expect to be delivered.
- Identify the upstream inputs and processes required to deliver on these whats. These become the "hows" on which upstream

suppliers focus, forming a chain of satisfaction measures with an ongoing customer orientation.

- Continuously monitor and improve the measures of satisfaction to ensure that they truly reflect the changing needs and expectations of target customers.

## *PROBLEM-SOLVING*

*"Our company is engaged in a process-improvement program, but we're having a difficult time reaching agreement among our functional units on how to prioritize the projects."*

Let your target customers give you direction. Your customer measurement system should provide all the data you need to make the decisions. It tells you what is most important to your current and potential customers and how you are currently doing from their point of view. You should concentrate on inputs and processes that will affect the important quality attributes on which your performance rating is lowest (i.e., your performance gap is greatest).

*"We seem to be doing an excellent job of improving and maintaining quality levels based on our internal quality measures, but our market share is slipping."*

Your measurement system is concentrating on doing things right (conformance quality), but obviously failing to do some of the right things from your target customers' perspective. You need a set of customer-focused external measures of performance that determine, and are closely linked to, internal processes/measures. Together they provide a winning combination of internal efficiency and customer satisfaction.

*"Our customer satisfaction rating continues to stay at an acceptable level, but our market share is declining."*

1. Your customer satisfaction measurement system is too narrowly focused on your present customers. It does not give you perceptions of potential customers, and in a growing market situa-

tion your competitors, with higher evaluations, can be capturing a greater share of accounts.

2. You are likely losing customers because "acceptable" customer ratings are no longer sufficient to keep customers. Your ratings need to move to "excellent" or "very satisfied," and you need to deliver unanticipated quality experiences to delight your customers, which will substantially improve your retention rate/market share.

## SUMMARY

- Customer satisfaction is a key objective of companies with world class status, and as a customer value-delivery process is clearly linked to customer retention and profitability. This means it must be measured if it is to be managed and improved.
- Too many measurement systems focus on internal performance measures—doing things right—at the expense of external customer-focused measures. As a result, they often end up not doing the right things.
- An effective system for measuring customer satisfaction includes the complete set of customers—downstream target external customers, internal customers, and upstream key suppliers (reverse customers). It also includes present, past, and future customers.
- Measures of customer satisfaction include quality attributes that are important to target customers and their evaluations of these attributes compared to key competitors, industry averages, and world class standards.
- A system of customer satisfaction measures provides direction to management in setting priorities and centers on value activities that ensure sustained customer satisfaction/delight, retention, and enhanced profitability.

## INFORMATION RESOURCES

*The Malcolm Baldrige 1993 Award Criteria,* National Institute of Standards and Technology, Gaithersburg, MD.

*Measuring Customer Satisfaction,* Bob Hayes, Quality Press, 1992.

"Identifying Your Customer, the First Step to Customer Delight," Charles O'Neal, *Target*, September–October 1992, pp. 8–12.

"Understanding Your Customer, the Most Critical Step to Customer Delight", Charles O'Neal, *Target*, September–October 1992, pp. 17–22.

*Managing Quality*, David Garvin, The Free Press, 1988.

*Delivering Quality Service*, Valerie Zeithaml, A. Parasurman and Leonard Berry, The Free Press, 1990.

## INTERNAL CROSS-REFERENCE

Your understanding of this topic may be enhanced by the following chapters:

    I–1. Hallmarks of Excellence

    II–1. Being a World Class Customer

    IV–3. Benchmarking the Best-in-Class

    VII–2. Performance Measurements That Support World Class Manufacturing

---

### About the Author

Charles O'Neal is an educator, author, and consultant specializing in time-based total quality systems (marketing implications). He has published extensively in *Journal of Marketing, Industrial Marketing Management, The International Journal of Purchasing and Materials Management, Target,* and other publications. Dr. O'Neal is co-author of *Developing a Just-in-Time Marketing Strategy* (1991). He has spent sixteen years in a variety of industrial marketing positions with General Electric and is professor of marketing (emeritus), University of Evansville in Indiana.

# VII-2

# Performance Measurements That Support World Class Manufacturing

*Thomas E. Vollmann*

## IN A NUTSHELL

Getting the right performance measurements is a critical issue in becoming a world class manufacturer. Companies need to develop the metrics that encourage the right kinds of actions—those that lead to enterprise well-being, competitive dominance, and financial prosperity.

The major improvements programs associated with world class manufacturing—Just-in-Time, Total Quality Management, Manufacturing Resource Planning, Quality Function Deployment, Employee Empowerment, Supply Chain Partnerships, and other programs—require that measures of company performance be consistent with the objectives of those programs. For example, when implementing world class manufacturing based on a Total Quality Management (TQM) approach, it is imperative that the evaluation of company activities be consistent with TQM objectives. TQM implementation must be the driving force, and performance measures need to support it. From the top of the company to the bottom, individuals must be evaluated with quality-based metrics. Measurements that run counter to a TQM-based organization—typically the financial metrics commonly associated with cost accounting systems—need to be identified and eliminated.

In changing performance measures, the company must understand the critical difference between "drivers" and "passengers." The drivers of long-term success are achievement of world class manufacturing capabilities and true customer focus, one in which the company continually exceeds its customers' expectations and sets the standard to which its competitors will be compared. The passengers are the financial results.

Cost is one of these passengers. It is the ante in the high-stakes game of modern manufacturing. Everybody watches cost, but mercilessly attacking cost, rather than the *drivers* of cost, will not win the game. Winning takes ongoing action programs to improve responsiveness to customer needs, rapid development of new products and services, flexibility, and second-to-none quality. None of these winning activities are the focus old of style performance measures.

Most traditional performance measures originate in cost accounting systems. For many manufacturers, these accounting measures fail to send meaningful signals as to the actual performance of operations. For more information on these shortcomings, see chapter VII–4.

## *Strategy and Performance Measures*

Performance measures need to encourage actions congruent with the company's business strategy. Unfortunately, while the strategies associated with world class manufacturing embrace speed, quality, product range, and service, in far too many firms the measures lag behind. Obsolete measures permit or even encourage incorrect actions. Leading-edge manufacturing companies are changing their strategic directions at an ever-increasing pace, and the measurement systems need to catch up so they can enhance this directional change.

Figure 1 shows the congruence that is required in strategy, actions, and measures. When a firm adopts a new strategic direction, its performance measures must be changed, first to support implementation of the new direction, and second to encourage optimum performance in achievement of the strategy. For example, if a company determines that Time-Based Competition is an appropriate strategy, then metrics to implement Time-Based Competition need to be established, as well as metrics to evaluate time-based performance. Time becomes the driving metric, and cost becomes a passenger. In fact, many measures of cost will need to be discarded.

Figure 1 shows the same congruence as required between actions and measures. If a company desires to implement Just-in-Time manufacturing practices, it must determine the proper metrics to support both implementation and operations under JIT. It also needs to find and eliminate those existing measures that can impede JIT. Measures to be eliminated include those that encourage the building of inventories or those that focus on capacity utilization rather than throughput times.

A closely related concept is that of Activity-Based Management (also see chapter VII–4). The basic idea here is to understand the underlying drivers of cost, to identify those that add little to the customer's perception of value, and to develop measures that lead to their elimination or reduction. Traditionally, the primary focus of work has been on transactions and the hidden factory—the one that pushes numbers into computers rather than the factory that makes

**FIGURE 1. CHANGING MANUFACTURING PERFORMANCE MEASURES**

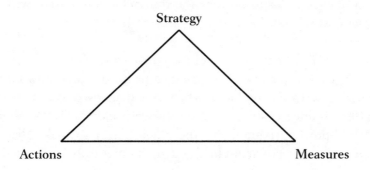

products and services. Where there are transactions there are uses of people, time, and other resources that can be saved.

Activity-Based Management is not the same as Activity-Based Costing—which attempts to carry these ideas into the costing of individual products based on their transactions and other activity drivers. Activity-Based Management generally is less concerned with product-costing issues, which can get quite arbitrary. Rather, the emphasis is on nonfinancial metrics that deal directly with the drivers and, as a result, are more easily changed to create congruent evolution in strategy, actions, and measures.

Changing performance measurements requires the involvement of the accounting/finance members of the organization. Once they understand the difference between drivers and passengers they can be of enormous help. Once they recognize that long-term profits are achieved through internal metrics that encourage implementation of world class manufacturing, the company's ability to replace the traditional cost-based measures will be increased.

## *The Four Phases of Changing Performance Measurements*

The path from traditional accounting-based metrics to those congruent with implementation of world class manufacturing takes a company through four phases:

***Phase 1. Frustration*** Inappropriate performance measures result in frustration and more than a few horror stories. Hewlett-Packard, for example, found it needed to shut down a JIT operation an hour early each day in order to process the transactions required by its job-order costing systems.

***Phase 2. Tinkering*** A manufacturer of large industrial machines found itself losing money on spare parts. So an accounting firm was called in to fix the problem, which was diagnosed as a need to get better product costing. The spares were older designs. Built on general-purpose equipment, they took longer to make than new parts, which were manufactured on numerically controlled machines. Since product costs were tied to direct labor hours, overhead rates on spares kept increasing—partially because of the depreciation expenses for the new equipment! The accounting firm devised a new, more fair system. Voilà! Spares now made money. But on the bottom lines of operating effectiveness and customer satisfaction, nothing changed—except that overhead was increased by the cost of the accounting study.

***Phase 3. Cutting the Gordian Knot*** The company makes a radical break between internal and external reporting. Northern Telecom gave up absorption costing (allocating overhead to inventory). Hardly the panacea of reform, but now, at least, one cannot increase profits by filling warehouses with inventory. Digital Equipment cut a different Gordian knot by abandoning traditional capital budgeting for a large sum of money that was to be devoted "to achieve manufacturing excellence." Cutting the Gordian knot requires a fundamental reexamination of the internal performance measurement system. A joint attack by manufacturing and finance is usually required to align strategy, actions, and measures.

***Phase 4. Embracing Change*** In this phase—still largely unpracticed—the company builds evolution into its performance measurement process. Measures are expected to change continually to support and drive evolution in strategy and actions. Eliminating measures is at least as important as adding them. A medical equipment manufacturer changed measures to support a much higher degree of factory automation and JIT. When it found itself with significant overcapacity, new measures were implemented to support development and introduction of new products, and several measures that encouraged high utilization of plant and equipment were dropped.

## *Using the Performance Measure Questionnaire (PMQ)*

The Performance Measurement Questionnaire (developed by Rob Dixon, Fred Nanni, and Tom Vollmann) has proven to be a useful tool for many companies trying to implement measures that directly support world class manufacturing. The PMQ collects the opinions of a wide set of managers on the match between current measures and what they see as important to succeed in the marketplace. By examining this data, management can find the anomalies in their current system of measures and identify areas where new metrics are needed and obsolete metrics need to be removed. Differences of opinion between various management levels and/or functional areas over what is important, and whether or not the system measures it, can tell management how dissimilar groups are (perhaps inconsistently) interpreting the strategy. Resolving these differences can get the whole company executing the strategy as a team.

Part I of the PMQ asks managers to rate the importance of improving quality, labor efficiency, machine efficiency, new product development, throughput time, etc., on a seven-point scale. Using a similar scale, respondents indicate alongside these questions the degree to which the current set of performance measures in the company either supports or inhibits improvement.

Part II of the PMQ takes a detailed look at performance measurement per se. Again, using dual 7-point scales, respondents assess a list of measures such as inventory turnover, conformance to specifications, on-time delivery, etc., for both the importance of the measure and the degree to which the company currently emphasizes the measure.

Analysis of the data yields consistent patterns and anomalies. One critical issue is the extent to which Top Management's professed strategy is consistent with what the participants believe is important to improve. Another is what are called gaps and false alarms. These are determined by subtracting the response on one 7-point scale from the other. For example, if improving quality was highly rated (say a 6), and the current measurement system did not support improvement in quality (say a 2), then 6−2=4, which is a gap. On the other hand, if for example, a cost accounting measure such as labor variance was rated as relatively unimportant (say a 2), and the company measures it extensively (say a 7), then 2−7=−5, which is a false alarm.

Experience with PMQ is that companies generally identify the cost accounting–based measures as false alarms, and find gaps in areas such as new product introduction, customer satisfaction, and Employee Empowerment. A recent survey by Roger Schmenner and Tom Vollmann attempted to determine the extent to which this experience is general and what variations are attributable to industrial and other differences. Table 1 provides overall results for the 92 respondents in the survey, and Table 2 breaks out the data in terms of process versus assembly companies, and then in five industrial classifications. The differences tend to be more in terms of the gaps than in terms of the false alarms. The usual suspects (i.e., the cost accounting–based metrics) are almost uniformly seen as false alarms—needing to be eliminated.

**TABLE 1. RESULTS FOR ALL RESPONDENTS, ALL INDUSTRIES (N = 92)**

|  | Performance Measures | Mean Differences (Left-right-hand scales) | Standard Deviations of the Differences |
|---|---|---|---|
| Gaps | New product introduction | 1.483 | 1.972 |
|  | Customer satisfaction | 1.308 | 1.495 |
|  | Employee involvement | 1.256 | 1.650 |
| The Middle Half | Integration with customers | 1.187 | 2.091 |
|  | Overhead cost reduction | 1.077 | 1.711 |
|  | Volume flexibility | 1.022 | 2.005 |
|  | Throughput times | 0.670 | 2.028 |
|  | Quality | 0.637 | 1.764 |
|  | Computer systems | 0.593 | 1.644 |
| False Alarms | Machine efficiency | 0.044 | 1.617 |
|  | Labor efficiency | 0.011 | 1.847 |
|  | Direct cost reduction | -0.165 | 1.985 |

## Table 2. Results for Selected Industry Definitions

| Category | Gaps | False Alarms |
|---|---|---|
| Process Industries* (n=65) | New product introduction<br>Customer satisfaction<br>Overhead cost reduction | Direct cost reduction<br>Labor efficiency<br>Machine efficiency |
| Assembly (non-process) Industries (n=27) | Employee involvement<br>Customer satisfaction<br>New product introduction | Machine efficiency<br>Direct cost reduction<br>Labor efficiency |
| Food and Tobacco (n=27) | Customer satisfaction<br>Integration with customers<br>Employee involvement | Labor efficiency<br>Direct cost reduction<br>Throughput times |
| Chemicals and Metals (n=35) | New product introduction<br>Overhead cost reduction<br>Customer satisfaction | Direct cost reduction<br>Machine efficiency<br>Throughput times |
| Engineered Products (n=17) | Employee involvement<br>Volume flexibility<br>New product introduction | Machine efficiency<br>Labor efficiency<br>Direct cost reduction |
| Electronics-related Products (n=9) | Customer satisfaction<br>New product introduction<br>Throughput times | Computer systems<br>Direct cost reduction<br>Machine efficiency |
| Other (n=4) | Integration with customers<br>Customer satisfaction<br>Employee involvement | Machine efficiency<br>Direct cost reduction<br>Volume flexibility |

* Process industries include food, tobacco, lumber, pulp and paper, chemicals, petroleum, rubber/plastics, stone/clay/glass, primary metals, and some metal fabrication. Assembly (non-process) industries include apparel, furniture, printing, leather, most fabricated metals, machinery, electric and electronic products, vehicles and other transportation equipment, instruments, and miscellaneous manufacturing.

## KEY CONCEPTS

**Activity-Based Costing**: An approach to determining individual product costs based on the activities that drive the costs. Examples might be engineered products being costed by allocating cost in changes, or allocating sales and marketing costs based on the number of customers served, sales, orders, or some other indicator of that activity.

**Activity-Based Management**: Similar to Activity-Based Costing with one major exception: The focus in both is on the activities that *drive* costs—but Activity-Based Management does not attempt to allocate costs or to determine individual product costs. Rather, the emphasis is on understanding the drivers of costs and thereafter attacking them directly (i.e., programs to reduce the drivers).

**Cost accounting**: A system to determine costs in an organization. Overall cost determination is necessary to report fairly the financial position of the firm to outside entities. But cost accounting is also a system to determine individual product costs, and this requires an allocation of indirect and other overhead expenses to products.

**Drivers**: As used here, those activities that cause something to happen. There are cost drivers—which result in overall costs. The term "driver" is also used in contrast to "passenger," meaning that it is the drivers that truly cause things to happen, while the passengers are along for the ride. Thus, reductions in inventory, lead time, scrap, or setup times are drivers, and costs are the passengers that result from these actions.

**False alarm**: As used here, a measure not in tune with what the enterprise really needs. If, for example, the company desires to increase its quality, measures of cost may be false alarms. False alarms result when the emphasis on the measure is greater than it should be.

**Gap**: The opposite of a false alarm. A gap indicates that a particular measure is more important than the emphasis it is given.

**Passengers**: *See* **Drivers**.

**Performance measure**: An indicator of how well something is working. There are financial and nonfinancial performance measures. A fundamental tenet of this article is that it is better to measure the right thing inexactly than the wrong thing with great precision. In other words, it is preferable to be approximately right then exactly wrong.

## ACTION STEPS

- Form a cross-functional team of executives that includes manufacturing, finance, and someone with a keen view to customer needs.
- Agree that action will follow analysis. Performing a study like PMQ and then not making the changes that people tell you are needed will create major motivation problems.
- Identify the company strategy and the desired set of action programs required to achieve world class manufacturing status. Then determine the set of performance measures that will be most useful for implementation as well as for ongoing operations. Also, try to determine which current measurements will work counter to achieving your objectives.
- Identify transaction-based systems and other cost drivers. Evaluate their benefits in terms of providing value to the customer. Eliminate those that do not provide customer benefits. In general, many companies move away from command and control to one based on empowerment of employees with a presumption of trust.
- Determine the usefulness of a questionnaire-based approach such as PMQ, both in terms of gathering information and gaining consensus about needed changes.
- Maximize employee participation in developing new performance measures; avoid dictatorial decree.

## PROBLEM-SOLVING

*"We are too slow in bringing new products to the marketplace, and part of the problem is a lack of measures that support new product information."*

It is better to measure the right thing inexactly than the wrong thing with precision. Metrics such as the percent successful, the concept to market throughput time, initial versus long-run cost, and percent of revenues generated by products less than two years old have been successfully implemented.

*"Employee involvement is a key issue for us in implementing world class manufacturing. How do we measure success in this area?"*

It is difficult to obtain concrete measures of employee involvement or empowerment. At the same time it can be dangerous to measure activity that may or may not be correlated with results. Even so, some companies are measuring the training cost per employee, the number of cross-trained employees, aspects in which they are cross-trained, the number of suggestions, the number of improvement teams, and savings generated through employee suggestions.

*"Improved customer satisfaction is perceived as an outcome of world class manufacturing. What are companies doing to improve measurements in this area?"*

The primary requirement is to identify all the sources of information about customer satisfaction: complaints, market focus groups, surveys, order-entry information, and any other contacts with customers. There must be a systematic way to collect this information, distribute it, and act upon it. New metrics include measures of time elapsed between customer requests and deliveries, customer measures of your company relative to competitors, complaint data, surveys, and market share information.

## *SUMMARY*

- Performance measures must support implementation and operations of world class manufacturing activities. When they do not they must be changed. Moreover, these changes are best seen as proactive; one needs to think through the metric changes concurrently with world class manufacturing implementation, not as an afterthought or as a response when problems become acutely visible.
- Nonfinancial measures are replacing financial measures in

state-of-the-art companies. They can be more directly related to desired results, are easier to comprehend, are easier to evolve, and less subject to abuse. Nonfinancial measures become the drivers for excellence, and the financial measures become the passengers.

- Strategy, action, and performance measures must be congruent. The measures must evolve as new strategic directions are identified and new action programs are undertaken. Any major shift in strategy should create an expectation of significant changes in performance measures.
- Activity-Based Management focuses on the underlying activities that drive costs, separating those that create value from the customer's point of view. The intent is to clearly identify potential savings in transactions and other cost drivers and to make them quite visible with metrics that encourage significant improvement.
- Accounting and financial personnel must play a key role in the process of changing performance measures. They can and should help the organization to better understand the fundamental distinction between drivers and passengers. They also can help the company in its need to change its focus toward nonfinancial measures.

## INFORMATION RESOURCES

*The New Performance Challenge: Measuring Operations for World Class Competition,* J. Robert Dixon, Alfred J. Nanni, Thomas E. Vollmann. Dow Jones-Irwin/APICS Series in Production Management, 1990.

"Performance Measures: Gaps, False Alarms, and the 'Usual Suspects,'" Roger W. Schmenner and Thomas E. Vollmann, Manufacturing Executive Report Number 7, May 1993, International Institute for Management Development (IMD), Lausanne, Switzerland.

*Measuring Up: Charting Pathways to Manufacturing Excellence,* Robert W. Hall, H. T. Johnson, and Peter B. B. Turney, Business One Irwin/APICS Series in Production Management, 1991.

## INTERNAL CROSS-REFERENCE

Your understanding of this topic may be enhanced by the following chapters:

I–1. Hallmarks of Excellence

IV–1. Total Quality Management (TQM)

IV–3. Benchmarking the Best-in-Class

VII–1. Measuring Customer Satisfaction

VII–4. Activity-Based Costing: Driver for World Class Performance

### About the Author

Thomas E. Vollmann is professor of manufacturing management at IMD in Lausanne, Switzerland, and director of its manufacturing 2000 research project. He is the author/co-author of nine books, most recently *Manufacturing Planning and Control Systems*, Third Edition, and *Integrated Production and Inventory Management,* as well as more than seventy-five journal articles. Professor Vollmann has served as a consultant to many firms on manufacturing and information systems, has lectured in executive programs throughout the world, and is certified at the fellow level (CFPIM) by APICS.

# One Set of Numbers: Integrating Operating Data and Financial Systems

*Jim Burlingame*

## IN A NUTSHELL

When material moves, money moves. This suggests that an interface between manufacturing and financial reporting should be part of a company's formal operating system. The operating system should be capable of providing the information needed by these two very different business functions. Fortunately, the set of tools known as Manufacturing Resource Planning, or MRP II, (see chapter I–6) provides this interface. It results in what some call a "single number system"; this refers to the fact that there is only one set of numbers used within the company, but that these numbers can be expressed in different units of measure for different purposes.

Figure 1 details the relationship between the financial system and the manufacturing operating system, showing how Production Plans and operations are linked to Business Plans and financial reporting.

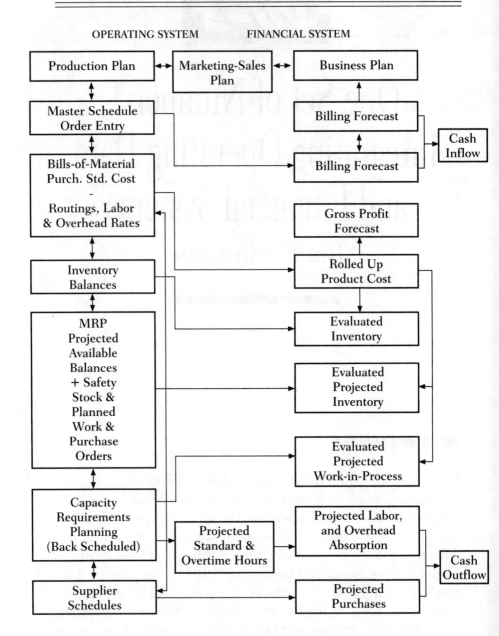

FIGURE 1. MRP II FINANCIAL PLANNING INTERFACE

As first glance, the feasibility of this one system's providing information for two very different business functions seems questionable. Accounting and manufacturing, after all, speak different languages: Manufacturing needs information described in physical units (pieces, pounds, gallons, etc.), while financial reporting systems require information in money (dollars, pounds, yen, etc.). Nevertheless, it's as easy to convert these units of measure as it is to restate pounds of steel bar stock (for purchasing) into feet and inches (for manufacturing).

The interface between manufacturing and accounting is logical and easy if the MRP II transaction system supports the general ledger. One of the challenges to this interface, described later, is the very rapid pace of change in modern manufacturing. Simplification and shortening of manufacturing processes are becoming the rule, with the result that manufacturing is giving up much of the detailed information it formerly generated and used. The question is: Can, or should, the financial system also relinquish this detail?

## MRP II—Accounting Integration

Three fundamental sets of data within Manufacturing Resource Planning are:

1. The routing
2. The bill-of-material (BOM)
3. Inventory balances

MRP II needs all three to operate, and so does the accounting system. The BOM is needed for material cost, the routing for labor cost, and the inventory balance to value the inventory.

All three pieces of information must be accurate. In fact, MRP II's requirements for accuracy are far greater than those of accounting. This is because errors in dollars (the language of accounting) can offset each other, but errors in units (the language of operations) must stand alone.

The routing can be used both to determine standard labor cost and, with the plant schedule, to value work-in-process (WIP) inventory. The plant schedule knows where all material is located, the routings know what the standard times are, and the labor reporting system knows the actual time. These three sets of data can be used to calculate labor cost.

Overhead (burden) can be calculated from labor cost or hours and, with the material cost added, yield the value of WIP at both standard and actual cost. Figure 2 depicts this valuation process.

Figure 3 shows the result of receiving the 30-piece work order due the week of 7/16 into finished stock. It shows how the accounting entries are a mirror image of the operational transactions being fed to the plant scheduling part of MRP II.

**FIGURE 2. VALUING WORK-IN-PROCESS**

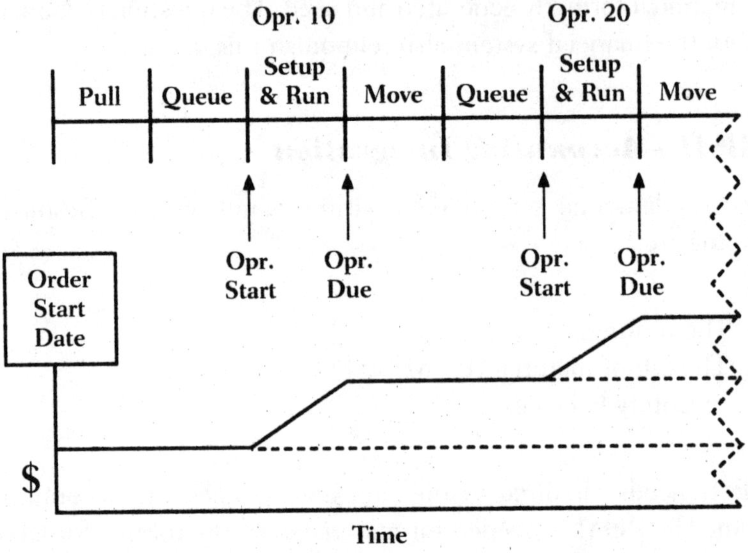

**Operating System:** Move 360 pieces from Opr. 10 to Opr. 20

**Accounting System:** DR WIP, CR Labor recovered & overhead recovered

## Figure 3. MRP Format. Work-order Receipt

|  |  | Allocation | SS | Scrap |
|---|---|---|---|---|
|  |  |  | 0 | 0% |
| Part No. | Description | On-hand | LT | Order Quantity |
| 350 | FRAME SUB-ASSEMBLY | 0 | 1 | LFL |

| Week Beginning | Past Due | 7/16 | 7/23 | 7/30 | 8/6 | 8/13 | 8/20 |
|---|---|---|---|---|---|---|---|
| Projected Gross Requirements |  |  | 30 |  | 25 | 35 |  |
| Scheduled Receipts |  |  | 30 |  |  |  |  |
| Projected Avail. Bal. |  | 0 | 0 | 0 | 0 | 0 | 0 |
| Planned Order Rel. |  |  |  | 25 | 35 |  |  |

## Figure 4. Recording Receipt of Work Order into Stock

| Operating System | Dr | Cr |
|---|---|---|
| Receive Finished Frames | 29 |  |
| Relieve WIP Inventory |  | 30 |
| Scrap | 1 |  |
|  | 30 | 30 |
| **Accounting System** | $ | $ |
| Component Inventory | 3190 |  |
| Scrap | 110 |  |
| WIP Inventory |  | 3300 |
|  | 3300 | 3300 |

The advantages of integration include:

1. Data needs to be entered into the information system only once. This cuts down on the chance for error and saves money.
2. When errors occur they are corrected by those who know most about the error (e.g., receiving errors are corrected by receiving personnel).
3. Teamwork is enhanced because manufacturing and accounting both have a stake in accurate numbers.
4. On-the-floor involvement by accounting personal is unnecessary because line manufacturing people are policing the accuracy of the numbers.
5. Manufacturing Resource Planning requires highly accurate and verifiable inventory figures. This eliminates year-end surprises and the need for an annual inventory.
6. Numbers are both timely and accurate. Huge multinational companies can (and do) close their books in several working days. Managers have results in time to make adjustments to operations in the current month.

## *Avoiding Unpleasant Surprises*

One of the worst things that can happen to a business is to have unpleasant surprises late in the fiscal year, when too little time remains to organize and execute adequate responses. Examples include below-forecast sales, higher-than-anticipated materials costs, and order-inventory imbalances.

However, these are rarely surprises to the entire organization. People close to the action know—or at least suspect—that there'll be a problem, but senior management is in the dark. Often, the basic reason for this is the failure to reconcile the Sales and Operations Plan (S&OP—see chapter I–5) to the Business Plan at the close of each accounting period. It may be human nature to put off unpleasant actions and hope that things will get better, but in business the sooner something is known the less damaging it will be. The translation of the Sales and Operations Plan into financial terms helps to avoid unpleasant surprises.

Sales and Operations Planning is the process of balancing the demand plan, the bookings plan, the Production Plan, the inventory plan, and the sales (shipment) plan with each other and with the overarching Business Plan. The Business Plan, in units and money, is both input to and output from S&OP. There is no good reason to maintain a Business Plan that cannot be supported by the Sales and Operations Plan. A year-end surprise is the result. S&OP with no tie back to the Business Plan is only half a plan.

## *Budgeting*

Budgets are one of the most important tools of management accounting, and represent one of management's best controls over the business. Budgets are used for planning, controlling, measuring, and reconciling. Integration between operating and financial systems makes budgeting easy and accurate. Some examples are:

1. The material budget is the planned orders plus the scheduled receipts of purchased materials or parts.
2. The labor budget is the same thing for manufactured materials using the routing to extend the quantity of material from MRP by the times and the labor rates.
3. Overhead items are prorated by the amount of labor.
4. The cash budget is easily derived as shown in Figure 1.
5. Capital needs can be determined in part by entering forecasted Production Plans into MRP II and using the system to do traditional Capacity Planning.

Budgets also give a company the opportunity to flex the budget by the volume of production, simulate different business scenarios, and, as stated above, work with one set of numbers.

## *Implementation*

The best opportunity to integrate financial and operating systems occurs when a new operating system is being installed. This makes the implementation process simple and straightforward. In these cases the needs of finance are studied in the software selection process, and implementation is simply a portion of the larger project. Finance is also be represented on the steering committee and on the project team and has its own spin-off task force.

Computer software is one area in which serious problems result when finance is brought into the project late. The results are: software with an incompatible chart of accounts facility, absence of flex budgeting, too few fields to track the classes of inventory, yield allowances, and others. Therefore, the most important implementation requirement is to have finance involved from the very start when a new operating system is being installed. There are cases in which a company chooses not to use the general ledger that comes with its software. A common reason is that the business unit installing the program is a part of a larger company that has standard accounting requirements. These requirements will not be waived under any circumstances.

Two practical approaches exist to overcome this block. One is to program outputs from the MRP II system into the standard general ledger; the other is to use the software's general ledger and program it to output to the standard corporate general ledger. Either of these will work. The latter has the advantage of making use of all the error protections that software vendors build into their products.

## Challenges in the Current Manufacturing Environment

An earlier section of this chapter discussed the evaluation of work-in-process. There is a very real question as to whether this is good practice or not. Manufacturers are doing their best to flatten bills-of-material and to use fewer routing steps—all in the name of greater operating efficiency. A negative aspect of these efficiencies is that detail needed to evaluate inventory in the traditional way is lost. But do we need to evaluate WIP in the traditional way? If the velocity of manufacture is high, it may just as valid to evaluate all WIP as *half done*, or not to evaluate WIP at all—adding value only as work is completed. The people who do process accounting have known this for years; it is time for discrete manufacturers to learn it.

Over the years, most of the accounting that has been done using the financial interface took a traditional approach to costing; it assumed that overhead will be absorbed into inventory in some proportion to direct labor. Overhead has never varied in proportion to direct labor, and modern manufacturing is making this method of distributing overhead increasingly invalid. Therefore, leading-edge companies today are moving to Activity-Based Costing (see chapter VII–4). The good news is that the kind of approach advocated here—operationally integrated financial reporting—supports this trend superbly.

## KEY CONCEPTS

**Activity-Based Costing (ABC)**: A method of measuring the causes, performance, and results of work. Unlike conventional standard costing, it assigns cost to activities based on their use of resources, and assigns cost to products and customers based on their level of activities.

**Burden**: *See* **Overhead**.

**Financial data**: Data in dollars.

**Financial integration**: The deriving of financial data from operating data. This is done by translating unit data into dollar terms.

**Financial interface**: *See* **Financial integration**.

**Operating data**: Data in units (not dollars) generated in the ongoing operation of the business (e.g., production, scrap, shipments, receipts).

**Overhead**: Costs that cannot be directly related to individual products produced. Examples include maintenance supplies, utility costs, and the plant manager's salary.

**Single-number system**: A synonym for a financially integrated system.

## PROBLEM SOLVING

*"We always get surprises, and most of them are bad. Things never seem to work out the way the Business Plan and budget say it will."*

Companies that have integrated their financial reporting with their operating data—after having made the operating data highly accurate—have virtually eliminated these kinds of bad surprises.

*"We spend a lot of time in meetings debating whose numbers are accurate."*

A single number system means that everyone is "singing off the same sheet of music." In a choir, some of the scores are for basses, some for tenors, some for sopranos; the notes are different but they're all derived from the same source. So it is with financial integration.

*"We need more people in the accounting department to handle the increased volume of transactions. They're getting swamped."*

Don't hire more people. Rather, implement a financially integrated approach. Capitalize on the data that already exists in the operational side of the business, and thereby eliminate the need for accounting people to reenter the same transactions (shipments, production, receipts, etc.) into their system.

## SUMMARY

- An interface between manufacturing and financial reporting should be part of the company's formal operating system. Manufacturing Resource Planning (MRP II) provides this interface, capturing nearly all of the information needed to support manufacturing operations and to provide the necessary feeds to the financial system.
- One of the challenges to this interface is the rapid pace of

change in modern manufacturing. Simplification and shortening of manufacturing processes are becoming the rule, with the result that manufacturing is giving up much of the detailed information it formerly generated and used.

- Routings, bills-of-material, and inventory balances are three basic items of information that both MRP and the accounting system need to operate. All three pieces of information must be accurate.
- Unpleasant surprises late in the business year are damaging, and usually reflect the lack of integrated data between the operations and finance functions.
- Integration of operating and financial systems makes budgeting easy and accurate. It also gives a company the opportunity to flex the budget by the volume of production, simulate different business scenarios, and work with one set of numbers.

## INFORMATION RESOURCES

*Manufacturing Resource Planning: MRP II,* Oliver Wight, Oliver Wight Publications, 1981.

*MRP II: Making It Happen,* 2nd edition, Thomas F. Wallace, Oliver Wight Publications, 1990.

## INTERNAL CROSS-REFERENCE

Your understanding of this topic may be enhanced by the following chapters:

I–6. Resource Planning: For Manufacturing, the Business, and the Enterprise

VII–2. Performance Measurements That Support World Class Manufacturing

VII–4. Activity-Based Costing: Driver for Continuous Improvement

## *About the Author*

Jim Burlingame is an independent consultant associated with the Oliver Wight group. He specializes in MRP II implementation and strategic manufacturing planning. He has held the positions of executive vice president at Twin Disc Inc. and president at Simon-Duplex, Inc. He is a fellow and past president of the American Production and Inventory Control Society.

# Activity-Based Costing: Driver for World Class Performance*

*Peter B. B. Turney*

## IN A NUTSHELL

Activity-Based Costing (ABC) is a method of measuring the causes, performance, and results of work. ABC differs from conventional standard costing in scope and method in that it assigns cost to activities based on their use of resources, and assigns cost to products and customers based on their level of activities.

ABC provides easy-to-understand information about problems and opportunities, and by reporting accurate product cost it leads to a better understanding of product and customer profitability. It also provides information about activities that managers can use in focusing and accelerating improvement efforts.

ABC helps answer a number of key strategic questions about which markets to focus on, which products and services to sell,

---

* Copyright © 1994 Peter B. B. Turney. All rights reserved. Used by permission of the author.

which customers to serve, which prices will ensure a profit, and what technologies are best suited to the goals of the company. In addition to high-level strategic issues, ABC also helps answer important operational questions, such as choosing between alternative improvement programs, deciding how to allocate scarce resources to their most productive use, investing capital for maximum impact on performance, and selecting from make-or-buy alternatives based on cost, time, and quality impacts.

ABC adds a new incentive for becoming a world class manufacturer—improvement of the bottom line. Total Quality Management (TQM) and other tools of the world class company may yield improvements in quality, delivery, service, and customer satisfaction, but they sometimes fail to improve profitability. With ABC, world class companies can add best-in-class profitability to their accomplishments.

In its earliest applications, ABC was used to allocate overhead cost more accurately to products. It was viewed as a timely replacement for poorly performing accounting systems in which standard costs often erred by hundreds or even thousands of percent. Today, ABC has evolved into a common language of work that facilitates communication between individuals, across functions and processes, and between customers and suppliers. In addition to improving the accuracy of product costs, ABC supplies useful information about many aspects of work, including its cost, time, and quality. Experience has shown that ABC can be successfully applied by workers everywhere, regardless of industry and culture. This success has been achieved even where workers have limited formal education.

The most recent extension of ABC is Workforce Activity-Based Management (WABM), which applies ABC information to the process of Continuous Improvement. WABM focuses efforts to adapt business strategies to meet competitive pressures and to improve business operations, and to answer strategic and tactical issues such as what prices to set, what product mix to sell, and which improvements to make.

## Benefits

Successful ABC and WABM implementation offers numerous important benefits. Among the most important, the entire workforce is focused on achieving the company's goals. This focus includes improvements in profitability, in addition to quality and time. The WABM group process and ABC information combine to enhance Employee Empowerment and build team skills.

The costs of ABC and WABM depend on the type and size of the organization, the nature of the implementation plan, and the level of development of the workforce. Internal costs include the time of managers, staff, and workers, as well as systems resources. External costs include training and software.

## The ABC Model

An ABC system contains cost and process information. Cost information explains the cost of work and its use. Process information explains why the work is done and how well it is performed, and describes relationships with customers and suppliers.

Figure 1 shows a graphical representation of activity-based information called the two-dimensional model or "ABC Cross." Each type of information in the cross has a defined role in the Continuous Improvement process.

Information about activities (the center of the cross) enhances work teams' understanding of their work and the cost of doing it. This information is used to identify high-cost activities and to reveal nonvalue-added work. Information about objects of work (the bottom of the cross) explains how work and its cost are affected by the volume, lot size, design, or requirements of each product or customer. It helps the work teams plan workload and resource requirements, as well as identifying problem products and customers. At the company level, product cost and customer cost are useful for making strategic decisions.

Cost drivers (the left of the cross) describe the causes of work. Some causes are positive, such as a customer order that presents an opportunity to serve. Other causes are negative, such as errors in

**FIGURE 1. ABC CROSS**

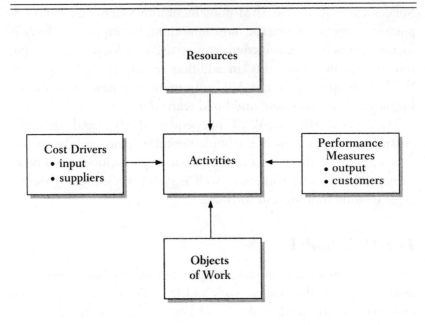

documentation that cause rework. Negative cost drivers explain why work requires excess cost and time, and result in poor quality, and why their removal is the key to permanent improvement.

The identification of inputs and suppliers helps reveal the causes of waste (the cost drivers), as well as the entities that must be involved if those causes are to be eliminated. This is essential because the root cause of a problem often exists within a supplier's operation, requiring the involvement of the supplier in its resolution. For example, errors in customer specifications (the input) received by engineering may originate in the sales department (the supplier).

Performance measures (to the right in Figure 1) explain how well the work is done. They cover the cost, time, and quality of the work. Performance measures are used to determine the baseline for Continuous Improvement, and can be compared with external benchmarks. They are also used to set targets for improvement.

Customers (and the outputs they receive) are important because they are affected by changes in work practices. The involvement of customers and suppliers in the WABM process ensures that priorities for improvement are set based on the process-wide impact of the changes.

## *Implementation*

Successful WABM implementation requires the following:

1. *Leadership commitment.* Management must articulate how WABM contributes to the goals of the company, develop a WABM charter for work team implementation, and provide resources for facilitation, resource availability (such as systems development), and training.

2. *Training.* Training is important to the success of any initiative that requires management, staff, and worker involvement. It helps build worker understanding and ownership, and increases the likelihood that improvements will be continuous. In addition to the WABM process itself, training should develop an understanding of the business, and further financial, computing, and communication skills.

3. *Wide availability of ABC information.* The availability of ABC information to the workforce plays an important role in Continuous Improvement by removing barriers to communication, serving as the sole source of information about cost, time, and quality, and demonstrating how everyone can contribute to an organization's goals. When ABC information is widely available, every employee is able to accept financial responsibility for the success of the organization, and decision making can be made on the basis of common factual knowledge.

4. *A group process.* WABM uses a group process to develop and apply ABC information. Workers are divided into teams using storyboards—workspaces for attaching cards, dots, yarn, and other items that visually represent information about a team and its work—to help document and organize ABC information. Storyboards help teams brainstorm key issues and resolve problems.

The group process is effective for several reasons. First, the people who do the work have the most knowledge about what they do.

Since WABM is a bottom-up process, the work teams develop and maintain the activity-based information, which instills a sense of ownership Moreover, all employees participate in WABM and share the experience of communicating and solving problems with a common language, so that WABM soon becomes an integral part of a team's daily work. Finally, WABM allows everyone to function as his own accountant, eliminating the need for large numbers of staff to develop and maintain systems, and changing the staff's primary role from that of technician to one of coach.

## KEY CONCEPTS

**Activities**: Work performed within the organization. Examples include placing a purchase order, shipping a package, writing a program, or servicing a customer.

**Activity-Based Costing (ABC)**: A method of measuring the causes, performance and results of work. Unlike conventional standard costing, it assigns cost to activities based on their use of resources, and assigns cost to products and customers based on their level of activities.

**Cost drivers**: Causes of work. They explain the current level of performance of work, and identify opportunities for improvement.

**Customers**: Users of outputs. Customers may be internal or external to the organization.

**Inputs**: Items or information received by an activity or process, such as credit guidelines or a purchase order.

**Objects of work**: Something to which, or for whom, work is applied. Objects include products and customers. For example, assembly is done to a product. Process engineering is done for a process (an internal customer).

**Outputs**: Something produced, transformed, or completed by an activity or process. An activity or process may have many outputs, including a product or service, paperwork, and transactions.

**Performance measures**: Indicators of how well work is done in terms of cost, time, and quality. They reflect the contribution of each team or process to the organization's goals.

**Resources**: Items used to do the work—people, facilities, equipment, supplies, materials, technology, and so forth—along with their associated cost. Measurements of the cost of these resources are typically generated by an accounting system, such as the general ledger.

**Suppliers**: Providers of inputs to an activity or process. Suppliers may be internal or external to the organization.

## ACTION STEPS

- Train management in the WABM concepts, terminology, process, and tools. Train staff and workers to implement them.
- Plan the implementation, including determining the specific purpose for WABM, creating focus, and chartering the work teams.
- Develop communication, problem-solving, and other people skills as necessary.
- Develop the communication and information systems that make pertinent information available to everyone in the organization.

## PROBLEM-SOLVING

*"We don't know which products, services, or customers are profitable."*

Use Activity-Based Costing to measures how resources and activities are used in the organization. Accurate costs sharpen perceptions of profitability and improve the quality of strategic decisions.

*"We suffer from 'program-itis'—too many initiatives, too little time, and no clear results."*

Avoid the typical shotgun approach to improvement efforts. ABC will provide clear measurements of each program's impact on cost, time, and quality. This allows priorities to be based on the known impact on business performance. Resources can then be assigned to those projects that yield the largest measurable improvement.

*"We have a hard time getting different parts of the organization to work together—each part speaks a different language, works off a different database, and blames other parts of the organization for problems."*

ABC is a common language and database of ideas that breaks down barriers to cross-functional communication and problem-solving.

*"Accounting is a nonvalue-added function. Its role as traffic cop interferes with efforts to empower the workforce, and its information is useless or dangerous. Accounting simply isn't a team player."*

When you use WABM, accounting's role of "control" will be replaced by that of "partner"—providing technical assistance, training, and support to the rest of the organization.

*"Our workers don't understand how they contribute to the overall performance of the business. Consequently, they cannot take responsibility for their work."*

With ABC, every worker and every team knows how its performance affects cost, time, and quality. With this understanding, it is easy for everyone to be accountable for their contribution to the improvement of business performance—including their impact on profitability.

## *SUMMARY*

- Activity-Based Costing (ABC) measures the causes, performance, and results of work including its cost, time, and quality. It is a common language that provides easy-to-use information about problems and opportunities.

- In contrast to standard costing, ABC reports accurate and complete cost information.
- Activity-Based Costing allows decisions to be made and priorities to be set, based on profitability, time, and quality impacts.
- Workforce Activity-Based Management (WABM) is the process of applying ABC information to achieve focused Continuous Improvement. It uses a group process and a problem-solving tool called storyboards.
- Success with WABM requires leadership, training, and the communication of ABC information to those who do the work.

## INFORMATION RESOURCES

*Common Cents: The ABC Performance Breakthrough,* Peter B. B. Turney, Cost Technology, 1992.

*Workforce ABM,* Peter B. B. Turney, Cost Technology, 1993. *Focus on Profitability: Workforce ABM* (Video), Cost Technology, 1993.

*Johnson & Johnson Medical, Inc.: A Case Series,* Peter B. B. Turney, Cost Technology, 1993.

## INTERNAL CROSS-REFERENCE

Your understanding of this topic may be enhanced by the following chapters:

IV–1. Total Quality Management (TQM)

IV–4. Just-in-Time: Driver for Continuous Improvement

VII–2. Performance Measurements That Support World Class Manufacturing

## About the Author

Peter B. B. Turney is president and chief executive officer of Cost Technology, Inc., an activity-based training and consulting company based in Beaverton, Oregon. A pioneer in the fields of ABC and ABM, and the author of numerous publications on both subjects, Dr. Turney is responsible for many innovations, including Workforce Activity-Based Management (WABM). He was formerly Tektronix Professor of Cost Management at Portland State University in Oregon.

# INDEX

Abbott Laboratories, 46
ABC Cross, 463–66
*ABCD Checklist for Operational Excellence*, Oliver Wight, 65, 67, 68
Accuracy, of measurement process, 10
Activities, in ABC Cross, 463, 466
Activity-Based Costing (ABC), 438, 442–43, 457, 461–70
Activity-Based Management, 437–38, 443
Advanced Manufacturing Research (AMR), 333–35
Advanced manufacturing technologies, 357–58
 *see also* Computer-Aided Design/Computer-Aided Manufacturing; Flexible Manufacturing Systems; MRP II; specific systems
Affinity Diagram, for Total Quality Management, 227, 228–30
*Age of Unreason, The* (Handy), 146
Aggregate planning, in Sales and Operations Planning, 47, 51
Aggregation of the forecast, in Sales and Operations Planning, 51
Agility, *see* Flexibility
All-hands meetings, 184, 186
American Society of Quality Control (ASQC), 305
Ames Rubber, 282

ANSI/ASQC, 293, 294
Anthony, Michael, 119
Approach, Baldrige Award and, 283, 285
Architecture of manufacturing systems, 329–30, 333–39
AT&T, 82, 154, 282
Attitude surveys, 185
Audit
 compliance, 306, 309
 first-party, 297, 299
 for ISO 9000 registration, 297, 298, 299, 300–301, 302
 performance, 306
 quality, 305–12
 risk-assessment, 306
 second-party, 298, 299
 surveillance, 297, 298, 299, 301
 third-party, 298, 299, 302
Automated material handling, 319, 321
Automated Storage and Retrieval Systems (ASRS), 321, 331
Automated test equipment, automation and, 319, 322
Automation, 317–27
 in time-based competition, 22

Backlog, Sales and Operations Planning and, 51, 54
Backlog levels, *see* Target inventory
Balanced measurements, excellence requiring, 7–9, 10, 12

471

# 472 INDEX

Baldrige, Malcolm, National Quality
Award, 281–91
customer satisfaction and, 424
to Xerox, 258
Bar chart, for Total Quality
Management, 239–42
Barbabba, Vincent, 87
Barnard, Bill, 26
Basic Flow Chart, for Total Quality
Management, 234–37
Batch processes (decoupled line flow),
352, 353, 354, 355, 358
Bean, L.L., 260
Bearley, William L., 167
Bell-shaped histogram, 249, 250
Benchmarking, 257–65
performance outcomes evaluated
with, 10, 12
for time-based competition, 18–19
Benchmarking partner, 259, 260, 262
Best-in-class
benchmarking, 257–65
performance outcomes evaluated
with, 10, 11
Bias, in forecasting, 111
Board of Examiners, for Baldrige Award,
283, 285
Boeing, 329
Boston Consulting Group, time-based
competition and, 18
Bottleneck, 358
Boundary crossing, teamnets and, 173,
174, 177
BP (Best Product, Best Partner, Best
Position), 78, 80–81
Brainstorming, for Total Quality
Management, 226–28
Broad banding, 193, 196, 198
Budget, 455
Sales and Operations Planning and,
54, 55
Bulletin boards, 185, 186
Burden, *see* Overhead
Business Plan
MRP II and, 61
Sales and Operations Planning and,
47, 48, 49, 52, 54, 454–55
Business Process Reengineering (BPR),
394
Business Resource Planning (BRP), 59,
66–67

Business Resource Planning (BRP)
(*continued*)
*see also* MRP II (Manufacturing
Resource Planning)
Business strategy, 25–26, 30, 32
improvement process needing, 11, 12
Buyers, in supplier scheduling, 410–13,
414

Cadillac, 26, 282
Capacity Planning
MRP II and, 61, 63, 64
Sales and Operations Planning and, 52
Capital need, budget and, 455
Cash budget, 455
Catch-ball, in Hoshin Planning, 39, 40, 41
Cause-and-Effect Diagram, for Total
Quality Management, 253–55
Champion, for Just-in-Time success,
273, 275
Champion of change, for employee
empowerment, 155, 157
Change, drivers of, 198
Changeovers
focused factory and, 347
in Just-in-Time, 270, 274
Charts, *see* Total Quality Management
Choice Modeling, voice of the customer
identified by, 88, 89, 90, 91
Chrysler, 86
Class A companies, MRP II and, 65, 67
Closed-loop MRP, 62–63, 64, 67
Co-location, High Performance Teams
and, 167, 168
Co-opetition, teamnets and, 175, 178
Column Flow Chart[sm], for Total Quality
Management, 230–33
Commodity team, Supplier Quality
Management and, 403, 404, 405
Communication
functional, 181, 186
open, 187, 189
organizational, 181–92
strategic, 181–83
Communications training, of High
Performance Teams, 167, 169
Company's voice, Quality Function
Deployment capturing, 27, 30
Comparative quality measures, customer
satisfaction measured with, 426–27
Compensation, 193–203

Competition, *see* Time-based competition
Compliance, in quality auditing, 306, 309
Compliance audit, 306, 309
Computer-Aided Design/Computer-Aided Manufacturing (CAD/CAM), 329, 331, 357, 359
Concurrent Engineering, 123–24, 331
  New Product Development and, 118, 122, 125
Conformance quality, 432
Connected line flow, 353, 354–55, 359, 360
Continuous-flow processes, 353, 354–55, 359, 360
Continuous Improvement
  as Baldrige core value, 285
  companies seeking excellence having, 6
  inventory level and, 47
  ISO 9000 and, 301
  Just-in-Time and, 269–70, 274
  Workforce Activity-Based Management and, 462
Continuous Replenishment Planning (CRP), 330, 334
  *see also* Efficient Consumer Response
Conventional factory, 343, 347, 349
Core/product/service attributes, 430
Core skills, 199
Core values, in Baldrige Award, 284, 285–87
Corning, 154
Corporate responsibility and citizenship, as Baldrige core value, 285–86
Corrective action, in quality auditing, 307, 310
Corrective Action Request (CAR), 306–7
Cost accounting, 441
  performance measures and, 436, 443
Cost drivers, in ABC Cross, 463–64, 466
Cost of quality, 13
Cross-functional training, High Performance Teams and, 164, 169, 170
Customer, 427
  in ABC Cross, 465, 466
  Efficient Consumer Response and, 93–103
  world class, 75–84, 402, 405
  *see also* Voice of the customer
Customer-driven quality, as Baldrige core value, 286
Customer expectations, performance outcomes evaluated with, 10
Customer focus, as Baldrige category, 286
Customer "in", in Hoshin Planning, 41
Customer-Oriented Manufacturing Management Systems (COMMS), 332–35, 338, 339
Customer satisfaction
  as Baldrige category, 286
  measuring, 423–34, 445
Customer service
  information technology improving, 330
  Sales and Operations Planning and, 46, 47, 52, 54
Customer-supplier partnership
  Supplier Quality Management and, 401–7
  Total Quality Management and, 214–15, 216
  world class customer and, 76–78, 82
Customer value (CV), 427–28
Customer wants, in Quality Function Deployment, 27, 28, 30
Cycle time, new product development and, 118
  *see also* Lead time
Cyclical influences, in forecasting, 111

Database module, of forecasting system, 108, 109, 110
Defect-Free Performance quality, in Total Quality Management, 212–13
Deficiency, in quality auditing, 306, 310
Deficiency finding, *see* Corrective Action Request
Demand
  dependent, 95, 98, 113, 114
  independent, 95, 99, 113, 114
Demand data module, of forecasting system, 108, 109, 110
Demand filters, forecasting and, 111, 115
Demand Management, MRP II and, 61

# INDEX

Demand pull, *see* Kanban
Demand pull lines, *see* Manufacturing cells
Demand-pull production, 274, 277
Demand/supply balance, in Sales and Operations Planning, 47, 48, 51, 52
Deming, W. Edwards, 244
Deming Wheel, *see* Plan-Do-Check-Act Cycle
Dependability, measuring, 7
Dependent demand
 Efficient Consumer Response and, 95, 98
 forecasting and, 113, 114
Deployment, Baldrige Award and, 283, 286
Design for Manufacturability (DFM), new product development and, 120, 122
Design for "x", new product development and, 120, 122
Design quality and prevention, as Baldrige core value, 286
Dialogue meetings, 184, 186
Digital Equipment, 439
Disaggregation of the forecast, Sales and Operations Planning and, 52
Dispatch list, *see* Work-to-list
Distributed Control Systems (DCS), automation and, 320, 322, 332, 334
Distribution, Efficient Consumer Response and, 93–94, 96, 99
Distribution Resource Planning (DRP), 95, 96–98, 99
 forecasting and, 114
Dixon, Rob, 439
Drivers
 of change, 198
 changing performance measures and, 436, 443
 companies seeking excellence using, 6, 9, 11, 12
 *see also* Cost drivers
Drucker, Peter, 85

Eastman Chemical, 282
Education, for learning organization, 149, 150

Efficient Consumer Response (ECR), 93–103
80/20 rule, 246–47
Electronic bulletin boards, 185
Electronic Data Interchange (EDI), 330, 334
Electronic mail (E-mail), 185, 186
EMC Corporation, 79
Employee development, as Baldrige core value, 286
Employee empowerment, 153–61, 167–68
 compensation and, 194, 198
 as hallmark of excellence, 5
 measures of, 445
Employee involvement
 in Just-in-Time, 274, 275
 measures of, 445
 in Total Quality Management, 213–14, 216
Employee participation, as Baldrige core value, 286
Empowerment, *see* Employee empowerment
Empowerment Profile, 167–68
Enterprise Logistics Management (ELM), 391–99
Enterprise Resource Planning, 59, 67
 *see also* MRP II (Manufacturing Resource Planning)
Entitlement mind-set, compensation and, 193, 198
Environmental soundness, measuring, 8
Excellence, hallmarks of, 5–14
Expectation mind-set, 196, 198–99
Expediting, for scheduling, 377, 381, 384
External quality, measuring, 7

Facilities focus, 358, 359
Factory within a factory, 344–45, 348
False alarms, performance measurements and, 440–41, 443
Fast response, as Baldrige core value, 286
Feature/Characteristic quality, in Total Quality Management, 213
Federal Express, 189
Feedback control system, automation and, 318
Fieldbus, automation and, 320, 322

# INDEX

*Fifth Discipline: The Art and Practice of the Learning Organization, The* (Senge), 146
Finance, Distribution Resource Planning and, 98
Financial results, measuring, 8, 13
Financial systems, operating data integrated with, 449–60
Finite Scheduling, 379–80, 381
First-party audit, ISO 9000 registration and, 297, 299
Fishbone diagram, *see* Cause-and-Effect Diagram
Flexibility
  automation improving, 318–19
  measuring, 7–8
Flexible Manufacturing Systems (FMS), 357, 359
Flow charts
  Basic, 234–37
  Column, 230–33
Flow lines, *see* Manufacturing cells
Flow shop, 366, 367, 371
  Just-in-Time, 365–76
Focus groups, 185
Focused factory, 343–50
Ford Motor Company, 26, 86
Forecasting
  Efficient Consumer Response and, 95–96
  elements of, 106–7
  methods, 105
  systems, 105–16
Forecasting module, of forecasting system, 108, 109, 110
Functional communication, 181, 186
Functional myopia, in learning organization, 148, 149, 150
Functional strategies, 30

Gain sharing, *see* Performance-based rewards
Gaps, performance measurements and, 441–42, 443
General managers meeting, Sales and Operations Planning and, 46–47, 50, 52, 54
General Motors, 321
Giant Foods, 94, 95–96
Gillette, 82

Globe Metallurgical, 282
Goeppinger, Kathleen H., 167
Granite Rock Company, 282
Group Technology (GT), 358, 359

Handy, Charles, 146
Hay, Ed, 22
Hayes, Robert, 356
*Hearing the Voice of the Market* (Barabba and Zaltman), 87
Hewlett-Packard, 9, 26, 82, 86, 154, 438
High performance enterprise, compensation for, 193–203
High Performance People Systems Process, 194–96, 199, 201
High Performance Teams (HPTs), 163–71
Histogram, for Total Quality Management, 249–52
Honda, 78
Horizon, Sales and Operations Planning and, 52
Horizontal bar chart, 241
Hoshin Planning (HP), 35–43
  as organizational communication, 181
House of Quality, in Quality Function Deployment, 27, 28, 30
  *see also* Relationship Matrix
Hows, *see* Measures
"Huddle" meetings, 186–87
Human capital, 149
Human Resources
  as Baldrige category, 286
  measuring, 8
  in Total Quality Management, 213–14, 216

IBM, 282
*Improshare*, 197
Improvement process, companies seeking excellence having, 6–7
  *see also* Continuous Improvement; Reengineering
In-context Customer Visits, 131
  voice of the customer identified by, 88, 89, 90, 91
In-House TV network, 184

Independent demand
  Efficient Consumer Response and, 95, 99
  forecasting and, 113, 114
Indicators, of excellence, 11, 12
Informal systems, MRP II and, 64, 67
Information, in Baldrige model, 283, 286
Information systems, for manufacturing, 324–25, 329–41
Innovation, measuring, 8
Inputs, in ABC Cross, 464, 466
Integration, Enterprise Logistics Management and, 391, 393
Internal controls, in quality auditing, 306, 310
Internal quality, measuring, 7
ISO 9000, 82, 293–304, 306
ISO/Technical Committee (TC) 176, 293, 297

Job shop (jumbled flow), 352, 353, 355, 359, 361, 365–66, 371
  conversion to Just-in-Time flow shop, 365–76
Johnson & Johnson, 82
Jones, John E., 167
Juran, Joseph, 247
*Just-in-Time: Making It Happen* (Sandras), 269
Just-in-Time distribution, *see* Efficient Consumer Response
Just-in-Time flow shop, converting from job shop to, 365–76
Just-in-Time (JIT), 267–79
  performance measurements for, 437
  supplier scheduling and, 411, 416
  time-based competition and, 16–17, 20, 22
Just-in-Time/TQC, Distribution Resource Planning and, 96

*Kaizen*, 269, 274
  *see also* Continuous Improvement
Kanban lines, *see* Manufacturing cells
Kanbans, 268–69, 274, 276, 277, 343, 346, 348, 381, 383
  flow shop and, 366, 371–72
  focused factory, 346–7
  manufacturing cell and, 368
  supplier scheduling and, 411, 416

Kanbans (*continued*)
  *see also* Pull system
Kellogg, 95–96
*Kintori amay*, 79, 81
  *see also* "Same face"
Knowledge assets, in learning organizations, 145–46, 149
Kotler, Phillip, 88

Labor budget, 455
Lead time, as driver, 9, 11, 13
Leadership, in Baldrige model, 283, 287
Lean production, 358, 359–60
Learning organizations, 145–52
Line chart, for Total Quality Management, 242–46
Line processes (connected line flow and continuous flow), 353, 354–55, 360, 361
Live video town meeting, 184
Local Area Network (LAN), 332
Logistics management, Enterprise Logistics Management and, 391, 393, 397–98
Long-range outlook, as Baldrige core value, 287

McGrath, Michael, 119
MAD (mean absolute deviation), forecasting and, 107, 112
Magazines, 185
Management by fact, as Baldrige core value, 287
Management by objectives (MBO), Hoshin Planning versus, 36
Management by Policy and Strategy Deployment, *see* Hoshin Planning
Management information systems (MIS), 330, 337, 338
Management of Process quality, as Baldrige category, 287
Management Product, Quality Function Deployment and, 26, 30, 32
Managerial interface and interaction module, of forecasting system, 108, 109, 110
Manufacturing
  Distribution Resource Planning and, 98
  Efficient Consumer Response and, 96
  focused factory and, 343–50

Manufacturing (*continued*)
  information systems for, 324–25, 329–41
  Just-in-Time flow shop and, 365–76
  operating data integrated with, 449–60
  process choice in, 351–62
  scheduling in, 377–85
  steps for automating, 317–27
  *see also* Advanced manufacturing technologies
Manufacturing cells, 346, 349
  for job shop to JIT conversion, 366–69, 372, 373–74
Manufacturing Execution Systems (MES), 331–36
Manufacturing pipeline, 99
Manufacturing Resource Planning, *see* MRP II (Manufacturing Resource Planning)
Manufacturing system architecture, 329–30, 333–39
Market-driven product development, 121, 122
Market-perceived quality and value, 428–29
Market research, voice of the customer identified by, 88–91, 90
Market satisfaction, 430
Market segmentation, voice of the customer identified by, 88, 90
Marketing, distribution resource planning and, 97
Marlow Industries, 282
Martin Marietta, 154
Master Production Schedule (MPS), 378–80, 381–82, 396–97
  MRP II and, 61, 63
Material budget, 455
Material handling, automated, 319, 321
Material planner, supplier scheduling and, 410, 414
Material Requirements Planning, *see* MRP (Material Requirements Planning)
Matrix analysis, in Quality Function Deployment, 27, 28
Maturity index, 11
Measures, in Quality Function Deployment, 27, 30, 131, 136
Media, comparison of, 184–85

Meetings, types of, 184, 186–87
Microelectronics technology, automation benefitting from, 318, 322
Milliken & Company, 282
Mitsubishi, 26
Monsanto, 154
Motorola, 76, 78, 82, 86, 154, 258, 282
  Six Sigma quality standard of, 9, 76–77
MRP (Material Requirements Planning)
  Enterprise Logistics Management compared to, 392–93, 394
  MRP II and, 63, 67
  software for, 396–97
  supplier scheduling and, 410, 414
MRP II (Manufacturing Resource Planning), 59–70, 358, 359, 381
  Distribution Resource Planning and, 96
  Enterprise Logistics Management compared to, 392–93, 394
  Finite Scheduling, 379–80
  as interface between manufacturing and financial reporting, 449–60
  Sales and Operations Planning and, 46
  software for, 396–97

Nabisco, 95–96
Nanni, Fred, 439
National Institute of Standards and Technology (NIST), Baldrige program administered by, 282
Natural pull, in Efficient Consumer Response, 94–95, 99
Needs, of customers, 86, 87, 88, 89, 90
Networks, *see* Teamnets
New product development (NPD), 117–28
  Quality Function Deployment and, 118, 123, 125, 130
  voice of the customer integrated with, 86–87
*NewComp*®, 193, 201
Newsletters, 185, 186
Nonconformities, for ISO 9000 registration, 300–301
Northern Telecom, 439
Numerical controls (NC/CNC), automation and, 319, 322–23
Nypro, 82

# 478　Index

Objects of work, in ABC Cross, 463, 466
*Oliver Wight ABCD Checklist for Operational Excellence*, 65, 67, 68
OMNI-Circuits, 78
Open communication, 187, 189
Operating data, financial systems integrated with, 449–60
Operational business objectives, 194, 199
Operational dimensions, of Total Quality Management, 212–13
Operational skills, 200
Order-push production, 274, 277
Organization as ecosystem, employee empowerment and, 155–57
Organizational communication, 181–92
Organizational dimension, of Total Quality Management, 213–14
Organizational priorities, in Hoshin Planning, 41, 42
Outliers, forecasting and, 111, 112, 114
Output module, of forecasting system, 108, 109, 110
Overhead, 457
　budget and, 455
　calculating, 452, 457

Pareto Chart, for Total Quality Management, 246–48
Pareto, Vilfredo, 246–47
Partners in merchandise flow, *see* Efficient Consumer Response
Partnerships, as Baldrige core value, 287
　*see also* Customer-supplier partnership
Passengers, changing performance measures and, 436, 442
Pay, 199
　*see also* Compensation
Pay-for-skills, *see* Skill-based pay
People are the "A" item, in MRP II, 64, 68
People Systems Process, 197, 199
　*see also* High Performance People Systems Process
Performance audit, 306
Performance-based rewards, 196–97, 199
Performance Measurement Questionnaire (PMQ), 439–41

Performance measurements, 435–47
　in ABC Cross, 464, 467
　excellence requiring performance, 7–12, 13
　time as, 19
Physical distribution, Distribution Resource Planning and, 98
Pie chart, for Total Quality Management, 237–38
Pilot manufacturing cell, for JIT production flow conversion, 372, 373
Plan-Do-Check-Act Cycle
　for Hoshin Planning, 41–42
　in Total Quality Management, 216, 217, 218
Plant and Supplier Scheduling, in MRP II, 64
Pneumatic systems, automation and, 318
*Practice of Management, The* (Drucker), 85–86
Pre-S&OP, 50, 52
Precision, of measurements, 11
Predictive modeling, *see* Choice Modeling
Pricing, Efficient Consumer Response and, 96
Prior performance, performance outcomes evaluated with, 9–10
Process analysis, in time-based competition, 20, 21
Process choice, in manufacturing, 351–62
Process control/management, in Total Quality Management, 209, 217
Process Control Systems (PCS), 332, 333–37
Process management, for new product development, 120–21, 122
Process mentality, of Hoshin Planning, 38–39, 41
Process owner, new product development and, 118, 122
Process performance measures (PPMs), new product development and, 118–19, 122–23
Procter & Gamble, 154
Product, voice of the customer integrated with, 86–87
Product audit, 306, 310

# INDEX

Product definition, for new product development, 120, 123
Product-dependent kanbans, 268, 269, 274
Product development, *see* new product development
*Product Development: Success Through Product and Cycle-Time Excellence* (McGrath, Anthony, and Shapiro), 119
Product family, in Sales and Operations Planning, 47, 49, 52–53
Product-independent kanbans, 268–69, 270, 275
Product life cycle (PLC), new product development and, 121, 123
Product-process matrix, 356–57
Product/service provider attributes, 430
Product success rate, new product development and, 119
Product velocity, Efficient Consumer Response and, 94, 99
Production flow, Just-in-Time, 365–76
Production Plan
  MRP II and, 61
  Sales and Operations Planning and, 48, 49, 53, 55
Programmable Logic Controller (PLC), automation and, 320, 323
Project retrospective (post-mortem), new product development and, 121, 123
Promotions, forecasting and, 114–15
Proven Path, MRP II and, 65–66, 68
Pull system, scheduling and, 379
*see also* Kanbans
Purchase order (PO), 409–10, 414
Purchasing, distribution resource planning and, 98

Quality
  cost of, 13
  external, 7
  House of, 27, 28, 30
  information technology improving, 330
  internal, 7
  market-perceived, 428–29
  *see also* Baldrige, Malcolm, National Quality Award; ISO 9000; Quality auditing; Total Quality Management

Quality and operational results, as Baldrige category, 287
Quality attributes
  measuring, 431
  prioritizing, 430–31
Quality auditing, 305–12
Quality Function Deployment (QFD), 25–34, 129–40
  cascading, 27, 29
  new product development and, 118, 123, 125, 130
  voice of the customer identified with, 87, 90, 91
Quality Function Deployment (QFD) facilitation, 137
Quality manual, for ISO 9000 registration, 300, 302
Quality report, in quality auditing, 308, 310
Queues, JIT flow operation and, 370, 372
Quick response, 20
  *see also* Efficient Consumer Response

Rapid prototyping, new product development and, 120, 123
Real-time information, Enterprise Logistics Management and, 392–93
Redesign, in employee empowerment, 156–58
Reengineering, 396
  for companies seeking excellence, 6
  time-based competition and, 17, 18, 19, 20, 21
Registering body, ISO 9000 registration and, 296, 298
Registrar, for ISO 9000 registration, 296, 298, 300
Registration Accreditation Board, 296
Registration audit, for ISO 9000 registration, 300–301
Regulated quality, in Total Quality Management, 212
Relationship Matrix, 131, 132–33, 134, 135, 137
Relevance, 11
Relevant communication, 189, 191
Resource Planning, *see* MRP II (Manufacturing Resource Planning)

Resource use, measuring, 7
Resources, in Activity-Based Costing, 462, 467
Results, Baldrige Award and, 283, 287
Reverse engineering, benchmarking and, 261, 262
*Revolution in Manufacturing: The SMED System, A* (Shingo), 270
Reward systems, 193–203
Risk-assessment audit, 306
Robotics, 318, 319, 323, 331
Rough-Cut Capacity Planning, MRP II and, 61, 63
Rucker, 197
Run tests, line charts and, 244

Salary, *see* Compensation
Sales and Operations Planning (S&OP), 45–57
  Business Plan reconciled with, 454–55
  MRP II and, 61
Salmon, Kurt, Associates, Inc., 94
"Same face", world class customers and, 79, 81
Sandras, Bill, 269
Scanlon, 196–97
Scheduling
  in manufacturing, 377–85
  supplier, 409–17
Schmenner, Roger, 441
Schwarz, Jim, 78
Seasonality, forecasting and, 111, 112, 113
Second-party audit, ISO 9000 registration and, 298, 299
Segmentation, Quality Functional Deployment and, 135
Senge, Peter, 146
Setup-time reduction, time-based competition and, 16, 20, 22
Seven Drivers of Breakthrough Partnering®, 77, 81
Seven Management and Planning Tools, 168
Shapiro, Amram, 119
Shewhart (Deming) Wheel, *see* Plan-Do-Check-Act Cycle
Shingo, Shigeo, 270
Silence is approval, 68

Simultaneous engineering, *see* Concurrent Engineering
*Single Minute Exchange of Dies* (SMED), 270, 275
"Single number system," 449–60
Skill-based pay, 193, 199
Skills, 199–200
Skinner, Wickham, 343, 344
Slip rate, new product development and, 119
Smith, Roger B., 321
Software
  for MRP II, 396–97
  for Sales and Operations Planning, 51
Solectron, 282
Staff meetings, 186
Stalk, George, 18
Stand-alone videotapes, 184
Stand-up meetings, 184, 186
Standard deviation, forecasting and, 107, 112
Standardization, ISO 9000 registration and, 82
Standards, performance outcomes evaluated with, 9
Stock-keeping-units (SKUs), 96, 99
  forecasting systems and, 106
Stockless materials management, *see* Efficient Consumer Response
Strategic communication, 181–83
Strategic quality planning, as Baldrige category, 287
Strategy-based Pay®, 196, 197, 200
Supplier
  in Activity-Based Costing, 462, 467
  Enterprise Logistics Management and, 391–99
  ISO 9000 standards and selection of, 297
  quality audits and selection of, 311
  Supplier Quality Management and, 401–7
  *see also* Customer-supplier partnership
Supplier agreements, in supplier scheduling, 410, 414
Supplier certification, 402, 404
Supplier councils, world class customers and, 81, 82
Supplier Quality Management (SQM), 401–7

# INDEX

Supplier scheduler, in supplier scheduling, 410, 415
Supplier scheduling, 409–17
Supplier surveys, world class customers and, 81, 83
Supply, competing for, 403, 404
Support skills, 199–200
Surveillance audit, ISO 9000 registration and, 297, 298, 299, 301
System audit, 306, 310
  *see also* ISO 9000
System control and maintenance module, of forecasting system, 109, 110

Target inventory, in Sales and Operations Planning, 47, 48, 53
Teamnets, 173–80
Teams
  in employee empowerment, 155, 158
  High Performance, 163–71
  for learning organizations, 148
  for time-based competition, 19
  Top Management, 28, 30, 31–32
  in Total Quality Management, 214, 216
  *see also* Teamnets
Technical skills, 200
Technical target values, in Quality Function Deployment, 131, 134
Technological Capabilities, in Total Quality Management, 213–14
Technology-driven product development, 121, 123–24
Teleconferencing, 184–85
Tellabs Manufacturing, 166
Texas Instruments, 282
Third-party audit, ISO 9000 registration and, 298, 299, 302
Throughput, focused factory and, 347, 348
Time-based competition, 15–24
  Just-in-Time and, 16–17, 20, 22
  performance measurements for, 437
Time performance measures, 19
Time-to-market, time-based competition and, 17, 20
Top Management team, in Quality Function Deployment, 28, 30, 31–32

Total cost of ownership, Supplier Quality Management and, 405, 406
Total Quality Management (TQM), 209–24, 271, 275
  Affinity Diagram for, 227, 228–30
  bar chart for, 239–42
  Basic Flow Chart for, 234–37
  brainstorming for, 226–28
  Cause-and-Effect Diagram for, 253–55
  Column Flow Chart$^{sm}$ for, 230–33
  histogram for, 249–52
  line chart for, 242–46
  Pareto Chart for, 246–48
  performance measurements and, 435–36
  pie chart for, 237–38
  time performance measures for, 19
  tools for, 225–56, 271, 275
  *see also* Supplier Quality Management
Toyota, 16
Tracking signals, forecasting and, 112, 115
Traditional compensation systems, 193, 194, 200
Training, for learning organizations, 149, 150
Transformation Pathway, employee empowerment and, 155, 156, 158
Trends, forecasting and, 111, 112

U-lines, *see* Manufacturing cells
U-shaped cells, 369, 372
Uniform Code Counsel, 95
Unit of measure, in Sales and Operations Planning, 53

Value, market-perceived, 428–29
Value-added analysis, in time-based competition, 20, 21
Value Added Network (VAN), 332
Value-added ratio, 21
Vertical bar chart, 241
Video staff meeting, 184–85
Voice of the customer, 85–92
  in product planning, 130, 131
  Quality Function Deployment capturing, 26–27, 30
  in total quality management, 210, 211–12, 217
Vollmann, Tom, 439, 441

Wal-Mart, 94
Wallace, Tom, 346
Wants
  of customers, 86, 87, 88, 89, 90
  in Quality Function Deployment, 130–31, 132–33, 137
Waste, Just-in-Time eliminating, 267–68, 275, 276
Watson, Gregory, 36
Watt, James, 318
Westinghouse, 282
Wheelwright, Steven, 356
Wide Area Network (WAN), 332
Wilson Learning Corporation, 164, 165
Work-in-process (WIP), valuing, 452, 456
Work-to lists, 378–79, 382

Work-unit staff meetings, 184
Workforce Activity-Based Management (WABM), 462–63, 465, 468
World class customer surveys, 81, 83
World class customers, 75–84, 402, 405
World class manufacturing, performance measurements for, 435–47
World class performance, determining, 12

Xerox, 36, 258–59, 260, 282

Young, John, 9

Zaltman, Gerald, 87
"Zero errors" standard, performance outcomes evaluated with, 10
Zytec, 282